多元融合视角下的跨文化交流导论

A Handbook of Intercultural Communication from Diversified and Converged Perspectives

李炜炜 编著

中国纺织出版社有限公司 | 国家一级出版社
全国百佳图书出版单位

图书在版编目（CIP）数据

多元融合视角下的跨文化交流导论 / 李炜炜编著
. -- 北京：中国纺织出版社有限公司，2019.9（2025.5重印）
ISBN 978-7-5180-6495-3

Ⅰ. ①多… Ⅱ. ①李… Ⅲ. ①文化交流—高等学校—教材 Ⅳ. ① G115

中国版本图书馆 CIP 数据核字（2019）第 167523 号

责任编辑：姚　君　　责任校对：王花妮　　责任印制：储志伟

中国纺织出版社有限公司出版发行
地址：北京市朝阳区百子湾东里 A407 号楼　邮政编码：100124
销售电话：010—67004422　传真：010—87155801
http://www.c-textilep.com
E-mail:faxing@c-textilep.com
中国纺织出版社天猫旗舰店
官方微博 http://www.weibo.com/2119887771
河北晔盛亚印刷有限公司印刷　　各地新华书店经销
2019年9月第1版　2025年5月第4次印刷
开本：710×1000　1/16　印张：17.5
字数：190 千字　定价：98.00 元

本书是北京邮电大学研究生教学改革项目
"'双一流'和'新工科'背景下
研究生国际化职场英语能力培养模式的构建研究"和
北京邮电大学人文学院研究生教学改革项目
"多元融合视角下的跨文化交流研究"
的研究成果。

序

人类进行跨文化交流活动的历史源远流长。历史上张骞凿通西域、甘英出使大秦,丝绸之路上的众多遣唐使都是跨文化交流的生动写照。近十年来,迅速发展的中国正在改变全球地缘政治格局,喜迎开创百年国运的时刻。党的十八大以来,我们不仅以骄人的成绩书写了中华民族伟大复兴的壮美篇章,还创造性地提出"人类命运共同体"的价值与世界分享。"一带一路"沿线国家不仅共享了中国经济发展的红利,也越来越多地感受到中国文化的魅力,以及不同于西方话语体系的中国学派。

进入新时代,随着经济全球化进程的加速,跨国、跨文化的交往日益频繁,多元文化背景的交流与日俱增,给现代人的生存和发展带来了前所未有的张力,全球意识、密切的跨文化沟通变得日益重要。跨文化交流学已经成为一门显学,是一流大学的必修课。

传统的跨文化交流教学多遵循语言传统,通过教师对不同语言文化之间的对比(cross-cultural communication)来实现,主要侧重于习俗、社会等符号的静态对比;跨文化教学的互动性(interactivity)不够;会通式超越的"共同体建构"(the construction of a common community)成为难以企及的梦想。

作为一门跨学科的教材,传统跨文化交际教材在新时代的语境下需要与时俱进。本教材从跨文化交际、跨文化传播、跨文化沟通、跨文化哲学等多元融合视角出发,在编写中考虑到了新一代信息通信技术对于文化交流方式的影响,在理论与案例的指导下引导学生"人文化成",不仅提升学生的跨文化交流素养,也助力其国际化职场交流能力建构,为国际交往中心建设贡献绵薄之力。在世界多极化、经济全球化、社会信息化、文化多样化时代的跨文化传播中,依托中国软实力,以价值共享为愿景,讲好中国故事,推动全球构建人类命运共同体的意识。

《多元融合视角下的跨文化交流导论》(A Handbook of Intercultural Communication from Diversified and Converged Perspectives)融合了跨文化交际学、跨文化传播学等相关学科的理念,从多元视角来帮助非语言专业高年级本科生和研究生,尤其是理工类专业学生,在新时代语境下学习和运用跨文化的能力。本书作者基于北京邮电大学研究生英语跨文化交流课程五年的教学经验,凝聚成书,以教学任务设计和对比分析为基石,设计了"导入—理论—讨论—实践—拓展"(Lead-in—Theory preparation—Detailed analysis—Cultural practice—Derivative development)五个教学环节,力求将理论与实践相结合,在涵化学生跨文化交流素养的同时,也培养了学生的国际化职场交流能力。

《多元融合视角下的跨文化交流导论》一共分成八个章节,既涵盖了传统跨文化教学的主流领域,如言语交流(第二章)和非语言交流(第三章),又融合了社会学和传播学研究的相关成果,如从媒介化的角度来思考跨文化交际在媒介化时代的新方法(第四章),也从跨文化哲学的角度来反思主体与客体之间的视角转换(第五章)。第六章和第七章则从对外传播和跨文化商务交流的角度探讨了中国在新时代语境下跨文化交流的新路径。第八章是全书的总结,探讨了跨文化能力和共同体的建构。尽管没有隔阂的跨文化交流之路依然任重道远,但我们相信,以"博观"为手段,以"圆照"为态度,以转换视角为起点,以模式融合为策略,做点"识器""晓声"的工作,提升广大学生跨文化素养研究的理论范式和实践能力,一定能为中国文化大传播做出应有贡献。

在书稿的写作过程中,北京邮电大学研究生院和人文学院都给予了极大关怀和支持。在这里,作者想特别感谢人文学院谢永江副院长、陈真真副院长,外语系研究生英语教研室郝劲梅副教授、史金金副教授,中国传媒大学博士生导师王宇教授和北京第二外国语学院英语学院李国庆副教授。他们或殷殷期盼或谆谆嘱托,给予本书作者巨大鼓舞与动力。感谢中国纺织出版社的朱健桦老师和姚君老师的细心策划与编辑。

因为作者初入该学术领域,鄙陋自是无须多言,请各位专家和同学批评指正!

是为序。

李炜炜

于朝阳雅筑

2019 年 8 月

目 录

第一章 走进跨文化交流的世界
Chapter One
Introducing Intercultural Communication

Section 1 Lead-in

1.Question

（1）How many years have you studied English as a foreign language? After so many years of learning, what is hidden behind languages in your opinion?

（2）Why do we have to learn a course of intercultural communication? What is the justification of learning intercultural communication?

2.Picture（Figure 1）

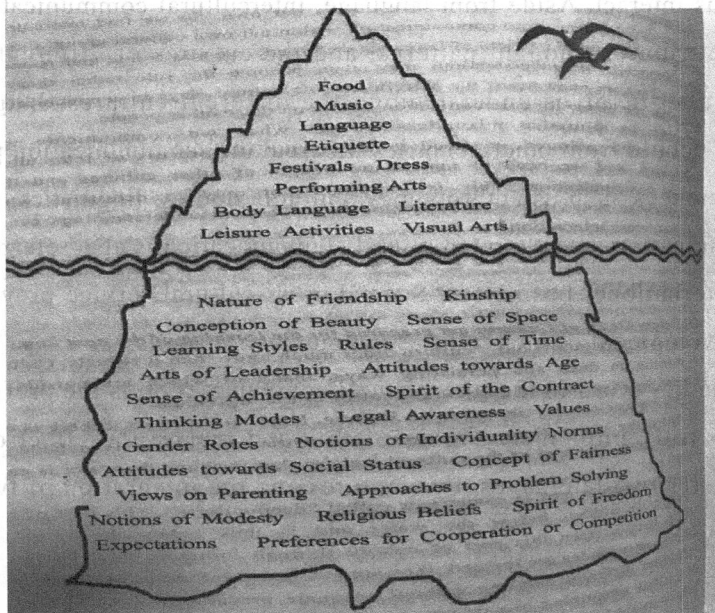

Figure 1   An Iceberg of Culture [1]

---

1   胡文仲 . 1999 /2018.《跨文化交际学概论》. 北京：外语教学与研究出版社，第 41 页 .

Section 2 Theory preparation

Theory preparation: the definition of intercultural communication

Intercultural communication (ICC for short in this course) is a discipline that studies communication across different cultures and social groups, or how culture affects communication. It describes the wide range of communication processes and problems that naturally appear within an organization or social context made up of individuals from different religious, social, ethnic, and educational backgrounds. In this sense it seeks to understand how people from different countries and cultures act, communicate and perceive the world around them. Many people in intercultural business communication argue that culture determines how individuals encode messages, what medium they choose for transmitting them, and the way messages are interpreted. [1]

With regard to intercultural communication proper, intercultural communication studies situations where people from different cultural backgrounds interact. Aside from language, intercultural communication focuses on social attributes, thought patterns, and the cultures of different groups of people. It also involves understanding the different cultures, languages and customs of people from other countries. Intercultural communication plays a role in social sciences such as anthropology, cultural studies, linguistics, psychology and communication studies. Intercultural communication is also referred to as the base for international businesses. Several cross-cultural service providers assist with the development of intercultural communication skills.

So, the key word in the intercultural communication is the prefix "inter-". In order to fully implement the denotation and realize the effect of ICC, we have to master two languages, two cultures and the integration of two cultures proficiently.

---

1 Lauring, Jakob (2011). "Intercultural Organizational Communication: The Social Organizing of Interaction in International Encounters". Journal of Business and Communication, 48 (3): 231 – 55.

Section 3 Detailed analysis

1.In-class task

Suppose you are asked to write a letter in this case:you listen to VOA for years (esp. VOA news and "Our World" program), and want its schedule and teaching material, so you write to VOA. What are you going to organize your letter? Please read the following letters written by students and share your comments on these two letters with the classmates. Which letter is better? Which letter could acquire higher scores? Which letter is a preferred style for you? And the reason?

（1）Letter 1 (a letter written by one Chinese student)

Respected VOA producers,

I have been a loyal listener to VOA news programs and to "Our world" for several years. I consider both programs to be extremely well produced.

Let me describe myself a little: I am a postgraduate student in Beijing University of Posts and Telecommunications. I am 22 and my home is in Qiqihar, Heilongjiang province, China. Because I like studying English, I therefore follow those programs closely. I get all my practice in listening comprehension and dialogue from your programs. This practice has been of great benefit.

As I progress, I am keenly aware that not having the teaching materials presents several difficulties. Because of this, I have taken time to write this letter to you, in the hope that I can obtain a set of VOA's English programs' teaching materials. Please let me know the cost of the materials. In addition, I hope to obtain a VOA program schedule.

Wishing VOA's programs more interesting.

Sincerely yours,

Li Jun

（2）Letter 2 (a letter written by another student)

Dear VOA producers,

I would be very grateful if you would be kind enough to send me teaching materials for your excellent English language teaching program. I am learning English from your program but am finding it difficult without the materials. I would also appreciate if you would be kind enough to send me a VOA program schedule.

Yours sincerely,

Zhou Ting

People tend to be entangled with the question that which letter is better in grammar, writing etc.However,regardless of the writing superiority of these letters, what is the **difference**? [1]

Let us try to analyze the difference from the following perspectives.

1.Purpose presenting

◆ Chinese:

General; make a good impression and write appropriately.

VS.

◆ Western:

Specific; convey information or persuade the intended reader.

2.Writing and speaking style

◆ Chinese:

Subjective; personal; poetic.

VS.

◆ Western:

Objective; impersonal.

3.Logic order

◆ Chinese:

Sentences reflect the process of natural thinking(from the known to the unknown, from the less important to the more important).

VS.

---

1 Tips: To identify "difference" is a very important mission of intercultural communication studies. Intercultural communication study generally pays more attention to the difference rather than superiority or inferiority of different cultures.

◆ Western:

Information is presented from the more important to the less important (from the unknown to the known).

4.Language and connectiveness

◆ Chinese:

Paratactic language (意合型语言).

Diffused, loose in structure, clauses or phrases are placed one after another without coordinating connectives relation usually implied in the context.

VS.

◆ Western :

Hypotactic language(形合型语言).

Compact, tightly combined with connectives or prepositions showing logical connections between sentences.

e.g.,

A typical English long sentence and its Chinese correspondent translation:

(English)

He had flown in just the day before from Georgia where he had spent his vacation basking in the Caucasian sun after the completion of the construction job (that) he had been engaged in the South.

(Chinese)

他在南方参加一项建筑工程，/ 任务完成后，/ 他就去格鲁吉亚度假，/ 享受高加索的阳光，/ 昨天才坐飞机回来。

5.Subject / actor of the sentence

◆ Chinese:

Personal; personal pronouns are used more frequently; dynamic, the Chinese language witnesses more verbs used in a single sentence.

VS.

◆ Western:

Impersonal structure is always used as the subject; static; agent nouns are frequently used to replace verbs.

e.g.,

(English) An idea suddenly struck me.

(Chinese) 我突然有了个主意。

(English) He is a good eater and a good sleeper.

(Chinese) 他能吃又能睡。

6.Language style

◆ Chinese:

General, vague, descriptive language showing emotions, frequent use of idioms, proverbs and sayings.

VS.

◆ Western:

Specific, concise, clear-cut, the argumentation is accompanied with evidence, creative use of language

After the detailed analysis of the differences of two languages, the next question is: what accounts for these differences?

Answer: **Writing represents thinking.**

The writing of different cultures will reflect the differences in thinking patterns used in those cultures（Figure 2）.

What is the difference between the two thinking patterns?

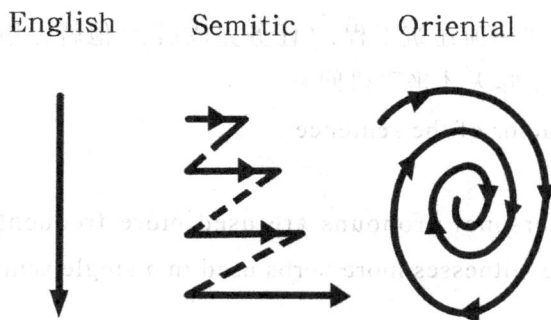

English   Semitic   Oriental

Figure2   Two thinking patterns

The English thinking pattern may be characterized by the following key words: linear, straightforward and direct presentation. However, the Chinese thinking pattern may be featured by other key characteristics: circular, stating positions in a roundabout or implicit way, definitive summary and the habit that statements of main arguments are delayed till the end.

If we say the thinking patterns are the very elements behind languages, cultures may be the very things behind thinking patterns. The English and Chinese cultures are characterized by "I" culture and "We" culture respectively.

"I" culture

① Each human is a rational being capable of making well-reasoned choices.

② Characteristics and differences are valued.

③ Communication is always linear and one way from sender to receiver.

④ Meaning is in the messages created by the sender.

⑤ Messages are detailed, clear-cut, and definite.

"We" culture

Social order and harmony, proper human relationships are valued.

① Group identity, uniformity and conformity are appreciated.

② The use of indirect communication is accepted as normative.

③ Meaning is in the interpretation, emphasizing sensibility to capture the under-the-surface symbols and to understand the implicit meaning.

（3）Conclusion

The relation of language surface structure and thinking pattern and culture may be drawn as follows（Figure 3）:

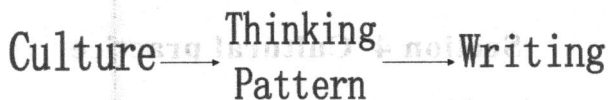

$$Culture \longrightarrow \underset{Pattern}{Thinking} \longrightarrow Writing$$

Figure3 "Language-thinking-culture" relation

In management, communication ability belongs to the domain of leadership, which is an important soft skill containing knowing the self and others, inspiring others etc. In many universities in the west, ICC course has been an optimal class for business schools in top universities.

We are now working in a global village where people from different backgrounds may work in the same team, especially in multinational companies. Even though you are not expected to work together with foreigners, you will definitely work with many guys with different or even contradictory values from yours. (west vs. east, north vs. south, dialects, localities, genders, majors, etc.)

College students need to search a lot of foreign literature in a fixed domain, which also calls for the ability of intercultural communication.Graduates are required to attend international academic conferences, which needs the ability of communicating with foreign experts and colleagues, too.

Intercultural competence is also widely employed in our life, traveling, entertainment, too.

Therefore, after so many years of learning the English language, we must turn from the language to culture to improve ICC effect.

By the way, in terms of the study of communication between different cultures, there are several different paradigms and hereby several different terms, for example, cross-cultural communication, intercultural communication and transcultural communication. This coursebook is going to adopt diversified and converged perspectives, thus not going to make a fine differentiation of these terms. Cross-cultural communication, intercultural communication and transcultural communication are used alternatively and synonymously.

Section 4 Cultural practice

Cultural practice :Discussion and role-play

You are a staff in a joint venture in Beijing. You are going to pick up an important foreign customer David (a CEO) of your company on the behalf of your boss Joseph for he is suddenly engaged in an urgent meeting.

Please work out this business airport pickup in an appropriate way. Your oral activity may start from the international arrival of the Terminal 3 of Beijing Capital International Airport (BCIA).

It is kindly reminded that this is not an artificial conversation in middle-school oral English class, but a real ICC practice!

Section 5 Derivative development

1.Film watching

Please watch the movie *Gua Sha* [1] (《刮痧》,2001)and tried to work out a short intercultural analysis of the story of the movie. In your analysis, can you give some suggestions on how to improve the communication effect based on the story of the film?

2.Extended reading

Culture

Culture is the social behavior and the collection of norms found in human societies. Culture is considered a central concept in anthropology, encompassing the range of phenomena that are transmitted through social learning in human societies. Cultural universals are found in all human societies; these include expressive forms like art, music, dance, ritual, religion, and technologies like tool usage, cooking, shelter, and clothing. The concept of material culture covers the physical expressions of culture, such as technology, architecture and art, whereas the immaterial aspects of culture such as principles of social organization (including practices of political organization and social institutions), mythology, philosophy, literature (both

---

1　《刮痧》是由郑晓龙执导，由梁家辉、蒋雯丽、朱旭主演，于2001年出品的一部电影。该片以中医刮痧疗法产生的误会为主线，讲述了华人在国外由于东西方文化的冲突而陷入种种困境，最后又因人们的诚恳与爱心，困境最终被冲破的故事。

written and oral), and science comprise the intangible cultural heritage of a society.

We believe that culture can be understood roughly into the following main dimensions:

① History and world view, including values, beliefs and religion

② Socialization, including education, enculturation and personal growth

③ Language

④ Non-verbal communication

...

The concept of "culture" in intercultural studies

Although culture may cover too many elements in the study of culture by itself, the concept of "culture" in intercultural studies is always referring to two major pairs, namely, objective culture and subjective culture, mainstream culture and subculture.

Objective culture refers to the social institution and artificial derivatives. Subjective culture refers to the psychological characteristics of culture, including conception, value and thinking mode. It must be reminded that subjective culture plays an overwhelmingly important role in intercultural communication. Intercultural communication experts such as Cusher and Brislin believe that a large amount of misunderstandings happen in the layer of subjective culture. Indeed, when people are communicating with people with different backgrounds, many obstacles, even conflicts in communication are originated from the sharp contrast in value system and thinking mode. Therefore, to systematically study the subjective culture will, to a great extent, will facilitate our competence in intercultural communication.

Mainstream culture refers to the culture manifested or controlled by the dominant groups. Subculture refers to minor culture features manifested by a small number of people or groups. In the United States of America, the mainstream culture is still the white culture, represented by White Anglo-

Saxon Protestants (WASP), but Asian-American, Latin-American and some other subcultures are also noticed in the country. We should be clear that the existence of the subculture does not deny the predominance of mainstream culture. However, with the popularization of the Internet, mobile Internet and social media, an increasingly number of subcultures become to attract distracted audiences and users in the network, which caused the appearance of many cyber subcultures.

In the field of intercultural communication, it is of great significance to draw a distinction between mainstream culture and subculture because people tend to draw a common and collective "picture" for all the people in one nation or one region regardless of the subtle differences inside the nation and the region. We always hear the stereotype that the Chinese nation belongs to the collective culture whereas the western culture is characterized as individualism. This stereotype may be true in a general sense. However, this may cause a phenomenon of cultural absolutism, which will of course hinder an effective communication interculturally. For the author of this book, we hold that growing attention should be paid to the diversification of different cultures, including subcultures and minor cultures.

A dominant culture exists in every society, but that collective is not monolithic. That is, within the dominant culture are numerous co-cultures and specialized cultures. We believe that the best way to identify these groups is with the term co-culture when discussing groups or social communities exhibiting perceptions, values, beliefs, communicative behaviors, and social practices that are sufficiently different as to distinguish them from other groups and communities and from the dominant culture. Co-cultures may share many of the characteristics of the dominant culture, but their members also exhibit distinct and unique patterns of communication. Co-cultural affiliation can be based on ethnic heritage, gender, age cohort, sexual preference, or other criteria.

Some important and commonly-acknowledged conclusions about

intercultural communication summarized by Chinese professor Hu Wenzhong [1] who advocates a multi-disciplinary study of intercultural communication.

① Culture exists everywhere, covering values, beliefs, thinking modes, literature, arts, music, architecture, verbal and nonverbal symbols. Culture is often unconscious; therefore, it is generally acquired in school education on one hand and in family and society on the other hand. For many people, such notions as values, beliefs, customs and behavioral modes are not deservedly conscious.

② Culture has both the characteristic of uniformity and the feature of continuity. Cultures diverse from nations to nations; therefore, it is full of variables. Every nation has a traditionally uniformed and collective culture which Benedict calls continuity. However, delicate differences also exist within a due nation or a social group or individuals. Subcultures are witnessed in every nation and country. The quickly-developed information and communication technology (ICT) makes human living and communicative modes modify rapidly.

③ Due to the fact of cultural unconsciousness, people tend to utilize their own culture as a criterion to judge another culture during cultural encounter, which will easily cause preconceivedculturalbias and ethnocentricity. It is of due difficulty to eliminate this influence of ethnocentricity. That is the reason why many people feel uncomfortable and unsatisfactory when encountering a new, especially a totally unfamiliar culture. In serious situations, that will even cause a culture shock for the people involved.

④ In order to improve cultural acculturation, it is of due significance to experience a transfer of standpoints from a low layer to a high layer. Hanvey [2] holds that intercultural sensitivity representation could be divided into four

---

1　胡文仲. 跨文化交际教学与研究 [M]. 北京：外语教学与研究出版社，2015：27-31.
2　Hanvey, R. G. 1979. Cross-cultural awareness. In Elise C. Smith and Louise Fiber Luce, eds. Toward Internationalism: Reading in Cross-cultural Communication. Cambridge, Mass.: Newbury House Publishers, Inc. Page 46-55.

phases: (1) identifying apparent and superficial cultural features; people will feel curious and alien in this phase. (2) identifying delicate and meaningful, virtually different elements from mother cultural features; people will feel unbelievable and unacceptable in this phase. (3) accepting similar or different cultures after a theoretical analysis. (4) sensing the other culture from the perspective of the other. An effect of empathy will be reached and every element in the target culture could be accepted based on being familiar with the target culture.

⑤ Experts design many ways to test and improve people's intercultural communicative competence. Intercultural Sensitivity (ICS) scale are hereby designed to meet this demand. Chen and Starosta [1] designed their ICS based on five factors, namely, communicative participation scale, difference identification scale, communicative confidence scale and communicative concentration scale. The scale of Chen and Starosta is of great influence among researchers in intercultural communication.

The concept of "communication" in intercultural studies

Similar as culture, communication itself also covers a lot. The concept of communication is a multi-dimensional notion which is used in many studies.

In mathematical communication, the term is regarded a linear process from the sender to the receiver mechanically according to Claude Elwood Shannon, who is an American mathematician, electrical engineer, and cryptographer known as "the father of information theory". Shannon is noted for having founded information theory with a landmark paper, *A Mathematical Theory of Communication* published in 1948. Shannon's diagram of a general communications system, which shows the process that produces a message, is always introduced in the social and humanity sciences study as an important reference (Figure 4).

1　Chen, G. M. & Starosta W. J. The Development and Validation of the Intercultural Communication Sensitivity. Human Communication. 2000(3).

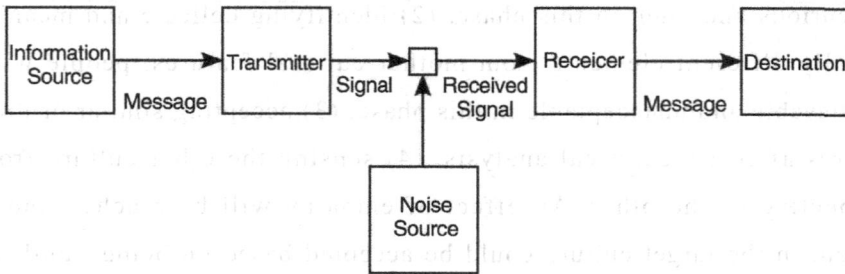

Figure 4　Shannon's diagram of a general communications system

In semiotics, communication is the process of symbolization and using symbols to share with others about our interior status. In journalism and communication areas, communication is a process of encoding and decoding, which is apparently originated from classical telecommunication technology. However, it is widely-acknowledged that communication in the layer of intercultural communication is not a simple message sending or receiving. It includes a dynamic negotiation and co-construction of meanings. If we use the term in telecommunication technology, the "noise" and "feedback" would be much more different than pure technical encoding and decoding.

In summary, intercultural communication means to build a meaningful negotiation and construction between different people and groups. It is a dynamic process of mutual communication and mutual influence, covering face-to-face interpersonal communication, group communication, mass communication, etc. A broad intercultural communication, of course, includes not only the communication between different nations and countries, but also the communication within a nation or a country, for example, between different ethnic groups or between different subcultures in a nation. However, in this course and in this textbook, we try to focus more attention on the intercultural communication between different nations, countries and cultures.

Three recommended scholars who contribute to the field of classical intercultural communication studies:

① **Bronisław Kasper Malinowski** (1884—1942) was an anthropologist whose writings on ethnography, social theory, and field research were a lasting influence on the discipline of anthropology.

② **Edward Twitchell Hall, Jr.** (1914—2009) was an American anthropologist and cross-cultural researcher. He is remembered for developing the concept of proxemics and exploring cultural and social cohesion, and describing how people behave and react in different types of culturally defined personal space. His famous book on intercultural communication is *The Silent Language* (1959).

③ **Eugene A. Nida** (1914—2011) was a linguist who developed the dynamic-equivalence Bible-translation theory and one of the founders of the modern discipline of translation studies.

Knowing more cultures about ourselves (1): the family culture

Before we introduce ourselves to the others, the first and foremost thing is to have a correct and profound cognition of ourselves. In the ends of all the eight chapters, we add some basic knowledge of ourselves which are divided into eight sections, namely, the family culture, the food culture, the education culture, the marriage culture, the medical culture, the art culture, the consumption culture and the cyber culture respectively. We hope to help both audiences from other cultures and ourselves to have a better cognition of Chinese cultures. During these parts, the author of this book not only summarizes the traditional essence of these sections, but employs a diachronic perspective and includes the up-to-date changes.

Our family cultures

In the history, China has been in the period of feudal society for over 2,000 years. This time duration is extremely long and rare in the whole world, thus laying an indelible influence on the family culture values for Chinese.

The Chinese feudal society is characterized by the centralization of authority, which leads to a feudal patriarchal system combining family power and political power together. The emperors, the fathers and the husbands are of superior positions in the society. The principle of hierarchy (social order) is overtly and covertly embedded into people's mind as a common norm. The popularity of Confucianism, to a certain extent, aggravate this tendency. The authoritarian policy is closely associated with social hierarchical orders. However, this value system is not completely disadvantageous. For example, the elder people are highly respected in China. As is said in one famous folk saying, the old person in a family is a treasure.

The system of strict social hierarchical orders is manifested in various domains.

Firstly, the overestimation on the male while underestimating the female is an overwhelmingly dominant in many places in China, even now. The sense of superiority of men and the inferiority of women are manifested bluntly in the formation of some Chinese characters such as "奸" (meaning wicked) and "妒" (meaning jealous) and folk sayings such as "女子无才便是德" (meaning that a woman without talent is virtuous). It is a shame that even now, some people with male chauvinism also believe in this principle deeply. Some companies have a favor of male employees in job-hunting even though they do not mark this evidently in their job advertisements. The road of the total equality is still filled with twists and turns.

Secondly, we pay more attention to the equality in marriage. A marriage between families of equal social rank is always preferred. The story of Cinderella in which the ordinary girl marries the prince is rare to be heard in the Chinese history. Surprisingly, the marriage partners are always selected by the parents of the brides and grooms. Freedom in love and marriage has been inspired after the foundation of the People's Republic of China. However, this marriage customs do not completely disappear in many places. In the modern society, people also judge and assess a ready marriage person, normally men, by their social status, materialistic foundation, etc.

Thirdly, it is almost impossible for the children to pose a challenge to the authority of fathers. The Chinese society is famous for its highly-developed self-efficient agriculture. A father farmer in the agricultural world is considered an experienced and sophisticated example who can help and guide the children in all dimensions. In traditional Chinese family, parents will make many, if not all, decisions, for their children, who, to a certain extent, lose their freedom for individualistic choice.

Fourth, in terms of the relation between the couple, the wife is always in the inferior position and subordinated to the authority of the husband. The husband-wife relation, in some cases, is not as important as father-son relation in the family. Even now, the husband is deservedly considered as the breadwinner to support the family in the mind of some Chinese. However, the role of wife has greatly improved in current society. They begin to study, work, shoulder the same responsibility and hold up half the sky as the husbands.

Fifth, when the communication scale is beyond the nuclear family, the differential effects by sequential patterns is common. According to Professor Fei Xiaotong, whether to implement the social communication and the frequency of social communication are closely related much sequential factors such as blood relation, geographical relation, academic relation and social ranks.

Sixth, the Chinese family culture emphasizes the group identity while western family gives more attention to the development of individualism. Face, or the honor, of the family is of great significance in many areas in China.

However, stepping into the modernization and post-modernization society, greatly spurred by the information and communication technology, we also witness several notable changes to the traditional family values. With the emergence of post-figurative culture, cultural repaying becomes increasingly common in modern society. Many young people in China teach their parents how to use mobile phones, social media and mobile payment. The authority of fathers in agricultural period hereby collapsed because their experience in agricultural and industrial phases is no longer used under the tendency of the society of information and artificial intelligence.

Furthermore, the convenience of transportation aggravates the mobility of the society, not only in China, but also in the whole globe. Therefore, traditional time value and space value are reconstructed. We can easily access to the Internet, mobile Internet, high-speed Wi-Fi almost everywhere. This ubiquitous status causes the scene that people will never be "offline" if they want. In a highly-mobilized modern China, people are separated from the family members due to the work and study. But they are connected on the Net via various social network sites and instant message sending systems.

Our country has been accessed to the Internet for more than 25 years since 1990s. It is noticed that the Internet does not change our family cultures fundamentally and many customs still are prevailing now in real China and virtual China. It is believed that a deep understanding of our family cultures will definitely be beneficial to intercultural communication practice.

第二章　重建巴别塔：言语交流
Chapter Two
Rebuilding Babel Tower: Verbal Communication

Section 1 Lead-in

1.Question

① Chinese Proficiency Test (HSK), an international standardized test of Chinese language proficiency, assesses non-native Chinese speakers' abilities in using the Chinese language in their daily, academic and professional lives. Compared with popular langauge proficiency tests such as The Test of English as a Foreign Language (TOEFL), International English Language Testing System (IELTS) and College English Test (CET), which test would be more difficult for non-native language learners?

② Which translation is more difficult, English-Chinese translation or Chinese-English translation? Why?

③ Have you ever noticed that it is difficult even impossible to translate some Chinese words, phrases or sentences into English? Give us some examples.

④ Have you ever heard the story of the Babel tower?

2.Case

Li Hongzhang, one of the top officials in the Qing Dynasty, was invited to visit the United States. He was warmly welcomed. One day, Li was hosting a banquet for the American officials in a popular restaurant. As the banquet started, according to the Chinese custom, Li stood up and said, （今天承蒙各位光临，不胜荣幸。我们略备粗馔，聊表寸心，没有什么可口的东西，不成敬意，请大家多多包涵……）"I am very happy to have all of you here today. Though these dishes are coarse and not delicious and good enough to show my respect for you, I hope you will enjoy them...".

The next day, the English version of his words was shown in the local newspaper. To his shock, the restaurant owner flew into a rage. He thought it was an insult to his restaurant and insisted that Li should show him the evidence of which dish was not well-made and which dish was not delicious. Otherwise, Li intentionally damaged the reputation of the restaurant, and he should apologize to the restaurant. All the fuss made Li rather embarrassed.

What Li said is just some formulaic polite expression common in China; almost all Chinese people know this and could be heared that nearly everywhere. As far as the literary meaning is concerned, Li's words are inappropriate, but they do convey the meaning of respect. The language form is different from its content, which is a phenomenon easily noticed in the Eastern culture. If Li used another linguistic way of presenting his modesty, the effect could be much more different. Here comes an interesting question of the relation between language and culture. This belongs to the domain of the study of verbal communication in intercultural communication, the theme of this chapter.

Section 2 Theory preparation

1.Theory preparation: the Sapir – Whorf hypothesis

The relation between language and culture is always one of the most interesting topics among various scholars represented by linguists. It has long been recognized that language is an essential and important part of a given culture and that the impact of culture upon a given language is something intrinsic and indispensable. Sociolinguists and anthropologists naturally are more interested in the relationship between language, culture and society, among whom Edward Sapir and Benjamin Lee Whorf are overwhelmingly renowned for their research—the Sapir–Whorf hypothesis.

The Sapir–Whorf hypothesis holds that the structure of a language affects its speakers' world view or cognition. This principle is often defined to include two versions: the strong hypothesis and the weak hypothesis:

The strong version says that language determines thought and that linguistic categories limit and determine cognitive categories.

The weak version says that linguistic categories and usage only influence thought and decisions.

Although this is a hypothesis, it does show that language is one of the most important symbols in culture. Therefore, we will mainly talk about verbal communication (communication using languages) in chapter two. In this chapter, we highlight the importance of verbal skills in communication and study translation from the intercultural perspective.

Section 3 Detailed analysis

1.Daily verbal communication

Chinese and English are different in daily verbal communication in greeting, addressing, conversation topics, etc.

Greetings in English:

① Good morning/afternoon/ evening.

② How are you?

③ How are things going?

④ How are you getting on?

⑤ How are things (with you)?

⑥ How's everything?

⑦ How's life?

⑧ Hello. / Hey. /Hi.

⑨ What's up?

⑩ What is the weather like today?

Greetings in Chinese:

① Where are you going?（你 / 您这是要去哪儿？）

② Where have you been? (你／您去哪儿了？)

③ Have you had your meal? (你／您吃了吗？)

The contrast of these cases in greetings shows that Chinese people and western people diverse in choose greetings. Western people may take it for granted that Chinese have a special interest into people's privacy, which will consequently cause some inconvenience and unhappiness in the intercultural communication. Indeed, Chinese prefer to a long and fixed relation with the people known. The greetings always happen among the familiar. Therefore, what is habitual and natural in one culture may be considered an intrusion into people's privacy in another culture. "When in Rome, do as the Romans do" seems a feasible way, but it is firmly suggested that more attention should be paid to the concrete context in which the communication is happening. An inflexible and mechanical utilization will cause an improper communication, too.

Addressing in Chinese in public:

①虚拟中国人名 1：张小龙,男,40 岁,某公司总经理。

张总、张先生……

②虚拟中国人名 2：王达蔓,女,50 岁,某高校党委书记。

王书记、达蔓书记……

Addressing in English in public:

① Fictitious English name 1: Steven Plant, male, 35, a CEO of a company.

Mr. Plant / Steven / ……

② Fictitious English name 2: Amanda Lewis, female, 50, a professor.

Ms. Lewis / Amanda / Professor Lewis / ……

"Surname + given name", "surname + title", "surname + career" are commonly noticed in China. However, English words seldom put titles or positions in addressing except such titles as professors and doctors. "Given name + middle name + surname" are normal. If it is not in a very formal occasion, addressing the given name itself is quite habitual in western countries.

Nevertheless, western people do use "title + surname/ full name" in addressing very important person (VIP).

① Ambassador（大使）

② Duke（公爵）

③ Marquis / Marquess（侯爵）

④ Count / Earl（伯爵）

⑤ Viscount（子爵）

⑥ Baron（男爵）

⑦ Sir（爵士）

Furthermore, in order to show respect, the following ways are also employed to address people in special occasions, for example, in the opening or closing ceremonies:

① Your Honor, title / Mr. / Ms. + full name/ surname,

② Your Excellency, title / Mr. / Ms. + full name/ surname,

③ Your Highness, title / Mr. / Ms. + full name/ surname,

④ Your Majesty, title / Mr. / Ms. + full name/ surname,

To be sure, generally, Chinese people lay great emphasis on blood relation, geographical relation, academic relation, people's title, people's social status, etc. Compared with this group identity orientation, western people attach more importance to the individual self. It is generally not a tradition to call a person by his or her social status or position except addressing doctors and professors in western environment.

There are also some differences in initiating a conversation topic between two cultures.

Common conversation topics in Chinese:

① Age

② Money/Salary

③ Health

④ Family

⑤ Marriage status

⑥ Place of birth

Common conversation topics in English:

① Hobbies

② Holidays

③ The weather

④ Jobs

⑤ Films/Books

⑥ A local or national event

As we say in the previous part of greeting differences, western ideas of privacy are somewhat different from those of the Chinese. Honestly speaking, Chinese ways of initiating topics generally have no intentions of being hostile or offensive. Chinese people try to show their concern to shorten the distance between people in this way. Phrases like "put on more clothes and drink plenty of water to recover quickly" have protective, parental overtones, and hence may sound inappropriate to westerners. We should bear in mind the saying that a casual remark sounds significant to a suspicious listener. We should be more careful in daily verbal communication because a good beginning in the daily communication is half the battle of the whole communication. The effect of intercultural communication, to a certain extent, is not dependent on what you say, but how you say it.

2.Intercultural verbal translation

If the two parties in the communication speak different languages, they will resort to translation for help. Therefore, translation and interpretation of culturally-loaded words, phrases and sentences are of great significance for the people who intend to improve intercultural communication competence. Different from daily verbal communication which could be easily noticed and hereby improved, it is difficult to enhance intercultural verbal translation. In this part, we will analyze the differences in the bilingual cultural translation and provide several feasible strategies for learners.

First, let us have a glance of a Chinese poem and its translation.

寻隐者不遇

贾岛（唐）

松下问童子,言师采药去。

只在此山中,云深不知处。

Seeking Hermit [1]

When I questioned your pupil, under a pine-tree.

"My teacher," he answered, "went for herbs,

But toward which corner of the mountain,

How can I tell, through all these clouds?"

It could be easily noticed that the English version of translation differs significantly from the original Chinese poem. This single comparison shows that the Chinese language lacks strict grammatical prescriptions, thus having a natural sense of being poetic. The language of time and space is different from that in English and the time and the space are open for readers (decoders). Therefore, Chinese poems endow us with abundant space for imaginative reading on one hand. On the other, they reflect the Chinese way of observing, sensing and interpreting the outside world. In this sense, a good intercultural person must learn translation; a good translator must acquire intercultural competence.

3.Correspondence between Chinese and English

（1）Total correspondence (not common):

e.g.,

一箭双雕 to kill two birds with one stone

趁热打铁 Strike while the iron is hot.

祸不单行 Misfortunes never come singly.

One eye witness is better than ten hearsays. 百闻不如一见。

to have one foot in the grave 风烛残年

papertiger 纸老虎

---

1 秦洪武、王克非，“英汉比较与翻译”，外语教学与研究出版社，北京：2012. 第209页.

（2）Asymmetrical correspondence

e.g.,

龙（中文）：真龙天子、望子成龙、龙凤呈祥

Dragon (English): fierce, violent

（English）When she's angry, she becomes a dragon.

（中文）火一上来她就成了一个母夜叉。

（中文）望子成龙

（English）hope to see one's children have a bright future

（3）Zero correspondence (Cultural vacancy)

Cultural vacancy refers to the phenomenon that some culturally-loads may vacant in other cultures due to historical, geographical, political, social and economic reasons. Such Chinese as "粮票", "下乡", "旗袍" will be difficult for westerners for the lack of context. Chinese always prefer the number "eight" which means "good luck". Therefore, liberal translation and transliteration will always be used in dealing with cultural vacancy.

e.g.,

（中文）这是七月下旬,合中国旧历的三伏,一年最热的时候。

（English）It was toward the end of July of the Chinese lunar calendar, equivalent to the "**san-fu**" period of the lunar calendar — **the hottest days of the year**.

（中文）说曹操,曹操到。

（English）Speak of the devil,and he appears.

4.Literal translation（直译）

Literal translation, direct translation, or word-for-word translation is the rendering of text from one language to another one word at a time with or without conveying the sense of the original whole. Rhetoric is often used in a passage to make the passage more vividly. Therefore, literal translation would be an optimal choice because it retains the rhetoric of the original. Since literal translation keeps the original grammatical form of the source language, it, to a large extent, keeps the structure, the metaphor, and hereby the cultural loaded in the original form.

e.g.,

(English) The love that lasts longest is the love that is never returned.

（中文）

①最长久的爱是不求回报的爱。（直译）

②永恒的爱不求回报。（意译）

③真爱无悔。（意译）

(English) God helps those who help themselves.

（中文）上帝帮助那些自己帮助自己的人。/ 天助自助者。/ 自助者天助之。

（中文）秀才不出门，全知天下事。

(English) Without stepping outside his gate, the scholar knows all the wide world's affairs.

（中文）子龙见妇人身穿缟素，有倾国倾城之色。

(English) Zilong saw that the woman was dressed entirely in white silk and her beauty was such as to overthrow cities and ruin states.

5.Liberal translation / free translation（意译）

Free translation is also called liberal translation, which does not adhere strictly to the form or word order of the original. Free translation is a skill of translation according to the meaning of the original, without pay attention or paying little attention to the details, translation would be more fluent and natural in the target language and culture. Compared with literal translation, free translation needs to focus the attention on how to conceptualize the symbolic meaning in the original texts. Borrowing, replacing are common skills noticed in free translation. However, there is no absolute distinction between literal translation skill and free translation skill. Two methods are used alternatively in translation. Free translation may be defined as a supplementary means to mainly convey the meaning and spirit of the original without trying to reproduce its sentence patterns or figures of speech. And it is adopted only when and where it is impossible for translators to do literal translation.

e.g.,

(English) Two is company, but three is none.

（中文）两个和尚抬水吃，三个和尚无水吃。

(English) Among the blind the one-eyed man is king.

（中文）山中没老虎，猴子称霸王。

(English) A hedge between keeps friendship green.

（中文）君子之交淡如水。

（中文）新官上任三把火。

(English) New broom sweeps clean.

（中文）己有过，勿正人。

(English) People who live in glass houses should not throw stones.

（中文）王婆卖瓜，自卖自夸。

(English) Every cook praises his own broth.

（中文）今年高考他又名落孙山了。

(English) This year he failed again in the entrance examinations for college students.

It must be noticed that the distinction between literal translation and liberal translation is not always clear-cut. We should study translation strategies both synchronically and diachronically. With the acceleration of globalization, a growing number of Chinese people begin to sense and celebrate foreign festivals such as St. Valentine's Day and western readers and audiences may notice the significance of "龙" for Chinese. Such terms as "Dragon-boat festival" becomes feasible and acceptable in many countries. Many foreigners will also join in the celebration in the coming of the Year of the Dragon of the Chinese lunar calendar. Therefore, our translation strategies should be more flexible and proper in accordance with different contexts. A careful preparation before intercultural communication will be of course the best strategy to avoid embarrassment. The author of this books puts forwards that a creative integration of both literal translation and free translation based on comprehension ("creation upon comprehension" strategy) could be used in intercultural translation to avoid Chinglish（Chinese English）or Euronese（Europ Chinese）.

e.g.,

包子 —— steamed bun with stuff / stuffed steamed bun

宫保鸡丁 —— diced chicken with cucumbers, carrots and peanuts

涮羊肉 —— quickly-boiled mutton slices in hotpot

Some commonly-acknowledged Chinese / English proverbs and their correspondent equivalents are listed as follows:

※ Practice makes perfect.（熟能生巧。）

※ Where there is a will, there is a way.（有志者，事竟成。）

※ Time and tide wait for no man.（时不我待。）

※ There is no royal road to learning.（学无坦途。）

※ A good beginning is half the battle.（良好的开始是成功的一半。）

※ Out of sight, out of mind.（眼不见心不烦。）

※ Fast bind, fast find.（锁得牢，丢不了。）

※ No pains, no gains.（种瓜得瓜，种豆得豆。）

※ Nothing ventured, nothing gained.（不入虎穴，焉得虎子。）

※ No rose without a thorn.（哪有玫瑰不带刺。）

※ No context, no text.（不要断章取义。）

※ No sweet without sweat.（先苦后甜 / 苦尽甘来。）

※ No dish suits all tastes.（众口难调。）

※ Once bitten, twice shy.（一朝被蛇咬，十年怕井绳。）

※ A stitch in time saves nine.（小洞不补，大洞吃苦。）

※ All that glitters is not gold.（闪光的并不都是金子。）

※ He who plays with fire gets burned.（玩火自焚。）

※ It's no use crying over spoiled milk.（覆水难收。）

※ A bird in hand is worth two in the bush.（一鸟在手，胜过两鸟在林。）

※ A rolling stone gathers no moss.（滚石不生苔。）

※ The early bird catches the worm.（笨鸟先飞。）

※ A man is known by the company he keeps.（观其交友，知其为人。）

※ A fall into the pit, a gain in your wit.（吃一堑，长一智。）

※ A new broom sweeps clean.（新官上任三把火。）

※ Spare the rod and spoil the child.（玉不琢不成器。）

※ You can't have your cake and eat it too. (鱼与熊掌不可兼得。)

※ It is a sin to steal a pin. (勿以恶小而为之,勿以善小而不为。)

※ Kill two birds with one stone. (一箭双雕。)

※ Haste makes waste. (欲速则不达。)

※ Constant dripping wears the stone. (水滴石穿。)

※ Rome is not built in one day. (冰冻三尺,非一日之寒。)

※ It never rains but it pours. (不雨则已,一下倾盆。)

Section 4 Cultural practice

In-class translation practice (Chinese to English translation)

六十整岁望七十岁如攀高山。不料七十岁居然过了。又想八十岁是难于上青天,可望而不可即了。岂知八十岁又过了。老汉今年八十二矣。这是照传统算法,务虚不务实。现在不是提倡尊重传统吗?老年多半能悟道。孔子说"天下有道"。老子说"道可道"。《圣经》说"太初有道"。佛教说"邪魔外道"。我老了,不免胡思乱想,胡说八道,自觉悟出一条真理:老年是广阔天地,是可以大有作为的。七十岁开始可以诸事不做而拿退休金,不愁没有一碗饭吃,自由自在,自得其乐。要看书可以随便乱翻。金庸、梁羽生、克里斯蒂、松本清张,从前哪能拜读?现在可以了。随看随忘,便扔在一边。无忧无虑,无人打扰,不必出门而自有天地。真是无限风光在老年。

Section 5 Derivative development

1.Film watching

Please watch the movie *Crazy Rich Asians* [1] (《摘金奇缘》,2018) and tried to work out a short intercultural analysis of the story of the movie.

1　*Crazy Rich Asians* is a 2018 American romantic comedy film directed by Jon M. Chu, from a screenplay by Peter Chiarelli and Adele Lim, based on the 2013 novel of the same name by Kevin Kwan. The film stars Constance Wu, Henry Golding, Gemma Chan, Lisa Lu, Awkwafina, Ken Jeong, and Michelle Yeoh. It follows a Chinese-American professor who travels to meet her boyfriend's family and is surprised to discover they are among the richest in Singapore. This movie has won many awards including the 76th Golden Globe Awards nominations.

Your analysis may be centered on two enlightening questions:

What accounts for the success of the all Asian-cast film?

Do you think that the Asians in the film represent the Chinese culture?

2.Extended reading

（1）Basic understanding of language

Language is an integral part of our life and humanity that too much about it has been taken for granted. At the most basic level, language is a set of shared symbols or signs that a cooperative group of people has mutually agreed to use to help them create meaning. The relation between the selected sign and the agreed meaning is quite often arbitrary.Webster's New World Dictionary offers that language is a means of verbal communication. Dai Weidong and He Zhaoxiong [1] hold that "language is a system of arbitrary vocal symbols used for human communication". It is instrumental in that communicating by speaking or writing is a purposeful act. It is social and conventional in that language is a social semiotic and communication can only take place effectively if all the users share a broad understanding of human interaction including such associated factors as nonverbal cues, motivation, and socio-cultural roles. Language distinguishes us from animals because it is far more sophisticated than any animal communication system. Language variations, including accents, dialects, argots and slangs will all lay an influence on the culture, thus affecting the effect of communication.

（2）Foreignization（异化）and domestication（归化）

If we continue to the discussion of literal translation and free translation, we will come to dispute of foreignization and domestication in intercultural translation. Historically, foreignization and domestication could be the extension of literal translation and free translation respectively, but these concepts also diverse. The pair of literal translation and free translation is centered on how to manipulate forms and meanings in the layer of linguistics.

1　戴炜栋、何兆熊主编，"新编简明语言学教程".上海：上海外语教育出版社，2003：第8页.

However, the pair foreignization and domestication go beyond the linguistic layer; it attaches great importance to factors such as culture and aesthetics.

Foreignization, similar as literal translation, refers to the initiative that translators keep the original language style and culture differences. Foreignization, to a certain extent, is to attract the readers of the target language to the source culture. This method of foreignizing is significant to transmitting ideas, customs, and cultures to the target world. However, it is of due difficulty for the readers who are unfamiliar with the source culture.

Domestication, similar as free translation, refers to domesticating the translation and making it easier to understand for the readers and audiences in the target culture. Translators using domestication must get closer to the target readers and use their readable words, phrases and sentences. Some scholars such as Venuti denounce this method of domesticating. They hold that this way is kind of centralism, forcing translators to give up the original form of the source language and pleasing the target readers.

（3）Untranslatability（翻译的无奈 / 不可译性）

Untranslatability is the property of text or speech for which no equivalent can be found when translated into another language. A text that is untranslatable is considered lexical gap. The term arises when describing the difficulty of achieving the so-called perfect translation. It is based on the notion that there are certain concepts and words that are so interrelated that an accurate translation becomes an impossible task. Some writers have suggested that language carries sacred notions or is intrinsic to national identity. Brian James Baer posits that untranslatability is sometimes seen by nations as proof of the national genius. He quotes Alexandra Jaffe: "When translators talk about untranslatable, they often reinforce the notion that each language has its own 'genius', an 'essence' that naturally sets it apart from all other languages and reflects something of the 'soul' of its culture or people".[1]

1　Baer, Brian James (2015). Translation and the Making of Modern Russian Literature.

（4）The story of Babel Tower

Babel Tower, or the Tower of Babel, is an origin myth meant to explain why the world's peoples speak different languages. According to the story in the Genesis [1], a united humanity in the generations following the Great Flood, speaking a single language and migrating eastward, comes to the land of Shinar. There they agree to build a city and a tower tall enough to reach heaven. God, observing their city and tower, confounds their speech so that they can no longer understand each other, and scatters them around the world. According to the *Bible*, the city received the name "Babel" from the Hebrew word which means to jumble or to confuse. Since it is hard to ascend to the top of the Tower of Babel, this story is always used in translation or intercultural communication to deliver people's beautiful wish to communicate with various people without any obstacles or misunderstandings.

（5）High-context culture and low-context culture

The approach towards the description of culture and communication in terms of high context or low context was proposed by Edward T. Hall in 1976, who organizes cultures by amount of information implied by the setting or context of the communication itself, regardless of the specific words that are spoken. Hall points out that every human being has to face different types of perceptual stimuli in everyday life, such as sights, sounds, smells, tastes, and bodily sensations, etc. It is not possible for us to pay attention and be equally sensitive to all the perceptual stimuli around us. He further argues that one of the basic functions of culture is to provide us with a screen that will divert our attention to the objective world. Therefore, our subjective perception and interpretation of the world is very much influenced by the selection made by the cultural screen, suggesting the important role of cultural context in communication.

---

1 Tips: The Book of Genesis is the first book of the Hebrew Bible (the Tanakh) and the Old Testament.[1] It is divisible into two parts, the Primeval history (chapters 1 – 11) and the Ancestral history (chapters 12 – 50).[2]

In Edward Hall's theory of high-context culture and low-context culture, he believes that any cultural transaction can be basically be divided into two communication systems: high-context and low-context.

High-context cultures can be seen to prefer the use of high-context messages, in which most of the meaning is either implied by the physical setting or presumed to be part of the individual's internationalized beliefs, values, and norms; very little is provided in the coded, explicit, transmitted part of the messages. Hall suggests that people from high-context systems tend to expect more of others to base their communication on common knowledge and mutual understanding. An illustration of high-context communication is the interaction among family members or between people who have maintained a long-term relationship. In such context, people involved in the communication are often able to interpret each other's message without the provision of explicit information. Communication can be based on shared understandings about their relation. Japan and China, for example, are typical examples of high-context culture.

Characteristics of high-context culture:

※Long-term relationships.

※People almost enjoy the same norms or values.

※Strong boundaries—who is accepted as belonging VS. who is considered an "outsider"?

※Dense, intersecting networks and long-term relationships, strong boundaries, relationships more important than tasks.

※Most of the information is in the physical world or individuals.

※Knowledge is situational and relational.

※People value group identity orientation and covert communication codes and maintain a homogenous normative structure with high cultural demand characteristics.

※Decisions and activities focus around personal face-to-face relationships, and often around a central person who has authority.

※A large portion of the message is left unspecified and needs to be accessed through the context.

※People judge what someone is talking about not only by what he is saying but also by the context in which the message occurs.

※In China, the meaning of the world "意思"（yisi, literally referring to "meaning" or "idea"）is very slippery and can be accurately interpreted only when it is used in a due context.

※ 什么意思 —— what meaning / What do you mean?

※ 好意思 —— good meaning

※ 这种话你也好意思说 ——How dare you talk like this!

※ 没意思 —— no meaning

※ 意思意思 —— little meaning

Low-context culture means that the mass of the information is vested in the explicit code. In low-context cultures, people prefer to use low-context messages, in which the majority of the information is explicitly presented in language in communication. Low-context cultures include German, Swedish, European American, and English cultures. In low-context cultures, the population is less homogeneous and therefore tends to compartmentalize interpersonal contacts. In low-context cultures, the verbal message contains most of the information and very little is embedded in the context or the participants.

Characteristics of low-context culture:

※More interpersonal connections of shorter duration.

※People enjoy different subcultures.

※Loose, wide networks, shorter term, compartmentalized relationships, task more important than relationship.

※Most of the information is in the transmitted message.

※People value individual orientation and overt communication codes and maintain a heterogeneous normative structure with low cultural demand characteristics.

※Messages are expected to be explicit and specific.

※People judge what someone is talking about mainly by what he is saying.

※Knowledge is more than transferable.

※Task-centered. Decisions and activities focus around what needs to be done, division of responsibilities.

※More knowledge is above the waterline—explicit, consciously organized.

(6) Knowing more cultures about ourselves (2): the food culture

Before we introduce ourselves to the others, the first and foremost thing is to have a correct and profound cognition of ourselves. In the ends of all the eight chapters, we add some basic knowledge of ourselves which are divided into eight sections, namely, the family culture, the food culture, the education culture, the marriage culture, the medical culture, the art culture, the consumption culture and the cyber culture respectively. We hope to help both audiences from other cultures and ourselves to have a better cognition of Chinese cultures. During these parts, the author of this book not only summarizes the traditional essence of these sections, but employs a diachronic perspective and includes the up-to-date changes.

(7) Our food cultures

"Food is the first necessity of the people" is a famous Chinese old saying, which reflects that Chinese have had paid much attention to food since the ancient times. The importance of food in people's daily life in China can be seen in the way they send greetings to each other: "Have you eaten?", which is far away from the way people greet in western countries and has been seen as a characteristic of Chinese culture. Staple food in China generally includes rice, wheat, buckwheat, corn, potato, sweet potato, beans and varieties of vegetables.

Chinese restaurants can be found easily in the whole globe with the footsteps of moving diligent Chinese. Many foreigners began to pay their attention to the Chinese culture via the food.

Generally, eight cuisines are renowned in China for their special ways of cooking and different features of tastes, namely, Sichuan cuisine, Cantonese cuisine, Shandong cuisine, Jiangsu cuisine, Zhejiang cuisine, Anhui cuisine, Fujian cuisine and Hunan cuisine. The cuisines provided in Chinese restaurants normally belong to these styles.

Advanced agricultural ability and vast territory provide diversified ingredients and seasonings for Chinese food.

Therefore, the first characteristic of the Chinese cuisine is the diversity of food sources and cooking techniques. The Chinese chefs are both classical and creative, who are proficient in cooking, boiling and frying by using different components in a mixed way. The frying techniques could also be further divided into pan-frying, deep-frying, spicy-frying, clear-frying and soup-frying. For example, the famous Chinese cuisine "满汉全席" (a full and formal feast in banquet, combining Manchurian and Chinese delicacies) contains 108 dishes with splendid delicacies. Some people may criticize for the overcooking technique and extravagant waste in a sense. However, this is an important part of the Chinese food culture and an important way of showing their hospitality.

The second characteristic of the Chinese cuisine is delicacy. The Chinese eaters pay attention to not only the taste, but also the aroma and the color of the food. It takes many years for an apprentice to grow into a chef in a restaurant. To a certain extent, to be a good chef in Chinese food requires not only techniques, but also some talents in food, and some artistic senses.

The third characteristic of the Chinese cuisine is an emphasis on the main food. People in the north generally take more wheat products, especially steamed bun and noodles as their main food while people in south China take more rice products. In the history of China, the proportion of meat is little compared with that the consumption of wheat, rice and vegetables largely due to the difference between nomadic groups and agricultural citizens. Even now, people tend to eat more vegetables than meat. A dish with too much meat is not the option for many Chinese. Chinese cabbages, potatoes and radishes are always seen in ordinary families. To a certain extent, the Chinese people pay attention to the balance of the food taken, which is very similar as the balance of yin and yang (the two opposing principles in nature according to the Chinese philosophy) in the Chinese culture. The Chinese people tend to keep a balance of the meat volume and vegetable volume. If they have taken much meat, they will eat more vegetables and fruits, to take more tea to keep a balance rather than taking tablets of vitamins which is the habit for many Americans.

The fourth characteristic of the Chinese cuisine is an association between food and traditional Chinese medicine (TCM). Many food in Chinese cuisine are endowed with the function to preserving health and nourishing life. For the Chinese food culture, there is no fine and clear distinction between food and medicine. Dietetic invigoration is of great significance in Chinese people's mind. A combination of medical therapy and diet is always recommended by TCM specialists.

Chinese eaters will use chopsticks, normally made by bamboo or wood, in most times. Spoon is also provided for the kids or for drinking soups. Since Chinese do not have the tradition of individual serving, when dining in Chinese restaurants now, a pair of public chopsticks will always be used in the dish for people to pick up food and people may use their own pair chopsticks in eating in their own plates. Children in China are always educated to respect the dining table, dishes, chopsticks and spoons. They are not allowed to make noises or point to other people by chopsticks.

As is mentioned before, Chinese people will provide more amount than the necessary amount to show their hospitality to the guests. Furthermore, the host will continue persuading the guest to eat and try more even though the guest may feel full. As is said in the Analects of Confucius, it is with great delight to have friends coming afar. China has a special and long-lasting tradition in reception. The number of dishes, the way of arranging dishes, the direction of dishes, the sitting postures are all emphasized to demonstrate our state of ceremonies. Apart from the food, liquor is always one of the important factors to enhance the dining atmosphere. Similar as the food, the liquor is also endowed with cultural connotations. Foreign people may say "Cheers!" and "For …" as a toast when drinking in dinner or parties. However, when Chinese people make a toast of "干杯", it generally means to finish the whole cup or glass of liquor. To the foreigners' surprise, the host will insist on drinking more than one cup or glass (normally three or two cups or glasses) with the guest to demonstrate the Chinese etiquette rituals. The sophisticated Chinese hosts, amazingly, will have many ways of persuading the guests to drink more without hesitation. The Chinese people prefer liquors with high degrees of alcohol. Champagnes and wines are not common in formal banquet. When pouring wine or liquor into a cup or glass, Chinese people will make it full to show the respect. When toasting for the elder people or the person with high ranks, it is an unwritten rule to have the host's cup or glass lower than that of the guest.

Apart from liquor, the Chinese people also lay great emphasis on drinking tea as a common beverage instead of coffee. In China, tea is more than a beverage. To many people it is a way of life and an incredibly important part of people's daily lives. According to legend, tea was first discovered in China by Shennong, an ancient Chinese chieftain and considered the father of Chinese medicine. Originally used as a form of medicine, tea drinking evolved until it became almost an art form. There are many different ways to brew tea with the most popular being Kung Fu Tea which uses smaller teapots and tiny cups. The Chinese vast territory is renowned for different configurations of the earth's surface and diversified climates, which are suitable for planting tea leaves ranging from green tea and black tea to oolong tea. The biggest tea family is the green tea family, which could be further divided into many sub-categories among which the tea from the West Lake of Zhejiang Province has a renowned reputation among tea lovers.

The most important feature and also the most distinctive difference between the Chinese and the Western food and drinking cultures is that we prefer to talk about business and other affairs by the table. The mix of food, socialization and business is also considered a special negotiation style in the westerners' eyes. Another sharp difference of the food culture between Chinese and American ways lies in the way of payment. "Going Dutch", which is extremely common in the world, is rare to see in China. As a matter of fact, it is a long-standing tradition for a person to pay the whole bill by himself or herself. The other people may pay the whole bill next time.

With the step of reform and opening-up, the Chinese food and drink culture is also globalized and absorbing the elements from other countries. Individual serving become available in some restaurants. A growing number of Chinese people begin to drink in bars and pubs. The drinking techniques are not so stubborn and become to be flexible and considerate in accordance with different people and situations.

第三章　无声的语言 :非言语交流
Chapter Three
The Silent Language: Non-verbal Communication

Section 1　Lead-in

1.Question

（1）How do you define "glamor"? Do you always define "glamor" by appearance, intrinsic value, inside wisdom, or something else（Figure 5）?

Appearance　　　　Intrinsic value　　　　Inside wisdom

Figure 5　Three representations of glamor

（2）Do you think that our body language also reflects our mind? If our body language does not conform with our verbal language, which should we follow?

（3）Is it necessary for us to learn nonverbal skills in intercultural communication?

2.Case

Katherine came to Beijing in 1998 and found a job as an English teacher in a foreign language institute. Soon after her classes began, she found that her students showed no interest in her teaching style. Quite a few of them avoided attending her class. She was feeling quite upset and discouraged so she decided to ask the Director, Professor Wang, for help. Prof. Wang reviewed his timetable and suggested they meet at ten o'clock on Thursday morning. When Thursday came, Katherine arrived at Prof. Wang's office at the exactly ten o'clock finding him talking with another teacher in Chinese. Seeing that she had come, Prof. Wang smiled and gestured her to sit down. Katherine sat down and the professor excused himself and continued to talk with the other teacher. After five minutes, he finished his conversation, and apologized to Katherine, and began to focus his attention on her situation. Prof. Wang showed great concern and asked her what the problem was. Just as she was discussing her problem, another Chinese teacher interrupted, with a form that required the Director's signature. The Director smiled, apologized to Katherine again, and turned to talk with the Chinese teacher in Chinese. Katherine became impatient, and wondered why their discussion should be interrupted since she had made an appointment. Also, she was upset and frustrated that they continued to speak Chinese in front of her. Although their talk continued, she was apparently unhappy about what had happened. [1]

The experience Katherine encounters indicates a sharp difference between Chinese and westerners in terms of the value of time, space and privacy. If Prof. Wang would respect Katherine's language of time and space and try another way of communication, the situation would not be too embarrassing.

Indeed, our language and its affiliated verbal symbols may promote or hinder the effect of intercultural communication. However, even though people are not talking or writing in any language forms, their nonverbal symbols will also facilitate or handicap the communicative effect, too. Here comes an interesting topic of intercultural communication—nonverbal communication.

Section 2 Theory preparation

Theory preparation: defining language from linguistic

1　汪福祥，马登阁编著．"文化撞击案例评析"．北京：石油工业出版社，1999：32-33.

perspective

Language is a set of shared symbols or signs that a cooperative group of people has mutually agreed to use to help them create meaning. The discipline of language is called linguistics. Ferdinand de Saussure, the famous linguist and the father of structural linguistics, held in his influential work Course in General Linguistics that there must be a discipline above linguistic which he called semiotics.

Semiotics, also called semiotic studies, is the study of sign process (semiosis). It includes the study of signs and sign processes, indication, designation, likeness, analogy, allegory, metonymy, metaphor, symbolism, signification, and communication. It is not to be confused with the Saussurean tradition called semiology, which is a subset of semiotics.

The semiotic tradition explores the study of signs and symbols as a significant part of communications. Different from linguistics, semiotics also studies non-linguistic sign systems. Therefore, non-linguistic and non-verbal symbols will also be of great significance in denoting the meaning.

Larry A. Samovar et al [1] propose that nonverbal communication involves all those nonverbal stimuli in a communication setting that are generated by both the source and his or her use of the environment, and that have potential message value for the source and/or receiver. Nonverbal communication is a multidimensional activity where nonverbal messages can serve as substitutes for verbal messages. However, verbal and nonverbal messages often work in unison. The interfacing of the verbal with the nonverbal is reflected in a number of ways. For example, you often use nonverbal messages to repeat a point you are trying to make verbally. You could place you index finger over your lips at the same time you were whispering "please don't yell" to someone who was shouting.

A study implemented in the United States showed that in the

---

1   Larry A. Samovar, Richard E. Porter, Edwin R. McDaniel, Carolyn S. Roy. "Cross-cultural Communication". (Eighth Edition) Beijing: Peking University Press, 2018. P171.

communication of attitudes, 93% of the message was transmitted by voice tone and facial expressions, whereas only 7% was transmitted by words.

Nowadays, with the popularity of the network and mobile phone, a growing number of users on the Internet use emojis (cyber emoticons) rather than linguistic forms in social network communication, which also amplifies the significance of studying nonverbal communication.

Section 3 Detailed analysis

1.Connotations of nonverbal symbols and nonverbal communication

Nonverbal symbols are both similar and diverse from verbal symbols in intercultural communication. Nonverbal communication will also have the functions of repeating, conflicting, complementing, substituting, moderating and regulating, which will be good supplements to the verbal communication. We may notice the following important characteristics of nonverbal communication.

Nonverbal communication behaviors may be conscious or unconscious. For some people, nonverbal communication behaviors may be the natural response or personal habits; for some others, nonverbal communication behaviors are implemented in an intentional way. When an unintentional behavior is interpreted as intentional act, a misunderstanding will possibly happen. For example, some westerners may misunderstand Chinese people and contend that they are quarrelling because they are speaking loudly in public. However, this high pitch may be just a kind of habitual way of speaking for some Asian countries such as China and Korea.

Nonverbal communication behaviors are always culturally conventional. There is no fixed and unchangeable connection between nonverbal communication symbols and the meanings. The meanings, to a great extent, are influenced by a due culture. In other words, each culture or subculture has their own designated meaning signifiers and rules. For example, shrugging shoulders is a common behavior in western countries which indicates "I don't know" or "unable to do anything". However, this act is not often noticed in Asian countries. In an extreme case, a nonverbal communication which is a matter of common and frequent occurrence in one culture may be considered a serious offence in another culture.

Nonverbal communication behaviors are dependent on the context. It, to a certain extent, is a hypercontextualized act. Therefore, it is meaningless to talk about or study nonverbal communication without considering context factors such as social class, status, education, gender, age, hobbies. Overgeneralization should be avoided in the intercultural communication involving nonverbal communication. Careful preparation will always be the best advice.

Nonverbal communication behaviors are more ambiguous. Compared with nonverbal communication, verbal communication will be much more clear-cut, thus reducing the possibility of misunderstanding. Part of the ambiguity associated with nonverbal messages is contextual, which can be seen if some brushes against you in an elevator: Was it merely an accident, or was it an opportunistic sexual act?

Although we try to focus on nonverbal differences across cultures, we need to point out that there are many similarities in how cultures employ this communication system. In other words, the study of nonverbal communication may also include cultural universals, too.

Generally, nonverbal communication study will broadly cover the following major domains.

Chronemics（时间学）: one of several subcategories to emerge out of the study of nonverbal communication; the study of the role of time in communication;the study of differences in viewing time, or the time language; often includes punctuality, promptness, time orientation etc.

Proxemics（空间学）: the study of human use of space and the effects that population density has on behavior, communication, and social interaction; often includes body distance and body touch; "the interrelated observations and theories of humans use of space as a specialized elaboration of culture" in Edward T. Wall's work "The Hidden Dimension".

Kinesics（身势学）：the interpretation of body motion communication such as facial expressions and gestures, nonverbal behavior related to movement of any part of the body or the body as a whole; the body language, often includes posture, stance, gesture, facial expression, eye behavior, appearance such as clothing, cosmetics; the most important part of nonverbal communication study.

Haptics（触觉学）: a branch of nonverbal communication that refers to the ways in which people and animals communicate and interact via the sense of touch;The sense of touch allows one to experience different sensations such as: pleasure, pain, heat, or cold. One of the most significant aspects of touch is the ability to convey and enhance physical intimacy. The sense of touch is the fundamental component of haptic communication for interpersonal relationships. Touch can be categorized in many terms such as positive, playful, control, ritualistic, task-related or unintentional. It can be both sexual (kissing is one example that some perceived as sexual), and platonic (such as hugging or a handshake).

Vocalics（副语言学）: also called paralanguage; a component of meta-communication that may modify meaning, give nuanced meaning, or convey emotion, by using techniques such as prosody, pitch, volume, intonation, etc.; often includes speed, volume, pause, silence, gasps, sighs.

2.Time language（时间学）

As is illustrated in the figure above, time is one thing that people usually take it for granted, but the lack of awareness of the difference of time language will result in confusion and even frustration. The way people treat time can also provide valuable cues to how members of that culture value and respond to time. Therefore, it is of great significance to master the cultural differences in the time value in the intercultural communication. Western people, especially Germans and Americans, will arrive at the venue punctually while Chinese may arrive either early or late.

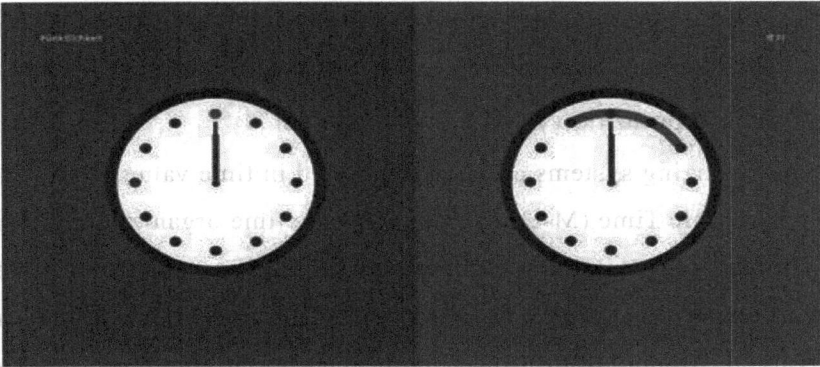

West VS. Chinese

Figure 6 A comparison between Chinese and western values of time

（1）Time Orientations (three orientations)

Three types of time orientations are always noticed in time value.

Past orientation: Some civilizations tend to look back because they have a long and strong history to memorize and boast about, such as Greek, French, British and Chinese cultures. They place much emphasis on tradition, since they have long histories that date back to thousands of years ago. They tend to use the past as a guide to make decisions and determine truth. History, established religions and tradition are extremely important to these cultures.

Present orientation: Cultures that concentrate on the present and don't worry about tomorrow are present oriented. Present-oriented cultures like Filipinos and Latin Americans place great emphasis on living for the moment. They tend to have a causal and relaxed lifestyle. It is not a tradition for these people to rush into a hurry.

Future orientation: Future oriented cultures encompass a preference for change. They have great faith in the better future. Americans, for example, belong to the future orientation. Although American ancestors did have strong spiritual links with their European roots, nowadays, many Americans already started anew. Their values of independence and individualism also drive them forward to build a brighter future. It is argued that most post-industrial cultures are future oriented because they place a lot of emphasis on the future, striving to ensure that the future will be better than the present.

（2）Time organizing systems (two systems)

Two organizing systems are always noticed in time value.

Monochronic Time (M-time): Monochronic time organizing system views time as linear, segmental and prompt. People with monochronic time value tend to do one thing at a time and may feel uncomfortable when their activity is interrupted. Monochronic time person place great emphasis on schedules. Visiting without any advanced appointment is considered impolite. More characteristics of monochronic time value may be seen as follows:

　　※ Focusing on one thing one time

　　※ Laying emphasis on promises on time

　　※ Low-context culture

　　※ Doing things according to the plan

　　※ Respecting others' privacy

　　※ Seldom borrowing personal property

　　※ Tending to build a short-term relation

Polychronic Time (P-time): polychronic time organizing system emphasizes the completion of transactions and tends to be more human-centered instead of strictly adhering to the clock. Comparatively speaking, people with polychronic time value are less rigid, less tangible and more flexible. They do things in a multi-task way. More characteristics of polychronic time value may be seen as follows:

　　※ More than one thing one time

　　※ Viewing promises on time as possible targets

　　※ High-context culture

　　※ Changing plans easily

※ Caring about the people close to them

※ Frequently borrowing and lending

※ Tending to build a long-term or a lifelong relation

3.Space language（空间学）

Space language refers to the study of human use of space and the effects that population density has on behavior, communication, and social interaction.

According to Edward Hall in his famous book *The Silent Language*, there are four major types of distances in American social and business circumstances, namely, intimate, personal, social and public.

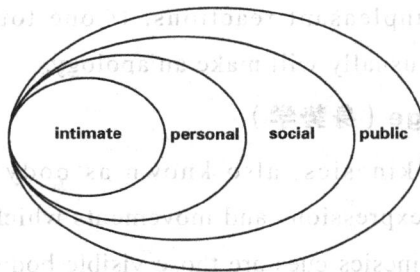

Figure 7　The language of proximity

※ Intimate Zone: physical touch to 45 centimeters

※ Personal Zone:45 ～ 80 centimeters

※ Social Zone: 1.3 ～ 3 meters

※ Public Zone: farther than 2 ～ 3 meters

In terms of the differences of the distance among communicating people in the world, it is reported that Japanese and Mediterranean Europeans prefer to a long distance whereas Latins and Mediterranean Arabs would prefer to a short distance. Therefore, when Arabs talk, the distance between the speakers could be so close that they can even smell each other. If we are speaking and communicating with an unfamiliar person from another unknown cultural background, it would be more feasible to keep a certain distance in order not to offend the speaker, for example, more than 90 centimeters.

Figure 8   Distance between people in intercultural communication.

In English-speaking countries, physical contact is generally avoided in conversation among ordinary friends or acquaintances. Touching someone causally may cause unpleasant reactions. If one touches another person accidentally, he or she usually will make an apology.

4.Body language（身势学）

Body language, kinesics, also known as body movements or body behaviors, include all expressions and movements which send communicative messages. In general, kinesics cues are those visible body shifts and movements that can send message about our attitude toward the other person, our emotional state and desire to control our environment. [1] Researchers lay great emphasis the following sections of body language study in intercultural communication: facial expressions, gestures, postures, eye contacts.

（1）Facial expression

The face in rich in communicative potential which could be considered an important supplement of our verbal expression. Many scholars believe that face expression is a primary source of communication information next to human speech. As a matter of fact, due to the delay of the decoding of the verbal symbols in trans-cultural environment, people tend to rely heavily on facial cues in the first impression when making significant interpersonal

---

1   Larry A. Samovar, Richard E. Porter, Edwin R. McDaniel, Carolyn S. Roy. "Cross-cultural Communication". (Eighth Edition) Beijing: Peking University Press. 2018. P179.

judgement.

However, we should be clear that facial expressions are not always true to our mind. Sophisticated and trained person may acquire to hide their true emotion and present a "mask" to the receiver, thus causing an effect which is called "post-truth". When people wear such a "mask", it is hard for others to read the poker face. People have to resort to other delicate testing instruments, for example, electroencephalograph or eye movement meter, to confirm whether the speaker is telling lies or not.

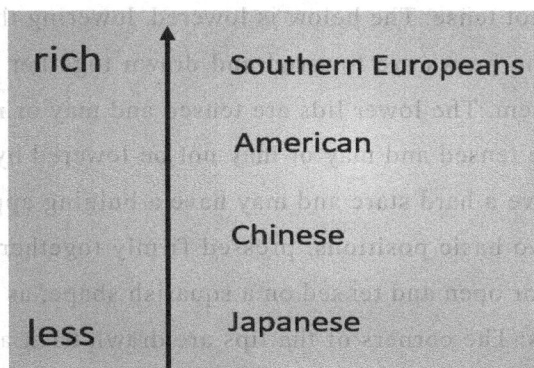

Figure 9　The facial expressions of different cultures

Due to the limit of text, in this course, we only discuss those facial expressions that are supposed to the true to the speaker's heart. Six basic emotions[1] showed below are judged with very high accuracy among observers in many studies, proposed by Judith Mark and other scholars.[2]

※ Surprise: The brows are raised so they are curved and high. The skin below the brow is stretched, and horizontal wrinkles go across the forehead. The eyelids are opened: the upper lid is raised, and the lower lid is drawer down; the white of the eye shows above the iris and often below as well. The jaw drops open so the lips and teeth are parted, but there is no tension or stretching of the mouth.

1　刘重宵、刘丽．"跨文化交际实训"．北京：对外经济贸易大学出版社，2018：104-108.

2　Mark, L. K. Judith A. H., & Terrence, G. H. (2014). Nonverbal Communication in Human Interaction. Wadsoworth: Cengage Learning. Page 279-281.

※ Fear: The brows are raised and drawn together. The wrinkles in the forehead are in the center, not across the entire forehead. The upper eyelid is raised, exposing the sclera, and the lower eyelid is tensed and drawn up. The mouth is open and the lips are either tensed slightly and drawn back or stretched and drawn back.

※ Disgust: The upper lip is raised. The lower lip is also raised and pushed up to the upper lip, or is lowered and slightly protruding. The nose is wrinkled and the cheeks are raised. Lines show below the low lid and the lid is pushed up but not tense. The below is lowered, lowering the upper lid.

※ Anger: The brows are lowered and drawn together and vertical lines appear between them. The lower lids are tensed and may or may not be raised. The upper lids are tensed and may or may not be lowered by the action of the brow. The eyes have a hard stare and may have a bulging appearance. The lips are in either of two basic positions: pressed firmly together, with the corners straight or down, or open and tensed on a squarish shape, as if shouting.

※ Happiness: The corners of the lips are drawn back and up. The mouth may or may not be parted, with teeth exposed or not. A wrinkle, the nasolabial fold, runs down from the nose to the outer edge beyond the lip corners. The cheeks are raised. The lower eyelids show wrinkles below them and may be raised but not tense.

※ Sadness: The inner corners of the eyebrows are drawn up. The skin below the eyebrows is triangulated with the inner corner up. The upper eyelid inner corners are raised. The corners of the lips are down, or the lips are trembling.

（2）Gesture and posture

Similar as facial expression, gesture and posture are supplements of our verbal expression, too. Gestures may perform many interpersonal and intrapersonal functions, among which arm and hands movements are mostly and overwhelmingly notices. Next, we are going to list several common gestures.

※ OK: With index finger and thumb held in a circle and the other three fingers extended, palm outward, people can easily pose an "OK" sign. However, this sign diverse in different cultural contexts. In America and Britain, it means "fine" and "great". In France, it means "zero" or "worthless". In Thailand, it means "yes". In Tunisia, it means "fool" and "stupid". In Greece, it has the offensive meaning. In China, this sign is a multi-meaning nonverbal symbol, meaning "zero" "three" "fine" or "no problem" in different situations.

※ Thumb-up: Thumb-up in North America always means "hitchhike". In Sri Lanka, Mexico and the Netherlands, it means "pray for good luck or blessing". In Japan and South Korea, it means "man" "your father" or "old man". In Greece, it means "enough". In Nigeria and Australia, it means "rude". In China, America and Britain, this sign has a similar connotation which means "great" "praise" and "incredible".

※ Finger-crossing: With index finger and middle finger crossed and curved thumb pressured on the ring finger and little finger, this finger-crossing sign may have totally different connotations in different contexts. In America, France, the Philippines, Malaysia, and Mexico, it means "pray for good luck or blessing". In Australia, it means "expectation". In India, it means "finished" or "done". In Sri Lanka, it means "evil". In the Netherlands, it means "swear" or "oath". In some European countries, it means "insult" or "hostility". In China, this sign means "number ten" "plus" or "good luck".

Apart from these signs of gestures, people sometimes use body movements to express their emotions. Posture and sitting habits offer insight into a culture's deep structure. Posture can indicate whether or not people are paying attention, the degree of status in the encounter, if people like or dislike each other, feelings of submissiveness, and even sexual intentions. The bow in many Asian countries is much more than a greeting. In some Buddhism nations, putting two palms together devoutly is also a way of greeting, appreciation and prayer for good luck.

　　The manner in which we sit also communicates a message. In the United States and some European countries, sitting casually is a habitual act. However, in China, how to sit, especially in a restaurant box or a car means significantly. For example, people have to careful about the position where they sit when they are sitting in a car. When sitting in a car driven by professional drivers such as taxi drivers, we can sit in the backseat. However, when sitting in the friend's car, it is better to sit in the copilot seat.

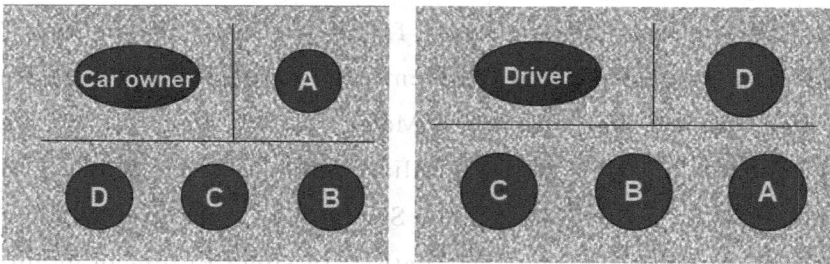

Figure 10　Position of sitting in a car

　　The seating language is pretty important in Chinese context not only in cars, but also in restaurants. In China, when dining in a box in a restaurant, the distinguished guests or very important person (VIP) will always sit in a position facing the door and having a good view through the window near the wall.

　　Nowadays, apart from facial expressions and postures, with the acceleration of Internet access, an increasingly large of people contact with other receivers via the Internet, mobile Internet and the social media. Similar as the communication in the real world, communication in the virtual network also includes two parts: verbal network communication and nonverbal network communication. An emoticon, short for emotion icon, known as emoji in Japanese and young Chinese, is a representation of nonverbal network communication. It is a pictorial representation of a facial expression using characters—usually punctuation marks, numbers, and letters—to express a person's feelings or mood, or as a time-saving method.Since the era of text messages to today's popular social network sites or media, emoticons became increasingly popular and were commonly used on text messages, internet forums and e-mails. Emoticons have played a significant role in communication through technology, and some devices and applications have provided stylized pictures that do not use text punctuation. They offer another range of "tone" and feeling through texting that portrays specific emotions through facial gestures while in the midst of text-based cyber communication.

	0	1	2	3	4	5	6	7	8	9	A	B	C	D	E	F
U+1F60x	😀	😁	😂	😃	😄	😅	😆	😇	😈	😉	😊	😋	😌	😍	😎	😏
U+1F61x	😐	😑	😒	😓	😔	😕	😖	😗	😘	U+F60B WINKING FACE	😛	😜	😝	😞
U+1F62x	😠	😡	😢	😣	😤	😥	😦	😧	😨	😩	😪	😫	😬	😭	😮	😯
U+1F63x	😰	😱	😲	😳	😴	😵	😶	😷	😸	😹	😺	😻	😼	😽	😾	😿
U+1F64x	🙀	🙁	🙂	🙃	🙄	🙅	🙆	🙇	🙈	🙉	🙊	🙋	🙌	🙍	🙎	🙏

Figure 11　Sample of emoticons from Official Unicode Consortium code chart

Unfortunately, emoticons in nonverbal network communication in the cyber world are also not uniform in the whole world. One emoticon meaning respect may be considered an offensive sign in another culture. According to the study of Wechat team, in China, people above 55 years old prefer to the emoticon 👍; people born in 1970s like 🤝; people born in 1980s like using 😁; people born in 1990s like using 💀; people born in 2000s tend to like 🚬.As is said in the widely-spreading slogan, when in Rome, do as Romans do. Therefore, we should be well-prepared not only in foreign languages but also in the nonverbal habits before the communication with people from different cultures.

Section 4 Cultural practice

Cultural practice

Discussion and presentation

You are going to invite an important guest to have a dinner in a Chinese restaurant box. Please work out an appropriate dialogue with the combination of proper body languages.

It is reminded that your reception has to be decent in etiquette. In order to show your intercultural consideration, you also need to explain the following points more clearly to your guest to avoid misunderstanding:

The way of sitting in a restaurant box.

The way of drinking alcohol in a Chinese dinner.

The differences between Chinese and western cuisines.

Section 5 Derivative development

1.Film watching

Please watch some episodes of *Friends* (《六人行》/《老友记》,1994—2004) [1] and the movie *Mr. Bean's Holiday* (2007) and work out a short intercultural analysis based on these two works. You may focus your attention on the secrets of the success of these comedies.

It will be more enlightening if you can compare some Chinese comedies, such as Zhao Benshan's comedy,with Friends' comedy and Mr. Bean's comedy and discuss why it is hard for the Chinese humor and comedy to be appreciated by audience from west countries.

Does it have a relation with our disadvantages that we are too heavily relying on verbal skills instead of nonverbal skills in presenting the sense of

---

1 Tips: Friends is an American television sitcom, created by David Crane and Marta Kauffman, which aired on NBC from September 22, 1994, to May 6, 2004, lasting ten seasons. With an ensemble cast starring Jennifer Aniston, Lisa Kudrow, etc., the show revolves around six friends in their 20s and 30s who live in Manhattan, New York City. It receives a great success not only in America, but also in the whole world.

humor? Would you please give several tentative strategies that may facilitate our communication effect in the future?

2.Extended reading

Braille

Braille is a tactile writing system used by people who are visually impaired. It is traditionally written with embossed paper. Braille users can read computer screens and other electronic supports using refreshable braille displays. They can write braille with the original slate and stylus or type it on a braille writer, such as a portable braille notetaker or computer that prints with a braille embosser.Braille is named after its creator, Louis Braille, a Frenchman who lost his sight as a result of a childhood accident. In 1824, at the age of fifteen, he developed a code for the French alphabet as an improvement on night writing. He published his system, which subsequently included musical notation, in 1829.

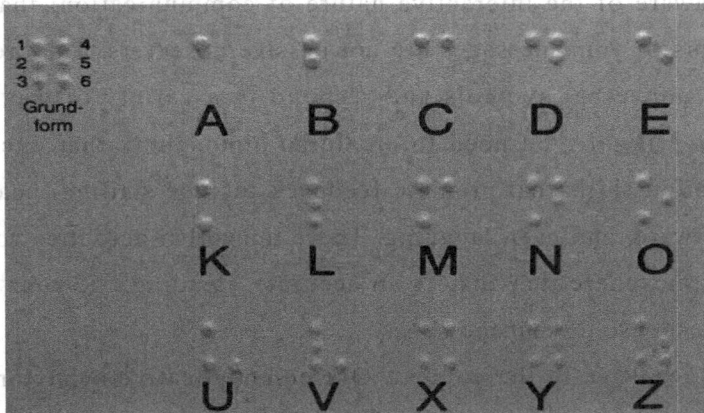

Figure 12　Sample of Braille

These characters have rectangular blocks called cells that have tiny bumps called raised dots. The number and arrangement of these dots distinguish one character from another. Since the various braille alphabets originated as transcription codes for printed writing, the mappings (sets of character designations) vary from language to language, and even within one; in English Braille there are three levels of encoding: Grade 1—a letter-by-letter transcription used for basic literacy; Grade 2—an addition of abbreviations and contractions; and Grade 3—various non-standardized personal stenography. Chinese administrations also work out our new and normative braille system and regulations since July 2018.

Improving nonverbal communication skills

Larry A. Samovar [1] offers a brief section on how we can exercise some control over that behavior to produce positive results.

※ Monitor your nonverbal actions. Although "know yourself" is an overused expression, it is, nevertheless, worth repeating. Our initial advice is to monitor your actions so that you better understand the experiences of others. By knowing how you present yourself you can gain insight into how people are reacting to the types of messages you are sending.

※ Monitor feedback. Using feedback is directly related to the preceding suggestion regarding the notion of self-monitoring. Both suggestions ask you to be aware of the interactive nature of communication; that is to say, the recipients of your messages are not passive observers. They receive your verbal and nonverbal symbols and respond in a variety of ways. Because feedback is critical, you need to create an atmosphere that encourages it. Communication skills that promote feedback include smiling, head nodding, learning forward, and even laughing. These nonverbal activities contribute to a relaxed atmosphere that fosters an accurate "reading" of your receiver's nonverbal response to your messages.

※ Be sensitive to the context. Our communicative behavior should be different as we move from place to place. Think of all the "rules" that are in operation in school rooms, courtrooms, churches, business meetings, parties, restaurants, sporting events, and the like. Each of these settings requires behaviors that you have learned as part of the acculturation process. When trying to improve nonverbal communication skills you need to understand

---

1　Larry A. Samovar, Richard E. Porter, Edwin R. McDaniel, Carolyn S. Roy. "Cross-cultural Communication". (Eighth Edition) Beijing: Peking University Press. 2018. P 204-205.

how each situation might influence meaning given a specific action. When trying to improve your ability to read nonverbal behaviors, ask yourself if the observed actions are appropriate for the setting.

※ Be aware of nonverbal ambiguity. Nonverbal messages can be intentional such as waving goodbye to a friend or unintentional such as frowning because you are looking into the sun and your friend believes you are upset. This multiple meaning dimension of nonverbal communication puts an increased burden on you whether you are the sender or the receiver.

※ Know your culture. The success of intercultural communication depends not only on the mastery of the target culture, but also on the familiarity of the mother culture. Our cultural inventory provides us with valuable insights for understanding our beliefs and attitudes, our values and assumptions. It is critical that we reflect on the various aspects of our own cultural identity and examine their positive impacts on our personal and professional development. Cultural affiliation influences both how you send messages and how other people react to those messages.

3.Knowing more cultures about ourselves (3): the education culture

Before we introduce ourselves to the others, the first and foremost thing is to have a correct and profound cognition of ourselves. In the ends of all the eight chapters, we add some basic knowledge of ourselves which are divided into eight sections, namely, the family culture, the food culture, the education culture, the marriage culture, the medical culture, the art culture, the consumption culture and the cyber culture respectively. We hope to help both audiences from other cultures and ourselves to have a better cognition of Chinese cultures. During these parts, the author of this book not only summarizes the traditional essence of these sections, but employs a diachronic perspective and includes the up-to-date changes.

4.Our education cultures

In the long history of Chinese feudal society, the opportunities of education are restricted to a small number of people due to the feudal patriarchal system. The education foundation was weak in old China. September, 1977 witnessed a return of National College Entrance Examination (Gaokao) to the education system. The year 1978 witnessed the return of the Entrance Exam for Postgraduate Study. The construction of the complete education system and the renewal of education value in China has reached astonishing and magnificent achievements in the past forty years.

The Chinese culture attaches great importance to the significance of education. Confucius, the great Chinese philosopher, holds that the congenital base for different people are similar so that we should provide education for all people without discrimination. He believes in the important function of education in the administration of the country. He also proposes the dialectical relation between teaching and studying, between in-class learning and extracurricular learning. The ancient wise scholars also pay high attention to the combination of intelligent education and moral education. Besides, the education of humanities, rituals, morals and classical arts are also highlighted in the process of educating.

In the modern China, although we made progressive achievements in the education theory and practice, the large population and the limit capacity cause a scarcity of teaching resources. The so-called test-oriented education system, which is always blamed by foreign criticizers, came into being. The scarcity of education aggravates the anxiety for parents. Millions of parents accompany their children to various extracurricular off-school classes of English, mathematics, Chinese and other selected courses. The mass media, to a certain extent, unwillingly, amplifies people's anxiety in education though repetitive agenda-setting and selected camera shots. It is unnecessary to completely stigmatize the Chinese education paradigm.

British Broadcasting Corporation (BBC) once launched a series of documentary about Chinese education for secondary school students named "Are Our Kids Tough Enough? Chinese School" in 2015. It records a four-week experiment of five Chinese teachers who are invited to teach in a middle school in Southern Hampshire in a Chinese teaching style. The Chinese teachers are in total charge of a 50-student grade 9 class, which is a contrast with Britain teaching. Students in this class have to study and behave as Chinese students in Chinese schools in the four-week test. They have to arrive at the classroom by 7 o'clock and stay in the school for 12 hours. BBC producers use the word "strong" because they doubt whether British students could endure this teaching pressure on one hand and they are curious of the result of this contrastive experiment on the other hand. To be honest, the Chinese teachers' class has no advantage over the British teachers' class because of the foreign language proficiency of the Chinese teachers and the cultural differences both for the Chinese teachers and British students. After four weeks, however, the Chinese teachers' class win this competition with a big margin of advantages in all subjects. A certain number of students, surprisingly, say that they benefit a lot from this teaching and learning experience.

The Chinese fundamental education is advantageous in cultivating the students' competence in calculation and discipline, which will lay a solid foundation for their future study and research. It is a great virtue to be rigorous and precise in many subjects such as science and technology. It is also unnecessary to draw a fine distinction between the Chinese education and the Western education. As a matter of fact, many Chinese young people go to top universities to continue studying and reach high peaks in their research after they complete the basic education right in China, which is a terrific example to renew our confidence in our way.

The reform of the Chinese basic education started almost at the same time as the path of the nation's reform and opening-up policy. Our education actively employs the latest inventions in information and communication technology. Computer-assisted teaching, task-based teaching, flipped classroom, mixed teaching and other forms continue promoting the teaching and learning effect. The gap between Chinese and Western literacy began to be narrowed quickly. Furthermore, our education studies, both in meta-educational theories and applied or empirical education studies, have reached many enlightening achievements in the past thirty years. On one hand, we succeeded the excellent education tradition originated from Confucius and Mencius; on the other hand, our education is integrated into the world education practice in a positive way.

The Chinese parents now belong to the generation born in 1980s and 1990s. These parents generally received high education in colleges and universities. Their studies competence (intelligent quotient) and emotional quotient are greatly improved in the lifelong learning environment. They are still in anxiety and are insecure about the uncertainty in the future. However, their family education arranged for their children are carried out more calmly and efficiently.

Of course, the education in China is not perfect. Like children in other countries, the information era witnessed a large trend of indulgence into the cyber myth and some children's world view are highly influenced by the information cocoon of the Internet.

The future progress lies in how to work out a harmonious combination between the interest and utilitarian target, between the Chinese tradition and the international standard, between the education for the mind and the education for the body.

第四章　当跨文化遇见媒介化：媒介化时代如何进行跨文化交流

Chapter Four
Intercultural Communication in the Era of Mediatization

Section 1 Lead-in

1.Question

（1）How long do you use your PC and mobile phone every day? Have you ever imagined the maximum time that you will be parted from these electronic devices?

（2）When people are communicating interculturally, they will easily shape a collective stereotype towards a person or a group? But where does the stereotype come from regardless of authenticity?

（3）How important is the role of medium for an individual in a modern society?

2.Case

Marco Polo was an Italian merchant, explorer, and writer, born in the Republic of Venice in 1254. His travels are recorded in *Book of the Marvels of the World*, also known as *The Travels of Marco Polo*, a book that described to Europeans the wealth and great size of China, its capital Peking, and other Asian cities and countries.This book inspired Christopher Columbus and many other travelers. However, some people, including some experts in European, doubted that what he described in his book was not real. Peking at the moment must not be that flourishing in economy and population. The prosperity of the city Peking is based on Marco Polo's fantastic imaginations.

It is not our interest to confirm this authenticity of the doubt and accuse of European experts. But Marco Polo's book did promote the communication interculturally, spreading the Chinese culture elements to the dots of Europe. Therefore, what interests us is the interdisciplinary study between inter-culture and medium (media).

Section 2 Theory preparation

Theory preparation: the proposal of the concept of mediatization

This chapter is a bit different from the traditional intercultural communication study. Broadly, traditional intercultural communication study prefers to a static cross-cultural and cross-language paradigm, paying little attention to the dynamic and newest elements in communication.

According to the latest data released by China Internet Network Information Center (CNNIC) on February 28th, 2019, in China, the scale of netizens has reached 829 million with the popularity rate reaching 59.6%. The popularity rate via the access of the mobile Internet has surprisingly reached 98.6%. Almost every adult's life except sleep is closely associated with various kinds of cyber applications, such as Facebook, QQ, Wechat, YouTube and Tik Tok. Everything and everyone seem to be mediatized quickly into a Net.Therefore, media ranging from TV to mobile phone have played an increasingly important role in modern cultural communication. Some experts call it "C@C", i.e. communication at the center. Communication becomes prior and vital in the society. It is of great significance to discuss what will happen when medium meets inter-culture.

In communication studies or media studies, mediatization is a theory that argues that the media shapes and frames the processes and discourse of political communication as well as the society in which that communication takes place. In this framework, an important aspect of modernization is the development of media,beginning with a change in communication media and proceeding to subordination of the power of prevailing influential institutions.

As a consequence of this process, institutions and whole societies are shaped by and dependent on mass media. Following the concept of media, mediatization has become the proper concept for capturing how processes of communication transform society, and designating large-scale relationships.

The current society witnessed a change of intercultural communication modes initiated by the new media based on the new-generation Information and Communication Technology (ICT). The Internet and the mobile Internet have been the major fronts of intercultural communication.

Under the background of turning from English for General Purposes (EGP) to English for Occupational Purposes (EOP), constructing the ability of tolerating heterogeneous languages and diversified cultures, and cultivating the integrated intercultural career ability not only respond to the mission endowed by globalization, but shoulder the responsibility of diverse demands from audiences.Mediatization hereby provides a new "motion energy" for intercultural communication competence cultivation. It would be a constructive and feasible attempt to initiate a mediatization-based intercultural teaching and learning mode under the support of task-based and flipped class.

Section 3 Detailed analysis

1.The world of mediatization

Since the birth of human beings, people always have great interest in seeking truth. Seeking truth and identifying truth have been the primitive motive for human communication. However, the reality that the audience sense is just one kind of reality (audience reality), two other realities in social science are always called objective reality (true world) and media reality (the world represented by the media). In the ideal situation, three realities are totally overlapped and the same. Nevertheless, in the history of the human communication, audience reality is always influenced by media reality and is not complete even distorted or biased.

Doctor Zhang kexu [1] holds that audience's cognition of the world, or known as audience reality, is acquiring objective reality via media reality. The relation is shown in the following figure of triangular

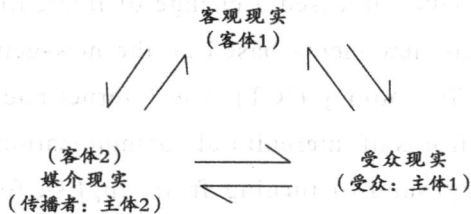

客观现实
（客体1）

（客体2）
媒介现实
（传播者：主体2）

受众现实
（受众：主体1）

Figure 13   Interactive relation among three realities

In modern society, media, by using its superpower, have dispelled the separation of the physical distance, thus reshaping people's time and space values. Ubiquitous network under the assistance initiated by intelligent algorithm, media has filled in every minute of people's life except sleep. Further, mediatization has also shaped people's cognition of other world, nation and culture. Therefore, media have been one of the most primary channels for people to know the indirect cultures.

Mediatization research investigates the interrelation between media communicative change and sociocultural change, understood as a meta-process, a conceptual construct designating long-term processes of change. Media do not necessarily cause the transformations but they have become co-constitutive for the articulation of politics, economics, education, religion, etc. For example, television, by showcasing know-how health specialists who promote quick individual changes in lifestyle, co-constructs the notion of health together with other institutions and broader cultural shifts in perceptions of the body.

Traditionally, we exert our great effort to eliminate the consequence caused by negative stereotype, prejudice and discrimination in intercultural

---

1   张克旭, 等. "从媒介现实到受众现实——从框架理论看电视报道我驻南使馆被炸事件" [J]. 新闻与传播研究, 1999（6）: 4.

communication. In the mediatized society, both the deepening and the eliminating of negative stereotype, prejudice and discrimination are happening in the evolution of mediatization. Mediatization and intercultural communication are closely intertwined which can be seen as follows:

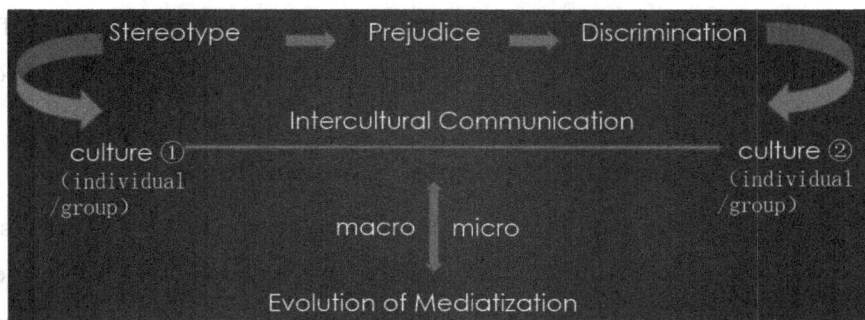

Figure 14　Interconnection between mediatization and inter-culture

The formation of mediatization, to a certain extent, relies on people's demands for information. In the primitive communication era, it is said that words from household are worth their weight in gold when the beacon fire has gone higher and higher in wartime. Modern society is, of course, characterized by an information-rich environment in which people's demands for information, unfortunately, are still not satisfied. The more we surf the Net, the more possible we will rely on the Net. Every step in the evolution of mediatization has been proved to affect intercultural communication effect, ranging from Marco Polo's travel book, to newspapers, TV, and the Internetmedia.

Previously, the image of other cultures always exists in the literature of other cultures, with comparative literature in the center. To be honest, this image in comparative literature is generally based on imaginative fancies, which could hardly be called true. However, nowadays, our impression of a due culture is, to a large extent, dependent on the image constructed by the media represented by the Internet. In the past, global village is the imagination beyond people's reach. Now the concept of global village is accessible to even a kindergarten student. Therefore, the competence of intercultural communication exists everywhere in the media ranging from TV dramas we watch to text messages, social media emoticons we send.

If we reach a consensus in the importance of media played in intercultural communication, the next question would be how to improve our intercultural competence in the mediatized world. The author of this course proposes that the critical point is to correctly identifying the notion of "medium / media" and the improvement of people's media literacy.

2.The improvement of people's media literacy

The key of mediatization in intercultural communication is first to shape a correct recognition of the medium/ media. We have to be clear-minded in the positive and negative effect of the media, so it is of great significance to improve people's media literacy, an ability vital in this mediatized world.

The study of media literacy traditionally belongs to the domain of communication study, especially mass communication study. However, since the title of this book is called *A Handbook of Intercultural Communication from Diversified and Converged Perspectives*, we would like to employ a converged perspective in discussing media literacy—a combination of both media and telecommunication technology. We are going to use a common term in telecommunication technology— "generation (G)" —to discuss media literacy.

Media literacy encompasses the practices that allow people to access, critically evaluate, and create media. Media literacy is not restricted to one medium. [1] This term could be traced back to Britain in 1930s. Scholars at that time want to deliberately distinguish elegance from vulgarity in movies, to keep the pure and high taste in culture. Elites with a strong complex of elegance looked down upon the mass culture initiated by mass media represented by TV. Therefore, media literacy at that time suggested a kind of immunity or superiority of elite culture. However, the following development of mass media go beyond the imagination of these elite experts. The influence

---

1 Potter, W. James (2010−11−30). "The State of Media Literacy". Journal of Broadcasting & Electronic Media. 54 (4): 675 – 696.

of broadcasting, TV and the Internet is overwhelming in shaping children's cognition of the world, setting agendas in public sphere and affecting the result of presidential election. The media literacy at the period is focusing on identifying fake news and criticizing negative effect of the media. After the acceleration and popularity of the Internet and mobile Internet, the media empower the audience in an unprecedented way, thus starting another media literacy research paradigm which lays emphasis on the relation between the sender and the receiver and the development the subjective initiative of the audience. Media literacy in modern society has been a basic literacy just like the ability of reading and writing. According to the report released by the United Nations Scientific, Educational and Cultural Organization (UNESCO) in December 2013, every citizen will need and should understand the rule of media and media information suppliers, opportunities and threats from virtual world, the mastery of information resources. [1]

（1）Media literacy in web 1.0 period (1G and 2G)

In the web 1.0 period, roughly in the time coverage from the first generation (1G) to the second generation (2G) mobile technology, the key word of media literacy is education. This phase is characterized by the exchange of voices and texts with little or no exchanges of data. Global village is still a fancy imagination for Marshall McLuhan [2], a Canadian philosopher with many enlightening works in the field of media theory. As a matter of fact, both broadcasting news and TV dramas in this period are scarce resources. Therefore, media literacy in this period functions as a basic education which may illuminate the space of communication and predict an era of cyberspace.

Education of media literacy in web 1.0 period is to guide audience correctly recognize media, understand the basic principles of media, cultivate

---

1　陶媛．"联合国教科文组织发布全球媒体和信息素养评估报告"．[J].《世界教育信息》，2014(3)：78.

2　McLuhan coined the expression "the medium is the message" and the term global village, and predicted the World Wide Web almost 30 years before it was invented.

a basic ability of immunity to protect people from the harm of the negative influence of media. It is reminded education of media literacy in web 1.0 is not out-of-date, but the people who needs the education may cover very young children.

(2) Media literacy in web 2.0 period (3G)

In the web 2.0 period, because the 3G technology becomes increasingly mature, a multi-media and multi-modal communication hereby comes to our world. The key word of media literacy research is cultivation. The improvement of the band width liberates people's communication potential. With the popularity of the interaction between the sender and the receiver, media literacy in this phase is centered on how to improve this interaction. It has to be noticed that in the period, people pay very little attention to the negative effect of media and tend to believe what is transmitted in the media.

Education of media literacy in web 2.0 period will be centered on the utilization of media in work, study and socialization. Education from offline to online, Massive Open Online Courses (MOOCs) and education cloud are typical products of this purpose.

(3) Media literacy in web 3.0 period (4G, 5G and beyond 5G)

In the web 3.0 [1] period, the key word of media literacy is culture—culturing the consciousness of using and criticizing media. Ubiquitous network under the assistance initiated by intelligent algorithm and media have filled in every minute of people's life except sleep. Our world, together with our interpersonal relation, is quickly mediatized. People soon notice that they are lost in the sea of information and data. Personalized recommendation technology, which is frequently employed in almost every mobile applications, microblogs, cyber-news, causes a phenomenon "information cocoon" — a situation which people are surrounded by homogenizing, even repetitive information. At this time, people began to realize the disadvantages of the network, thus reflecting the orgy of the Internet. In the early fourth-generation mobile era,

---

1   Web 3.0 is not a universally—acknowledged concept. Some experts doubt the justification of this notion. We hold that web 3.0 roughly covers the period from 4G, 5G to beyond-5G.

people's consciousness in rejecting fake or even harmful information is still weak. However, with the evolution of the mobile communication technology, especially spurred up the stimulus of 5G technology, people will never be "offline" if they want. In this case, people's media literacy has reached a new height and evolved from unconscious to conscious utilization.

Education of media literacy in web 2.0 period needs a rational criticism of the media. Bottoms-up and top-down interactions are both common and popular in communication. It predicts a more comfortable, harmonious utilization of media. Human beings, media, technology and society are listed in a harmonious and emotional circle. Since more users are showing their subjective initiative, the whole media will also improve the credibility and validity.

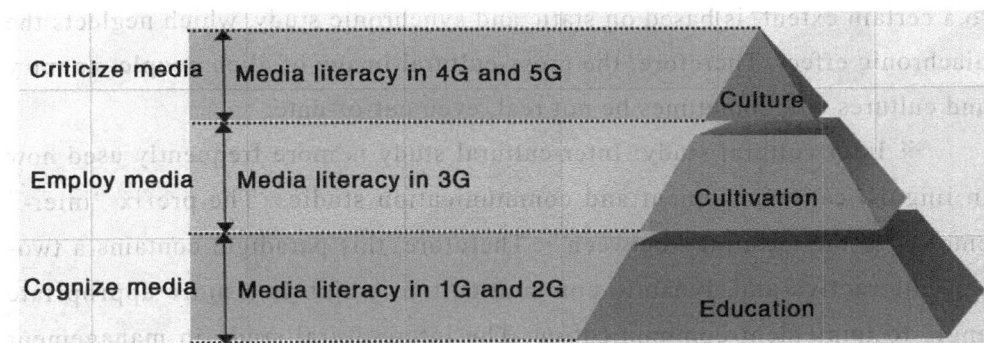

Figure 15 Evolution of media literacy

If traditional media literacy study, people focus on a connection between human beings and society, the media literacy in the 5G period in association with the Internet of Things (IOT), Big data (BA) and Artificial Intelligence (AI), initiates a connection between human beings, things and society. The intercultural competence based on media literacy seems easier than before in implementation because we can conveniently communicate with anyone via any apparatus such as car, wearable devices. This forever online and forever present feature will, of course, lays great emphasis on intercultural communication.

3.The improvement of people's intercultural literacy

Following the discussion of the improvement of people's media literacy, we will continue to talk the improvement of people's intercultural literacy in the fifth generation (5G) communication era from the integrated perspective between media and culture. The first key point is to shifting our research angles.

（1）Angle-shifting

"跨文化" is a translated word which has three English equivalents representing three research paradigms in the west.

※ Cross-cultural study: Cross-cultural study is the term used in early study, especially in foreign language research. It tries to make a comparative analysis on the differences in languages and cultures. However, this analysis, to a certain extent, is based on static and synchronic study, which neglects the diachronic effect. Therefore, the cross-cultural image of alien people, country and cultures will sometimes be not real, even out-of-date.

※ Inter-cultural study: Inter-cultural study is more frequently used now in linguistics, management and communication studies. The prefix "inter-" emphasize the meaning "between". Therefore, this paradigm contains a two-way interactive and dynamic communication, which is a more appropriate angle to implement communication. The intercultural study in management studies focuses on the communication between people in different business environments. The communication study focuses on interpersonal and mass communication activities between people from different environments. This communication, having an eye on cultural shock, culture conflict and cultural acculturation, is considered a main research school at present.

※ Trans-cultural study: Trans-cultural study makes a transcending leap of cultural communication possible. This term is obviously a hypernym word beyond different cultures. It has long been a dream for people to communicate freely and construct a harmonious beauty regardless of the differences in race, gender and ethnics. Trans-cultural study hereby exerts great effort to approach this dream by enlightening creative, and complementary dialogues.

It is in close association with soft power [1] instead of hard power. This word indicates the construction of a common community (consortium) with a shared future for all human beings, which belongs to the domain of the study of intercultural philosophy, thus more penetrating.

The relation between these three intercultural paradigms could be seen as follows:

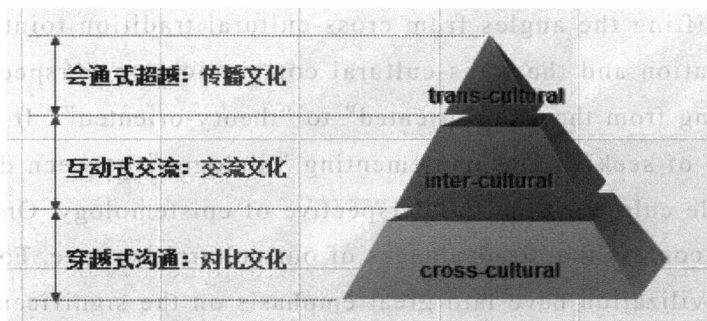

Figure 16 The relation between these three intercultural paradigms

On the basis of the above-mentioned analysis, we have to admit that the image of the other is rigid, even a distorted image in traditional cultural study, learning and teaching. One-direction expression is considered inefficient or a failure in many cases of international communication. This is the reason why we advocate a reciprocal understanding based on mutual respect. We look forward to a diversified cultural prosperity with different cultures. Therefore, we should transform our angles from the traditional cross-cultural path to intercultural path and trans-cultural path. Instead of telling directly and rigid what our Chinese culture is, it would be more feasible and flexible if we try to seek the common ways of communication and tell our Chinese stories in a universally-acknowledged principle.

Unfortunately, there is a kind of duality (binary opposition) between China and the West in the history of China. This duality has been surprisingly

---

1 Soft power is the ability to shape the preferences of others through appeal and attraction. Joseph Nye, a professor of Harvard University, explained that with soft power, "the best propaganda is not propaganda", further explaining that during the Information Age, "credibility is the scarcest resource."

severe when stepping into the recent Chinese history. [1] Since the Opium war in 1840s, China is belittled compared with powerful modernity of the West. Arrogant attitude, closed policy and geographical distinction suspended the possibility of dialogues. We will, of course, refuse to accept a totally westernized principle. However, we also reject an old, conservative and closed arrogancy which is characterized by Chinese ethnocentrism.

To shifting the angles from cross-cultural tradition tointer-cultural communication and the trans-cultural communication perspectives is to transforming from the "tool-oriented" to "theory-oriented". It indicates a possibility of seeking and implementing "dialogue" between different or even hostile cultures from the perspective of epistemology. On one hand, we should confess the disadvantages of our cultural heritage. For example, Chinese civilization have laid great emphasis on the significance of life. Early philosophers in China such as Confucius, Mencius and Lao-tzu have written many shocking and enlightening works exploring the ultimate meaning of life. However, our methodology is generally lagged behind in terms of mathematical ratiocination compared with western Greek tradition. On the other hand, it also has to be acknowledged that western methodology may not be the only or the most authentic paradigm in the world. It may be powerful in other dots of world, but it may lose its part of whole interpretive force in Chinese contexts. Therefore, western methodology of intercultural communication is never equal to the universally-acknowledged principle. According to Professor Shan Bo [2] in Wuhan University, we should go to the way of reciprocal understanding and construct the possibility of trans-cultural communication based on dialogue and cooperation. We should transcend the prejudices of the culture and eliminate the habit of looking at the other culture in an alien, novel and way. Professor Jin Xuemin holds that we should summarize the essence of the value of the common community of a shared

1　沈清松. 跨文化哲学论. [M]. 北京：人民出版社，2014，第 1 页.
2　单波. 论跨文化传播的可能性. [J]. "广东外语外贸大学学报"，2014(3)：7.

future for all human beings based on the Chinese experience of the Chinese Dream. [1] In general, an interactive, diversified and polyphonic resonance will be built instead of a single voice, no matter how big the sound is.

（2）Mode-converging

In order to fully implement the improvement of people's intercultural literacy, we must organically integrate three literacies (elements) into a trinity and enhance the whole trinity, namely, technology, symbol and emotion.

※ The element of technology in intercultural literacy. Although we refuse the concept of a strong technology view, which is to take technology as the most important motive in the world and believe blindly in the superpower of the technology, we still have to confess the meaning of technology in modern society because we are now living in a technology-driven or data-driven society. The level of manipulating technology, to a certain extent, will lay great influence on the effect of intercultural communication. Intercultural literacy, in this course, will first consider technology literacy including the ability of expressing the meaning appropriately in an appropriate instrument (web, mobile Internet, etc.). The improvement of technology is always the important power of communication evolution. According to the report released by the United Nations Scientific, Educational and Cultural Organization (UNESCO) in December 2013, every citizen will need and should understand the rule of media and media information suppliers, opportunities and threats from virtual world, the mastery of information resources.

※ The element of symbol in intercultural literacy. Communication will generally resort to two categories: verbal communication and nonverbal communication. Both communications belong to the study of symbols, or semiotics in the term of Ferdinand de Saussure. As is said in the famous saying, it is not what you say; it is how you say it. Correct utilization of diction, sentences, emoticons, pictures, videos will facilitate the effect of intercultural communication. The year 2010 witnessed a large-scale China's

---

1　荆学民. 国际政治传播中政治文明的共振机制及中国战略 [J]. 国际新闻界，2015（8）：6.

national image advertising video which was launched in New York city. Unfortunately, this direct and utilitarian expression of symbols did acquire the expecting effect. However, documentaries in the recent years, such as *A Bite of China* [1], did make an enlightening difference in spreading Chinse cuisine to many corners of the world.

※ The element of emotion in intercultural literacy. With the development of technology, it is increasingly easier for audiences to express their emotions. In the domain of intercultural communication, the amount of overt bias is declining. However, the covert bias still exists in a large amount under the disguise of news professionalism. The acceleration of media convergence and the appearance of the relation-basedcommunication endow new connotation to the study of media literacy. Traditional interpersonal relation has shaped into a "human-media-society" triangular. Therefore, people's emotional needs and emotional literacy will be of great significance in modern media structure. Audiences, on one hand, receive information from the Net; on the other hand, they also discharge overwhelming feelings via the Internet. Intercultural communication has to take literacy of emotion into careful consideration.

Furthermore, the American tradition of literacy has a pragmatical orientation whereas European tradition has a habit of criticizing. The Chinese intercultural literacy cultivation will learn but not fully copy these two traditions. On the basis of the Chinese characteristics, we hold that intercultural literacy cultivation in China does not only mean the ability of learning, speaking and translating. It contains an organic circle of trinity of three literacies with a close combination of mediatization. The relation of the trinity can be listed as follows:

---

1   *A Bite of China* is a Chinese documentary television series on the history of food, eating, and cooking in China directed by Chen Xiaoqing. The documentary has also been actively encouraged as a means of introducing Chinese food culture to those unfamiliar with local cuisine.

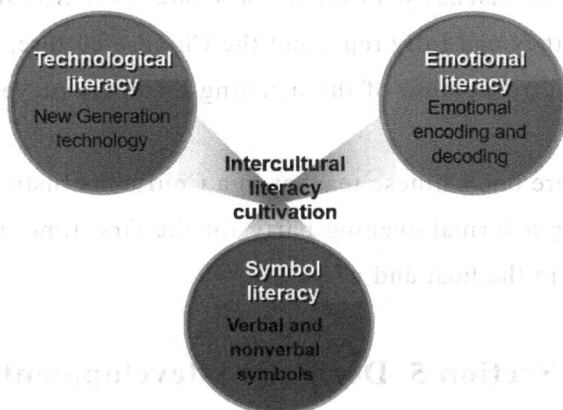

Figure 17　Trinity mode of three literacies in intercultural communication

In the trinity mode of three literacies in intercultural communication, technological literacy is the prerequisite, symbol literacy is the tool, and emotional literacy is the ultimate goal. We should improve all of the three literacies together. It is acknowledged that only audiences from other cultures draw an empathic resonance with our culture can we reach a harmonious intercultural communication. In order to realize this target of trinity, we should learn not only traditional research methodologies such as content analysis, corpus-based analysis, frame analysis, critical discourse analysis (CDA) and other kinds of emotional and semantic analysis instruments based on computer and Internet technologies.

Section 4　Cultural practice

Cultural practice

Discussion

① If a foreigner wants to know the Chinese culture, he or she may go to the online store of applications for mobile phones. They may possibly download some popular Chinese video sharing applications such as Kuaishou or Douyin [1]. Please discuss with other classmates how true these short videos are and whether they can fully represent the Chinese culture. The discussion is centered on the introspection of the meaning of media played in intercultural communication.

② If you were one Chinese teacher in a Confucius Institute in a European country attending a formal evening party for the first time, what cultural gift would you bring to the host and why?

Section 5 Derivative development

1.Film watching

Please watch the movie *The Joy Luck Club* [2] (《喜福会》,1993) and tried to work out a short intercultural analysis of the story of the movie.

Many people try to reflect of the social identification of Chinese Americans in the United States based on the story of this film. In this course, we are more interested in the inter-generation communication between sons and daughters and their parents.

With the popularity of base stations and mobile phones, different from western developed countries, China witnesses a sharp leap shifting Net-less (Internet inaccessible) society into mobile Internet society in an increasingly large number of areas, including many rural areas. A growing number of families, especially the families with rural migrant workers, communicate via the mobile Internet and many applications or social media. Inter-generation

---

1   Kuaishou and Douyin are popular short video sharing platforms in China and parts of the world. Users like recording and sharing their life and experiences in work, life and entertainment. These short videos are generally accompanied with music. Kuaishou and Douyin companies provide easy and accessible modules to produce these music videos in a short time.

2   The Joy Luck Club is a 1993 American drama film about the relationships between Chinese-American women and their Chinese immigrant mothers. The film is based on the eponymous 1989 novel by Amy Tan.Four older women, all Chinese immigrants living in San Francisco, meet regularly to play mahjong, eat, and tell stories. Each of these women has an adult Chinese-American daughter. The film reveals the hidden pasts of the older women and their daughters and how their lives are shaped by the clash of Chinese and American cultures as they strive to understand their family bonds and one another.

communication has increasingly become a serious headache for many families, especially between the children who were born from 1990s to 2000s and their parents.

What is your accounting for this phenomenon? Would you please explain this situation from the perspective of mediatization and provide several tentative and feasible suggestions to improve inter-generation communication in China?

2.Extended reading

（1）Marshall McLuhan

For the people out of the circle of culture, mass communication studies, Marshall McLuhan may be unfamiliar name. But for the students, teachers and scholars in cultural studies, communication studies, communication technology and technology philosophy, this name is so glowing that it enlightens and predicts a new paradigm. Many works and terms proposed by Marshall McLuhan were considered fantastic, weird and illogical in his period. However, his works have been the foundation of a discipline called "Media Ecology". Furthermore, his contributions are above and beyond media ecological study, which is the reason that he is called a thinker and a philosopher and is recommended by many teachers in various domains.

Herbert Marshall McLuhan was a Canadian philosopher. His work is one of the cornerstones of the study of media theory.Born in Edmonton, Alberta, McLuhan studied at the University of Manitoba and the University of Cambridge. He began his teaching career as a professor of English at several universities in the U.S. and Canada before moving to the University of Toronto in 1946, where he remained for the rest of his life.

McLuhan coined the expression "the medium is the message" and the term "global village", and predicted the World Wide Web almost 30 years before it was invented. He was a fixture in media discourse in the late 1960s, though his influence began to wane in the early 1970s.In the years after his death, he continued to be a controversial figure in academic circles.With the arrival of the Internet and the World Wide Web, interest was renewed in his work and perspective.

（2）Marshall McLuhan: The medium is the message.

"The medium is the message" is a phrase coined by Marshall McLuhan introduced in McLuhan's book Understanding Media: The Extensions of Man, published in 1964.It means that the nature of a medium (the channel through which a message is transmitted) is more important than the meaning or content of the message. McLuhan tells us that a "message" is, "the change of scale or pace or pattern" that a new invention or innovation "introduces into human affairs." McLuhan uses the term message to signify content and character. The content of the medium is a message that can be easily grasped. And the character of the medium is another message which can be easily overlooked. McLuhan says "Indeed, it is only too typical that the 'content' of any medium blinds us to the character of the medium."

The author of this course holds that the most important meaning of "The medium is the message" is draw people's attention in the media. To a certain extent, Marshall McLuhan also predicts the coming of the era of mediatization.

（3）Marshall McLuhan: Global village

The term global village represents the simplifying of the whole world into one village through the use of electronic media. Global village is also a term to express the constituting relationship between economics and other social sciences throughout the world. The term was coined by Canadian media theorist, Marshall McLuhan,and popularized in his books The Gutenberg Galaxy: The Making of Typographic Man (1962) and Understanding Media: The Extensions of Man (1964). McLuhan changed the way the world thought about media and technology ever since his use of the word in his book. McLuhan described how electric technology has contracted the globe into a village because of the instantaneous movement of information from every quarter to every point at the same time.

On the Internet, physical distance is even less of a hindrance to the real-time communicative activities of people. Social Spheres are greatly expanded by the openness of the web and the ease at which people can search for online communities and interact with others who share the same interests and concerns. According to McLuhan, the enhanced "electric speed in bringing all social and political functions together in a sudden implosion has heightened human awareness of responsibility to an intense degree." Increased speed of communication and the ability for people to read about, spread, and react to global news quickly, forces us to become more involved with others from various social groups and countries around the world and to be more aware of our global responsibilities.Similarly, web-connected computers enable people to link their web sites together.

（4）Knowing more cultures about ourselves (4): the marriage culture

Before we introduce ourselves to the others, the first and foremost thing is to have a correct and profound cognition of ourselves. In the ends of all the eight chapters, we add some basic knowledge of ourselves which are divided into eight sections, namely, the family culture, the food culture, the education culture, the marriage culture, the medical culture, the art culture, the consumption culture and the cyber culture respectively. We hope to help both audiences from other cultures and ourselves to have a better cognition of Chinese cultures. During these parts, the author of this book not only summarizes the traditional essence of these sections, but employs a diachronic perspective and includes the up-to-date changes.

（5）Our marriage cultures

Talking about the marriage, we must first touch upon the conceptualization of the family. In the traditional Chinese society, the family is the base of social institution and the basic cell for the society. the Chinese traditional society is a patriarchal system built on blood relations. The society and country are amplifying families in structure and function. The West society, however, pays more attention to the potential of individuals or the collection of individuals.

In China, the marriage is always considered as the connection between two families. A stable marriage means a stable family. In a traditional social context, once a husband and a wife become a couple, it means both parties will shoulder the responsibilities for the family, though the financial burden is put on the husband generally. Therefore, the Chinese marriage culture does not pay enough attention to the feelings of the individual. In the past, the marriage partners are always selected by the parents of the brides and grooms under the assistance of the matchmaker (a person known as the go-between between two families). The freedom of marriage is rare in the long history of feudal society and the total obedience in marriage is to demonstrate the filial piety, which is highly appreciated in society. The role of the wives in feudal society is the other that is under the gaze. The style of arranged marriage has led to many tragedies in many families. However, the matchmaker is still popular now in many places. Due to the status of mobility and the fast pace of the society, some people at the ready-marriage age lack the opportunities for effective communication. The matchmaker, in the information era, changes from middle and old-aged women into the website and various social network sites. Blind dating, including TV and cyber blind dating, is still prevailing in some parts of China.

In China, marriage is also closely related with the status of different genders. If a daughter is going to get married, a certain number of betrothal gifts is always needed from the bridegroom's family to the bride's family. When a daughter finishes the ritual of marriage, she is considered to merge into another family. Under this circumstance, the wife is hereby subordinated to her husband.

In the past century, China has undergone dramatic social, economic and cultural changes. Accordingly, the contemporary Chinese marriage customs pay more attention to the consequence of the marriage rather than its process. The procedures of the wedding rituals have been simplified greatly, and the wedding banquet has become the core of the whole ceremony. The following customs are normally needed for the contemporary Chinese marriage.

① Marriage certificate. When the two persons decide to get married, they have to register at the local government administrative agency, applying for the marriage certificate so as to become a legitimate couple.

② Wedding photos. Since 1990s, it has become a popular tendency for the young couples to take the wedding photos in professional photograph studios, which now has become a necessity for young couples. The enlarged wedding photos are usually hung up in the newlyweds' bedroom, reminding them of their happy moments which deserve to be shared with others.

③ Wedding banquet. In modern China, the wedding banquet is the most important procedure in the whole wedding ceremony. A formal marriage banquet usually serves the guest with more than twelve courses. In the wedding banquet, there will normally an anchor person hosting the ceremony with the common and local humor. The newlyweds will, of course, show their heartfelt thanks to the guests by words and toast.

As one of the most important rituals in the Chinese families, there are many customs to be considered in the ceremony. For example, the numbers "six" "eight" and "nine" are always favored by the marriage families and the couples themselves. Many families will choose a day with the lucky number of "eight" to hold the wedding ceremony. The procedure for the marriage ceremony is long and complicated. Normally, an old man with renowned prestige in the family will be recommended to chair the whole ceremony. Traditionally, people will celebrate the marriage ritual in the family. However, an increasingly large of families will choose to celebrate in hotels booked earlier. All the relatives, friends and acquaintances will be invited to attend the big ceremony and enjoy a magnificent feast or several feasts. It is always a long-standing habit for the people who attend the ceremony to prepare a "red envelope" beforehand in which their money is put. In different parts, there are even very clear prescriptions about the food, drinking, dressing and vehicles for the couple. It will be funny and interesting for foreigners to hear that people will put some Chinese dates, peanuts, longan and lotus seeds on the bed of the new couple, symbolizing "Zao Sheng Gui Zi" (wishing for the birth of a baby as early as possible).

A marriage between families of equal social rank is always preferred. The story of Cinderella in which the ordinary girl marries the prince is rare to be heard in the Chinese history. Freedom in love and marriage has been inspired after the foundation of the People's Republic of China. However, this marriage customs do not disappear in many places. In the modern society, people also judge and assess a ready marriage person, normally men, by their social status, materialistic foundation, etc.

The press and social network in China always witnessed a heated discussion about naked marriage. The proposal of the topic of naked marriage is an illustration of different states of mind in this issue.

The party who is in favor of naked marriage may hold that love and marriage are pure and saint free from any other elements. They have a strong belief in the virtue of marriage and normally optimistic in overcoming any difficulties in the after-marriage life through hard work.

The party who is against naked marriage believes that life is real and concrete and a marriage without a due amount of guarantee is fragile. A certain amount of materialistic preparation is a base and a responsible attitude for future life.

A phenomenon that deserves our attention is the decrease of the marriage rate as well as the birth rate. Pluralist trends of thought, financial burden, biological deficiency may account for this phenomenon. However, it is firmly believed a modern Chinese value on marriage will be built on the freedom and respect and a more harmonious relation between couples will soon be expected.

第五章 被"凝视"的他者：中国形象的国际媒介建构

Chapter Five
The Gaze of the Other: Media Construction of Chinese Image

Section 1 Lead-in

1.Question

British Broadcasting Corporation (BBC) launched a series of documentary about Chinese education for secondary school students named "Are Our Kids Tough Enough? Chinese School" in 2015. It records a four-week experiment of five Chinese teachers who are invited to teach in a middle school in Southern Hampshire in a Chinese teaching style. The Chinese teachers are in total charge of a 50-student grade 9 class, which is a contrast with Britain teaching. Students in this class have to study and behave as Chinese students in Chinese schools in the four-week test. They have to arrive at the classroom by 7 o' clock and stay in the school for 12 hours. BBC producers use the word "strong" because they doubt whether British students could endure this teaching pressure on one hand and they are curious of the result of this contrastive experiment on the other hand. To be honest, the Chinese teachers' class has no advantage over the British teachers' class because of the foreign language proficiency and the cultural differences both for the Chinese teachers and British students. After four weeks, however, the Chinese teachers' class win this competition with a big margin of advantages in all subjects. A certain number of students, surprisingly, say that they benefit a lot from this teaching and learning experience.

We are living in China and of course are educated in a Chinese teaching style. Would you please discuss with your partners and share your understanding of the advantages and disadvantages of the Chinese education style? Please notice that your comment should be objective.

2.Case

The New York Times is an American newspaper based in New York City with worldwide influence and readership. Founded in 1851, the paper has won 125 Pulitzer Prizes, for its excellent and professional news coverage and comment, more than any other newspaper. However, when covering China, it will use metaphorical and other designated words and pictures with negative connotations.

Both *The New York Times* and BBC in the lead-in part are world-famous media. However, in these two cases above, China and Chinese are both gazed from the perspective of the other. These two cases remind us of an interesting but embarrassing question: western media Construction of the Chinese Image, i.e., how do they look at us? Are the images of China (the Chinese environment and the Chinese education) genuine?

Section 2　Theory preparation

1.Theory preparation: the study of national image

An image is an artifact that depicts visual perception, such as a photograph or other two-dimensional picture, that resembles a subject (usually a physical object) and thus provides a depiction of it. National image is a mental "picture" of a nation or a country in foreign audiences.National image is the portrayal or impression of the history, status quo, behaviors, activities and exterior influence in the audiences in the international or a specific country. The construction and communication of image have a long history of over hundreds of years. In the early time, foreign audiences' and readers' national image about China always comes from the figurative and literal imagery from literary works, including poems, essays and novels, especially comparative novels. After media came into the center of the society, national image is always constructed by the media. How is the Chinese national image constructed, produced and transmitted in an intercultural context and how can we improve the spreading of the Chinese image? These concerns are the interior motive of this chapter.

Due to the inequality of the hard and soft powers between China and the west, national image or the media construction of the Chinese image have not been given too much attention to. In this sense, the national image we are going to explore and improve is to enhance our cultural confidence and cultural consciousness from equal and interactive intercultural perspectives. We hope that we can, on one hand, eliminate the overwhelming predominance of the west cultural superiority; on the other hand, join into the intercultural dialogue more voluntarily.

According to Sun Xiangfei, there are three dimensions in the study of national image. Firstly, the representation includes both self-expression and the representation by the other. These two representations are intersected and interacted. Secondly, the Chinese image will be portrayed as both Utopia or Hell in the past construction of western media. Thirdly, it should be clear foreign audiences with different standpoints or starting points may lead to different comments. Therefore, a set of symbolic representation system of Chinese national image in intercultural is to take the gaze of the other as a mirror and carry out a dynamic process of "the self-the other" and "domestic-alien" relations.

Section 3　Detailed analysis

1.The evolution of the Chinese national image

The national image is the result of judgement from different commentary subjects. Due to the restraints in social environment, lifestyles and cognitive structures, judging subjects may arrive at different comments on the same nation. The consequence of this factor is that every nation's image is multi-dimensional and full of changes.

China is a big country with a long and splendid history in east Asia. We tend to be very proud of our highly-developed civilization and achievements in the past. The publication of the famous book, *The Travels of Marco Polo*, in the late 13th century is considered the starting point of the Chinese national image. This book not only initiates the earliest collective memory of China for westerners, but also triggers a craze for seeking treasure in the east. Another book *Historia del Gran Reino de la China* by Spanish Fray de Mendoza in 1585 also depicted a decent and elegant image of China. China in this book is characterized as the area rich in wisdom and morality. This book had been translated into many European languages and was spreading to many dots of Europe. The open politics described in Mendoza's book presented a sharp contrast with the dark European doctrines before Renaissance. Represented by Confucianism, long history, delicate china, silk products, tea and other Chinese products, a distant country has been portrayed as a dream land or a Utopia for many Europeans at that time.

In the early and the middle sections of the Chinese history, China has a strong sense of superiority in comparison with the other kingdoms affiliated to it. Identity has never become a question for the old kingdom until the late Ming dynasty and the early Qing dynasty. With the acceleration of the communication between China and other countries, especially Western countries, this sense of superiority has lost its prestige gradually. The rising of the role "the Other" made China begin to reflect on the issue of the identity especially when we came into the crisis.

The consequence is the that the powerful position of the west doubted China's long-existing superiority and subjectivity. Blind pride was easily turned into the lack of confidence in military, economy and culture. China began to open the "gate" and tried to learn from "the other". The modernity of China hereby began. National image has been a harassment bothering

Chinese scholars for a long time. Some of them chose to turn to the west completely sacrificing our own heritage. "I" am homogenized by "the other". Since the collapse of the Chinese superior national image, the western's sense of superiority and advantages have reached a historical peak. Therefore, Chinese national image in comparative literature at this moment became belittled and stigmatized.

After the Renaissance, western's ethnocentrism is accompanied with a fast exploration of the globalization. Chinese national image began to fall down and was portrayed into a yellow devil which resists modern civilization in the late 18th century. After the Opium war, China, reluctantly, had to be emerged into the world order dominated by the west. The Chinese national image has come to the darkest period. Such insulting words as "Chink", "Chow" and "Chinee" began to be used by many Europeans.

Since the 1930s, "red China" has been a frequent word in describing the Chinese national image for Europeans and Americans. Although the foundation of the People's Republic of China has won many respects from developing countries since 1949, "red China" for the westerners, to a certain extent, is equal to distant, special and dim national feature.

The 1990s witnessed the initiative and the implementation of the famous reform and opening-up policy in China. China has tried to be more active in many international occasions and shouldered more responsibilities in the world. However, the Chinese national image among westerners, especially in France, Germany and Italy, has not been improved unfortunately. This consequence, to a certain extent, should be ascribed to the international media construction of China before, during and after 2008 Beijing Olympics.

Factors such as the consideration of economic profits, the distribution of international power and the heritage of history and culture all contribute to the formation of the Chinese national image. It is hard to point out very clearly which factor is more positively correlated with the evolution of the Chinese national image. However, what is clear-cut is that in the hundreds of years, many countries including less developed African countries and China are marginalized in the west-oriented tradition, are gazed as the other instead of the equal and interactive counterparts. Intercultural dialogue and communication become difficulty in the modernity of the west.

Stepping into the new century, the first two decades of the 21st century witnessed a quickly-rising and peacefully-rising China. Western countries are projecting increasing attention to the China national image, constructed by their international media organizations in a hospitable or hostile way. At the same time, a rising China also attaches growing importance to the construction of self-image based on its rising hard power and increasing soft power. Many researches in this domain are hereby proposed to provide strategies to improve China self-construction by mainly using our major media. The author of this course believes that it will be more significant for us to familiarize the generation of the Chinese national image in the literature of "the other" first before arriving at improving strategies.

2. The generation of the Chinese national image in literature of "the other"

Several influential studies and literature of the Chinese national image from the perspective of the west have to be mentioned here. Some missionaries came from England and other European countries to China since the Yuan dynasty (1271—1368). The communication between the west and China was recorded by these missionaries, which spurred up the interest of studying Chinese image. Raymond Dawson wrote the book *Chinese Chameleon: An Analysis of European Concepts of Chinese Civilization* in the beginning of the 20th century. Harold R. Isaacs wrote *Scratches on Our Minds: American Images of China and India* in the middle of the 20th century. The turning point between the 20th century and the 21st century witnessed several important works in this domain. American famous sinologist's monograph *The Chan's Great Continent: China in Western Mindsin 1998* had aroused influential power in the circle of the study of Chinese national image. Colin Mackerras, the British scholar, wrote *Western Images of China* in 1999. As Raymond Dawson wrote in his book, "chameleon" instead of "dragon" is the key word of the Chinese image in the westerners' eyes. These studies, represented by sinology, the Han school of classical philology, greatly triggered westerners' interest to explore China's economy, politics and culture, thus enhancing intercultural communication to a certain extent.

After the media came into the center of the communication of the society, international media construction of the Chinese national image has been the dominant channel for audiences to form a cognition of the Chinese image. The press such as *The Economist*, *The New York Times*, and *Times*, give its world-scale readers or audiences a constructed "China" and "Chinese". These media coverage, to a certain extent, stimulated China's self-reflection as a subject to rethink its image issue. Although these media coverage was implemented in the name of journalism professionalism, which perplexed many audiences, experts still used research methods such as critical discourse analysis (CDA) to unmask the hidden power ancestry and the covert discriminating attitude towards the development of China after news discourses. Van Dijk, Norman Fairclough, Ruth Wodak and other experts in the western world started from the linguistic analytic path and tried to reveal signs of power, ideology and bias in these discourses.

3. The spreading of the Chinese national image

Since the policy of the reform and opening-up and the stable growth in economy afterwards, China has been rising and has been the second largest country in the total volume of GDP since 2011. The invisible card "made in China" during and after the financial crisis from 2008 to 2010 has become overwhelmingly famous in the world. The rising of Chinese economy, however, does not have a corresponding improvement of the influence and the image. "Chameleon" is still the key and common concept describing the

Chinese national image for foreign journalists. Four tones of reporting, "the beauty of China", "the threat from China", "the collapse of China" and "the responsibility of China" are always noticed in the international media construction.

A rising China will naturally pay growing attention to the improvement of national image. Since the theoretical proposal of "peaceful rise" by Zheng Bijian in 2002, this conceptualization has won the approval of many officials, scholars and people. The peaceful rise has become one of the most important contradicting and protesting discourses for China, which is a different discoursal system from western centralism. This discourse system, together with the practice in international business and cultural exchanges contribute to a multi-dimensional spreading of the Chinese national image. Represented by "four new China's inventions" [1], Chinese products and services begin to go abroad and depicts a totally new and responsibly positive self-image in the globe. The December of 2001 witnessed China's participation into the World Trade Organization (WTO). After that, due to the benefit of globalization, products with the logo "made in China" has speeded Chinese image to countries ranging developed countries to many less developed or even impoverished countries. This hard power of economy and business has been an important internal core for the spreading of the Chinese national image.

If we search the key word "made in China" in the famous searching engine Baidu, we can reach over 43,300,000 results in a blink of eyes. Based on the logic of "taking commodities as a connection", the construction of national image has accomplished its first link during which the separation of communicating subjects has been got through. The commodity is, of course, is the invested with a nation's history and culture, thus becoming the carrier of the meaning. Although the implied meaning carried by the products may not

---

1   The phrase "four new China's inventions" is a web coinage which includes high-speed raiway, mobile payment, bicycle-sharing and cyber-shopping. Although these acts may not be invented in China, we highly popularize these acts and spread them to many dots of the world.

be positive all the time, this behavior (intentionally and unintendedly) does initiate a new move of actively spreading China in a voluntary way.

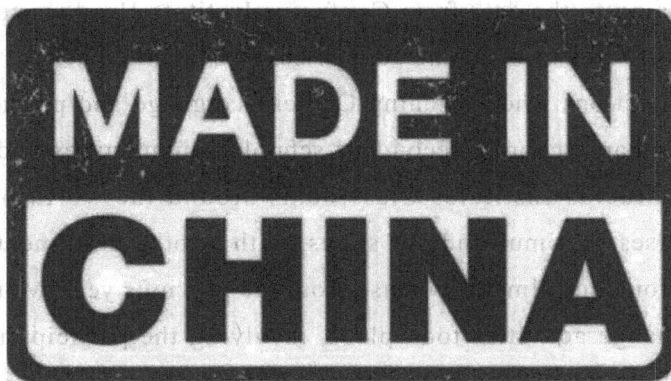

Figure 18 A logo of "made in China"

In accompany with China's exportation of products, Chinese advertisements, including TV and web commercials, national image advertisement, public service announcements, hard and soft advertising representations also spread the Chinese image to the globe. At the same time, an increasingly large number of Chinese tourists begin to show their footprints and "selfies" in the whole world, which is considered as another transmitting channel, too. The year 2017 saw over 130 million Chinese going abroad for traveling, spending 11.52 billion US dollars globally, according to the data released by Chinese Tourism Research Institute. As China's economy and exchanges with the world have seen rapid growth, there has also been a sharp increase in the world's demands for Chinese learning. Benefiting from the UK, France, Germany and Spain's experience in promoting their national languages, China began its own exploration through establishing non-profit public institutions which aim to promote Chinese language and the Chinese culture in foreign countries in 2004. These were given the name the Confucius Institute.Over recent years, the Confucius Institutes' development has been sharp and they have provided scope for people all over the world to learn about Chinese language and culture. In addition, they have become a platform for cultural exchanges between China and the world as well as a bridge reinforcing friendship and cooperation between China and the rest of the world and are much welcomed across the globe.According to the data from Confucius Institute Headquarters (Hanban), Confucius Institutes/Classrooms adopt flexible teaching patterns and adapt to suit local conditions when teaching Chinese language and promoting culture in foreign primary schools, secondary schools, communities and enterprises. In 2009, Confucius Institutes/Classrooms around the world offered 9,000 Chinese courses of a multitude of styles, with a total enrollment of 260,000, a 130,000 strong enrollment increase from the previous year. More than 7,500 cultural exchange activities took place, involving the participation of over 3 million reaching double the participation figures of the corresponding period of the previous year.These commodity exchanges, folk communications and language and culture cultivation all contributed to the public diplomacy of China, thus improving intercultural communication effect.

The Chinese leading official media groups, represented by China Global Television Network (CGTN) [1] in the center, are accelerating their footsteps of emerging in the center of the world and reporting China and telling good stories of China. Meanwhile, with the empowering of the media, the "microphone" has been delivered the individual citizens. A growing number of users began to generate contents in their favorite instant messages and social network sites. An increasingly abundant of information ranging from texts, pictures to videos about China are frequently noticed in Facebook, Twitter, YouTube, WhatsApp, QQ, Wechat, etc., transmitting the Chinese image to the audiences in the whole world. Due to the sharp difference in media tradition, foreign media and some foreign audiences are on their guard of the official information, user-generated content (UGC) hereby becomes an integral and important part to supplement the official and rigid content, thus

---

1   In March, 2018, the central committee of the Communist Party of China (CPC) canceled China Central Television (CCTV) / China Global Television Network (CGTN), China National Radio (CNR) and China Radio International (CRI) and built a new station named "China Media Group (CMG)". The original forms are remained in domestic China whereas "Voice of China" is used in the globe.

contributing to a multi-dimensional and more convincing China. UGC-based TV series and films of China have triggered growing attention in the west.

4. The new cognition of the Chinese image: sample of TV series and films

The year 1980 first witnessed a TV drama called *Wang Xiang Zhi Xing* (Star of Homesickness), a work co-produced by Chinese and Japanese companies, broadcasted in Japan. Since then, a growing number of TV series and films, such as *The Legend of Emperor Yongzheng*, *The Legend of Bruce Lee*, *The Story of Ji Xiaolan* and *Beautiful Life for Daughter-in-law*, have shown in many countries in the past three decades. The "going out" of Chinese TV series and films have been an important issue to construct the Chinese national image.

（1）Kungfu TV and film products and the imagination of Chinese image

Kungfu, or martial art, has been the most important symbol for foreign audiences in the globe when they are asked about the impression of Chinese movies in various surveys. *The Legend of Bruce Lee* in 2008 and *The Legend of Ye Wen* (Bruce Lee's Kungfu master) in 2013 reached a peak of the Kungfu Chinese in the west. These portrayals of actors, moves endow foreign audiences a fantastic imagination of the Chinese martial art, creating an atmosphere of oriental beauty. Spectacles of the Chinese Kungfu, the national spirit in front of invasions and the pursuit of harmony are manifested in the movies. The aesthetic pursuit and philosophical thinking of these movies go beyond fighting moves, presenting the glamor of the splendid and profound Chinese culture. Some foreign audiences are even greatly spurred up by these penetrating stories and magnificent scenes, and chose to go to China, for example, the Temple of Shaolin in Mountain Songshan in Henan province, to formally acknowledge Chinese Kungfu masters as their masters.

（2）Historical TV and film products and the construction of Chinese image

TV and film products such as *Emperor Nurhachi*, *First Emperor of Qin*,

Emperor Genghis Khan and *Emperor Hanwu* have their eyes on important emperors in the Chinese history. *Peace Talks in Peking* tells the story of the talk between the Community Party of China (CPC) and the Kuomintang (KMT) in 1949, in which the KMT did not accept peace talks and the CPC finally tided over the Yangtze River and liberated the whole nation. These historical TV series and films return to the original history and help foreign audiences to form a correct and genuine cognition of China's image.

The folk historical stories such as *The Pilgrimage to the West*, *The Story of Ji Xiaolan* and *The Romance of the Three Kingdoms* fulfill our Chinese collective imagination as a nation. The folk story-telling, as an important supplement of the official image-building, strengthen our social and group identification. It will be easier for people to construct the portrayal of China emotionally.

(3) Reality TV and film products and the construction of Chinese image

The past fifteen years witnessed a growing number of Chinese TV dramas and films with the story from real families and societies translated and broadcasted in other countries. *Beautiful Life for Daughter-in-law*, received warm welcome in many countries, especially in African countries. These TV dramas and films generally reflects the true evolution and transformations of the Chinse society, thus appealing interesting for many foreign audiences. Additionally, family is a mini-unit of the society, so the stories about family ethics, couple relations, relations between parents and children and relations between mother-in-law and daughter-in-law are somewhat universal topics in every country. Therefore, these TV dramas and films will easily cause a cultural resonance among foreign audiences. It is believed that family-country relation is the basic tone for story-telling in many movies. The popularity of Chinese reality TV and film products will of course assist the construction of a complete and human national image.

(4) Documentaries and the construction of Chinese image

A documentary film is a nonfictional motion picture intended to document some aspect of reality, primarily for the purposes of instruction, education, or maintaining a historical record.Western directors and producers have started to record China and portray the image of China in a documentary way many years ago, for example, Michelangelo Antonioni's *China* (1972), Joris Ivens' *How the Yukong Moved the Mountains* (1975) and *Wham! In China: Foreign Skies* (1986). During the inadequate emphasis on the documentary art form, Chinese documentaries, especially documentary films, have to show their figure in international film festivals, which provide important growing space for Chinese independent documentaries.

The past two decades witnessed an increasing number of documentaries both in China and abroad represented by Chinese director Chen Xiaoqing's *A Bite of China* (2012). China Central Television (CCTV) started a professional TV channel for documentaries (CCTV9 Documentary) from November 1st, 2011. The emergence and popularity of Internet platforms such as Sohu Video and Aiqiyi Video also provide a possibility for Chinese documentaries to enter into audience's vision more easily, though these documentaries may be under tough pressure of market and capital. Due to the limit of broadcasting channels, Chinese independent documentaries still have to resort to western film festivals. Some western film festivals controlled the generation and the discourse power of Chinese documentaries. They hided the ideological implications of the West and forced Chinese documentaries to accept their story and script logic, which became a heavy restraint for Chinese independent documentaries.

Regardless of the difficulty and dilemma of Chinese documentaries, they do provide a good opportunity for foreign audiences to know and construct the image of China. Furthermore, foreign audiences will choose to believe in the Chinese national image for its genuine reflection of China instead of official spreading and advertising. According to Stuart Hall's "encoding-decoding" theory, foreign audiences will feature a kind of contradictory interpretation of the official discourse.

In the beginning of the year 2016, British Broadcasting Corporation (BBC) produced and broadcasted 6-episode documentary *The Story of China*, which presented a panorama of the Chinese history of five thousand years. Apart from BBC, Discovery Channel and National Geographic Channels International (NGCI) also produced a large number of documentaries about China with the themes ranging from delicious food, Chinese Kungfu, Chinese porcelain to the Chinese social reality. Although documentaries are always criticized for their selective recording and editing, and their covert ideological biases, it is acknowledged that discourses from these documentaries have been important channels for foreign audiences to familiarize China. As we illustrate in Chapter Five, few foreign people have opportunities to come to visit China by themselves. Therefore, mediatization becomes a significant for them to construct the Chinese national image. TV and film documentaries hereby become more trustworthy resources for foreign audiences. In this sense, we should attach enough importance to the production and communication of documentaries. On one hand, we should take the exposure in these TV and film documentaries as a pressure and a motive to make us better, especially in environment and education. On the other hand, we ourselves, with our mainstream media in the center, should actively produce and spread high-quality and high-definition documentaries to other dots of the world. We can focus our eyes on the heated topics in documentaries, for example, the environment, the youth, the education, the product made in China, and endow a positive denotation to the objects that have been stigmatized by "the other". *A Bite of China I* has won 8.7 high points in Internet Movie Database (IMDb). The past fifteen years witnessed excellent Chinese documentaries such as *The Rise of the Great Nations* (2006), *Magnificent Instruments in Big Country* (2013) and *Splendid China* (2017), which won marvelous acclaim from the critics. *Hong Kong-Zhuhai-Macao Bridge*, casted in five years, was broadcasted in both CGTN and Discovery Channel in 2017, received many positive comments for its documentary story-telling and the Chinese image it reflected.

Section 4 Cultural practice

Cultural practice

Discussion

The research team in Beijing Normal University, chaired by professor Huan Huilin, started the research "International Communication of the Chinese Films" since 2011. They have carried out a large-scale quantitative investigation among foreign audiences to check foreign respondents' preference for varieties of the Chinese films which is shown in the following chart.

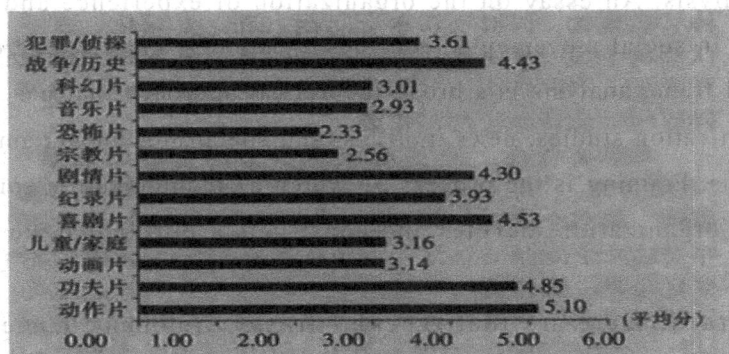

Figure 19 Foreign respondents' preference for varieties of the Chinese films

Would you like discuss with your partners and describe and interpret the chart? Based on what we learn in this unit, would you please give your comments and several tentative and feasible suggestions on how to improve the international communication effect of the Chinese films from the perspective of national image and intercultural communication?

Section 5 Derivative development

1.Film watching

Please watch the documentary *A Bite of China I* (《舌尖上的中国Ⅰ》, 2012) and tried to work out a short intercultural analysis of the story of the documentary.

In your analysis, please explore what is foreign audience's comment on the food presented in this documentary. If you are going to introduce one of the most delicious food to foreign guests, what would you introduce and why?

2.Extended reading

(1)Frame analysis

Frame analysis is a multi-disciplinary social science research method used to analyze how people understand situations and activities. The concept is generally attributed to the work of Erving Goffman and his 1974 book Frame analysis: An essay on the organization of experience and has been developed in social movement theory, policy studies and elsewhere.Framing theory and frame analysis is a broad theoretical approach that has been used in communication studies, news, politics, and social movements among other applications. Framing is the process by which a communication source, such as a news organization, defines and constructs a political issue or public controversy.

Generally, there are four types of frame alignment, namely, frame bridging, frame amplification, frame extension and frame transformation. [1]

① Frame bridging is the linkage of two or more ideologically congruent but structurally unconnected frames regarding a particular issue or problem.

② Frame amplification refers to the clarification and invigoration of an interpretive frame that bears on a particular issue, problem, or set of events. This interpretive frame usually involves the invigorating of values or beliefs.

③ Frame extensions are a movement's effort to incorporate participants by extending the boundaries of the proposed frame to include or encompass the views, interests, or sentiments of targeted groups.

④ Frame transformation is a process required when the proposed frames

1 Snow, David A., R. Burke Rochford, Jr., Steven K. Worden, and Robert D. Benford. 1986. "Frame Alignment Processes, Micromobilization, and Movement Participation." American Sociological Review 51: 464−481.

may not resonate with, and on occasion may even appear antithetical to, conventional lifestyles or rituals and extant interpretive frames. When this happens, new values, new meanings and understandings are required in order to secure participants and support.

(2) Knowing more cultures about ourselves (5): the medical culture

Before we introduce ourselves to the others, the first and foremost thing is to have a correct and profound cognition of ourselves. In the ends of all the eight chapters, we add some basic knowledge of ourselves which are divided into eight sections, namely, the family culture, the food culture, the education culture, the marriage culture, the medical culture, the art culture, the consumption culture and the cyber culture respectively. We hope to help both audiences from other cultures and ourselves to have a better cognition of Chinese cultures. During these parts, the author of this book not only summarizes the traditional essence of these sections, but employs a diachronic perspective and includes the up-to-date changes.

(3) Our medical cultures

With a history of 2000 to 3000 years, Traditional Chinese Medicine (TCM) has formed a unique system to diagnose and cure illness. The TCM approach is fundamentally different from that of Western medicine. In TCM, the understanding of the human body is based on the holistic understanding of the universe as described in Taoism, and the treatment of illness is based primarily on the diagnosis and differentiation of syndromes.

The TCM approach treats zang-fu organs as the core of the human body. Tissue and organs are connected through a network of channels and blood vessels inside human body. Qi (or Chi) acts as some kind of carrier of information that is expressed externally through jingluo system. Pathologically, a dysfunction of the zang-fu organs may be reflected on the body surface through the network, and meanwhile, diseases of body surface tissues may also affect their related zang or fu organs. Affected zang or fu organs may also influence each other through internal connections. Traditional

Chinese medicine treatment starts with the analysis of the entire system, then focuses on the correction of pathological changes through readjusting the functions of the zang-fu organs.

Evaluation of a syndrome not only includes the cause, mechanism, location, and nature of the disease, but also the confrontation between the pathogenic factor and body resistance. Treatment is not based only on the symptoms, but differentiation of syndromes. Therefore, those with an identical disease may be treated in different ways, and on the other hand, different diseases may result in the same syndrome and are treated in similar ways.

The clinical diagnosis and treatment in Traditional Chinese Medicine are mainly based on the yin-yang and five elements theories. These theories apply the phenomena and laws of nature to the study of the physiological activities and pathological changes of the human body and its interrelationships. The typical TCM therapies include acupuncture, herbal medicine, and qigong exercises. With acupuncture, treatment is accomplished by stimulating certain areas of the external body. Herbal medicine acts on zang-fu organs internally, while qigong tries to restore the orderly information flow inside the network through the regulation of Qi. These therapies appear very different in approach yet they all share the same underlying sets of assumptions and insights in the nature of the human body and its place in the universe. Some scientists describe the treatment of diseases through herbal medication, acupuncture, and qigong as an "information therapy".

The philosophical origins of Chinese medicine have grown out of the tenets of Taoism. Taoism bases much of its thinking on observing the natural world and manner in which it operates, so it is no surprise to find that the Chinese medical system draws extensively on natural metaphors. In Chinese medicine, the metaphoric views of the human body based on observations of nature are fully articulated in the theory of "yin-yang" and the system of Five Elements.

The direct meanings of yin and yang in Chinese are bright and dark sides of an object. Chinese philosophy uses yin and yang to represent a wider range of opposite properties in the universe: cold and hot, slow and fast, still and moving, masculine and feminine, lower and upper, etc. In general, anything that is moving, ascending, bright, progressing, hyperactive, including functional disease of the body, pertains to yang. The characteristics of stillness, descending, darkness, degeneration, hypo-activity, including organic disease, pertain to yin.

The function of yin and yang is guided by the law of unity of the opposites. In other words, yin and yang are in conflict but at the same time mutually dependent. The nature of yin and yang is relative, with neither being able to exist in isolation. Without "cold" there would be no "hot"; without "moving" there would be no "still"; without "dark", there would be no "light". The most illustrative example of yin-yang interdependence is the interrelationship between substance and function. Only with ample substance can the human body function in a healthy way; and only when the functional processes are in good condition, can the essential substances be appropriately refreshed.

The opposites in all objects and phenomena are in constant motion and change: The gain, growth and advance of the one means the loss, decline and retreat of the other. For example, day is yang and night is yin, but morning is understood as being yang within yang, afternoon is yin within yang, evening before midnight is yin within yin and the time after midnight is yang within yin. The seed (Yin) grows into the plant (Yang), which itself dies back to the earth (Yin). This takes place within the changes of the seasons. Winter (Yin) transforms through the Spring into Summer (Yang), which in turn transforms through Autumn into Winter again. Because natural phenomena are balanced in the constant flux of alternating yin and yang, the change and transformation of yin-yang has been taken as a universal law.

Traditional Chinese medicine holds that human life is a physiological process in constant motion and change. Under normal conditions, the waxing and waning of yin and yang are kept within certain bounds, reflecting a dynamic equilibrium of the physiological processes. When the balance is broken, disease occurs. Typical cases of disease-related imbalance include excess of yin, excess of yang, deficiency of yin, and deficiency of yang.

The practice of acupuncture and moxibustion is based on the theory of meridians. According to this theory, qi (vital energy) and blood circulate in the body through a system of channels called meridians, connecting internal organs with external organs or tissues. By stimulating certain points of the body surface reached by meridians through needling or moxibustion, the flow of qi and blood can be regulated and diseases are thus treated. These stimulation points are called acupuncture points, or acupoints.

Acupoints reside along more than a dozen of major meridians. There are 12 pairs of regular meridians that are systematically distributed over both sides of the body, and two major extra meridians running along the midlines of the abdomen and back. Along these meridians more than three hundred acupoints are identified, each having its own therapeutic action. For example, the point Hegu located between the first and second metacarpal bones, can reduce pain in the head and mouth.

In acupuncture clinics, the practitioner first selects appropriate acupoints along different meridians based on identified health problems. Then very fine and thin needles are inserted into these acupoints. The needles are made of stainless steel and vary in length from half an inch to 3 inches. The choice of needle is usually determined by the location of the acupoint and the effects being sought. If the point is correctly located and the required depth reached, the patient will usually experience a feeling of soreness, heaviness, numbness and distention. The manipulator will simultaneously feel that the needle is tightened.

The effectiveness of an acupuncture treatment is strongly dependent upon an accurate Chinese medical diagnosis. The needling skills and techniques of the practitioner will also influence greatly the effectiveness of the outcome.

Acupuncture can be remarkably effective in many conditions, but in the West, patients often use acupuncture as the last option for their long-term chronic problems. Therefore, we sometimes see the treatment as slow and in some cases of marginal benefit. With the gradual establishment of acupuncture as the treatment of choice for many people, the effectiveness of the approach with acute as well as with more chronic conditions is being recognized.

Acupuncture is often conducted in combination with Moxibustion. Moxibustion is the process where moxa sticks, made of dry moxa leaves (Artemisia vulgaris) is ignited and held about an inch above the patients' skin over specific acupuncture points. Moxa is available in a loose form that can be used for making moxa cones. Alternatively, moxa is packed and rolled in a long stick like a large cigar, about 15 ~ 20 cm long and about 1 ~ 2 cm in diameter. The purpose of this process is to warm the qi and blood in the channels. Moxibustion is most commonly used when there is the requirement to expel cold and damp or to tonify the qi and blood. A single treatment of moxibustion usually lasts 10 ~ 15 minutes. Needle-warming moxibustion combines needling and moxibustion by attaching a moxa stub (about 2 cm long) to an inserted needle. This method enhances the effects of needling and is often used to treat chronic rheumatism and rheumatoid arthritis.

第六章 用恰当的方式传播中国 :中国的"自塑"
Chapter Six
Introducing China in a Proper Way

Section 1 Lead-in

1.Question

（1）If you were one Chinese teacher in a Confucius Institute in a European country attending a formal evening party for the first time in this country, what cultural gift would you bring to the host and why?

（2）Why is it hard for the Chinese humor and comedy to be appreciated by audience from west countries?

（3）Can "four new China's inventions" (high-speed railway, mobile payment, bicycle-sharing and cyber-shopping) be a good intermediary to introduce China effectively?

2.Case

Nowadays, an increasing number of Chinese begin to celebrate foreign festivals. Meanwhile, some traditional Chinese festivals, including the most important Spring Festival, are losing their attractiveness and influence among young people.

Would you discuss about this phenomenon with your partners and work out possible factors that may account for this case? It is suggested that you should not oversimplify the matter and ascribe the reason to the attractiveness of the western festivals. Factors such as the trend of consumerism, the field of cyber culture, the advancement of technology should be given consideration, too.

Based on your analysis, try to figure out a better and a more efficient way to introduce Chinese festivals not only to foreign audiences, but ourselves.

Section 2　Theory preparation

Theory preparation: the concept of globalization and Chinese path

Globalization is the process of interaction and integration among people, companies, and governments worldwide. As a complex and multifaceted phenomenon, globalization is considered by some as a form of capitalist expansion which entails the integration of local and national economies into a global, unregulated market economy. Globalization has grown due to advances in transportation and communication technology. With the increased global interactions comes the growth of international trade, ideas, and culture. Globalization is primarily an economic process of interaction and integration that's associated with social and cultural aspects. However, conflicts and diplomacy are also large parts of the history of globalization, and modern globalization.Economically, globalization involves goods, services, the economic resources of capital, technology, and data. The expansions of global markets liberalize the economic activities of the exchange of goods and funds. Removal of cross-border trades barriers has made formation of global markets more feasible. These improvements have generated further interdependence of economic and cultural activities around the globe.

Academic literature commonly subdivides globalization into three major areas: economic globalization, cultural globalization, and political globalization. In 2000, the International Monetary Fund (IMF) identified four basic aspects of globalization: trade and transactions, capital and investment movements, migration and movement of people, and the dissemination of knowledge.Further, environmental challenges such as global warming, cross-boundary water, air pollution, and over-fishing of the ocean are linked with globalization.

Since the proposal of the reform and opening-up policy in 1990s, China began to converge into the trend of globalization. Areas along Zhujiang River Delta and Yangtze River Delta were the first places to join the global trade and manufacturing. Original Equipment Manufacturer (OEM), Original Design Manufacturer (ODM), Original Standardization Manufacturer (OSM) and Original Brand Manufacturer (OBM) are common ways to implement export-oriented business.

The December of 2001 witnessed China's participation into the World Trade Organization (WTO). After that, due to the benefit of globalization, products with the logo "made in China" has speeded Chinese image to various countries.

With the acceleration of Belt and Road Initiative (the Silk Road Economic Belt and the 21st Century Maritime Silk Road) in the beginning of 2000s, our Chinese economy and the Chinese culture are converged into the world culture map with more confidence.

However, the years since 2016 saw a stream of de-globalization or anti-globalization or counter-globalization, represented by some "post-truth" events such as Brexit. It is a social movement critical of economic globalization. Participants in these social movements oppose large, multinational corporations having unregulated political power, exercised through trade agreements and deregulated financial markets.

Another variant of globalization is a coinage called "glocalization", which is a combination of globalization and localization, and first appeared in a late 1980s publication of the Harvard Business Review. This term indicates simultaneous occurrence of both universalizing and particularizing tendencies in contemporary social, political, and economic systems. Glocalization indicates that the growing importance of continental and global levels is occurring together with the increasing salience of local and regional levels.

At the same time, we should be clear that globalization is different from uniformity. Many years ago, European scholars such as William Stead and David Held began to worry about and warn Europe off the overwhelming influence of the United States. People are afraid of being "too American", homogenized and heavily relied on American food, movies and culture. Although we cannot deny people's groundless worry and proved that they are ill-founded, we should be confident that the deep structure of a certain culture is always deeply-rooted and not easily-changed. As the author of this course talks with his young students jokingly in the class, "guys, you are so young. When you are old enough, you will believe that tea is a better drink than coffee and Chinese mahjong is a better game than computer games."

For many years, western cultures, represented by American culture with Hollywood films in the center, have poured into China and become a predominant phenomenon among Chinese citizens, especially young Chinese. However, this trend will be replaced by a new round of cultural convergence between the Chinese culture and western culture. Actually, our traditional culture has been favored by people all over the globe. The history ranging from the Silk Road to Zheng He, one of the pioneers in exploring the ocean engaging into inter-cultural communications in Ming dynasty demonstrated the glamor of our splendid culture. The past fifteen years also witnessed the great popularity and prosperity of our Chinese TV series such as "A Bite of China" and "Beautiful Life for Daughter-in-law," all over the world. We have every reason to believe that our Chinese culture was, is and will be enjoyed in the whole world.

The growing number of Confucius Institutes in various countries now provides a terrific opportunity for foreign people to keep track of our language and culture. However, the spreading of our culture and the convergence of different cultures will never be an easy task. We should exert all our effort to renovate and refurbish methods to fulfill the real cultural harmony.

Section 3 Detailed analysis

1.Before introducing China: knowing ourselves

It is believed that an efficient intercultural communication effect is, to a certain extent, dependent on the cognition of "I". Before introducing China to the world, it is of great significance to know ourselves, including such issues as what we have and who we are. The essence of the Chinese culture should be familiarized to shape a sense of pride. Although the studies of Chinese ancient civilization may have different interpretations, it is generally-acknowledged that basic knowledge about Chinese ancient civilization will benefit Chinese people greatly in intra and intercultural communication.

It is hard to arrive at a consensus on the definition, even on the research territory the studies of Chinese ancient civilization. But we can roughly agree that the studies of Chinese ancient civilization are a series of cultural systems which integrate the combination of Confucianism, Taoism and Chinese Buddhism as the center and conclude Chinese history, Chinese literature, Chinese arts, Chinese dramas, Chinese music, Chinese martial arts, Chinese customs and Chinese cuisines.

(1) The significance of knowing ourselves

The first significance is to make us more familiar with the Chinese history. Living in a modernized and mediatized society, people now find that it is easy to know the current or even the future situation whereas it is of due difficulty to know the history deeply. The latent obstacle may lie in the competence of reading and comprehending old Chinese, which is a good argumentation that we should read the history and study Chinese ancient civilization.

The second significance is to improve individual quality. The classics, knowledge and methodology in the studies of Chinese ancient civilization will make people increasingly and gradually refined. As Francis Bacon said in Of Studies, histories make men wise; poets witty; the mathematics subtle; natural philosophy deep; moral, grave; logic and rhetoric, able to contend. The ancient classics such as *The Analects of Confucius* are the origin of the Chinese culture which will enlighten not only Chinese generations, but the whole world.

The third significance is to develop and expand national spirit. The content in the studies of Chinese ancient civilization is an important and integral part constructing the Chinese national spirit and socialist spiritual civilization. A good manipulation of the Chinese culture is the pavement for developing and spreading the Chinese culture, too.

The fourth significance is to keep the status of subjectivity and independence of the Chinese culture in the globe. Every country never stops seeking their own and unique identity, especially in the identity of culture under the fierce impact of globalization and modernization. Although China is a great country with splendid history, we should also be more forward and prospective in keeping our unique subjectivity. If unique subjectivity does not remain, it is meaningless to talk an intercultural dialogue and a prosperity of converged cultures.

An online survey in June 2006 by China Renmin University and Baidu company revealed top 10 masters in the studies of Chinese ancient civilization: Wang guowei（王国维）, Qian Zhongshu（钱钟书）, Hu Shi（胡适）, Lu Xun（鲁迅）, Liang Qichao（梁启超）, Cai Yuanpei（蔡元培）, Zhang Taiyan（章太炎）, Chen Yinque（陈寅恪）[1], Guo Moruo（郭沫若）and Feng Youlan（冯友兰）. Apart from these figures, Liang Suming（梁簌溟）, Ma Yifu（马一浮）, Xiong Shili（熊十力）Zhao Yuanren（赵元任）and some other intellectuals are also referenced in the studies of Chinese civilization.

As for the reading list, according to Qian Mu (1895—1990), the famous thinker, philosopher, historian and educationist, every Chinese is required to read the following seven books, namely, *The Analects of Confucius*(《论语》), *The Analects of Mencius*(《孟子》), *The Analects of Lao-tzu*(《老子》), *The Analects of Zhuang Zhou*(《庄子》), *Platform Sutra of the Sixth Patriarch*(《六祖坛经》), *The Analects of Jinsi*(《近思录》), *The Analects of Chuanxi*(《传习录》). In 1923, Hu Shi, the famous thinker, philosopher, historian and educationist, wrote thirty-nine books which he called the minimum list of reading Chinese

---

1　The Chinese mandarin pinyin of "陈寅恪" is ambiguous. Some Chinese pronounce it as "Chen Yinke", but scholars and intellectuals generally prefer to pronounce it as "Chen Yinque". The author of this book chooses the second tradition.

classics upon the invitation of the students in Tsinghua University. We'd better read them all if possible, to have a deeper understanding of our own culture and civilization.

2.Before introducing China: intersubjectivity

Intersubjectivity is the psychological relation between people. It is usually used in contrast to solipsistic individual experience, emphasizing our inherently social being. Intersubjectivity is considered crucial not only at the relational level but also at the epistemological and even metaphysical levels. For example, intersubjectivity is postulated as playing a role in establishing the truth of propositions, and constituting the so-called objectivity of objects.

When comes to intercultural communication, the contrast between subject and object will not be propitious to a two-way interactive dialogue. George Macartney, the British diplomat, for example, paid an unhappy visit to Emperor Qianlong of the Qing Dynasty in 1793. Many factors, according to the study of historians, may contribute to this failure diplomatic communication. However, the arrogance of the Qing Dynasty due to the ignorance of the importance of intersubjectivity may be one of the reasons.

The shift of angles from cultural ethnocentrism to intersubjectivity is to transform from the tool-oriented to the theory-oriented methodology. A harmonious intercultural communication and a successful spreading of the Chinese culture will need to be more mutual in the communicative attitudes. Intersubjectivity means mutually reciprocal understanding under the Under the premise of admitting our disadvantages, thus making intercultural dialogues possible and feasible.

3.Introducing China in a proper way: speaking in a foreign language

Speaking in a foreign language, even with a poor accent, will soon shorten the distance between people in daily verbal communication.Professors Wang

Fuxiang and Ma Dengge [1] from Beijing International Studies University once mentioned a case in their book about foreign language and culture. In 1998, Frank came to China from Australia for research purposes. He chose Beijing as his first stop. In order to help his communications with the local people, he boned up on the Chinese language, which he had been studying at college and with which he could communicate fairly comfortably. After he arrived in Beijing, he began to talk to some of the local people to ask directions and advice. Although he used mostly Chinese in his communication, he noticed that people around him would sometimes giggle and answer him in English even if they knew very little English. He continued talking to various individuals but often, when he was trying to discuss a more complex and intricate idea, the people smile and encourage him to use English. When he was talking in Chinese, he found that they continued to laugh, grin, nod their head, and encourage him to continue in English. And when he was talking in English, he was not sure that he was perfectly understood.

According to the observation of the author of this book, the phenomenon the two professors mention is common and true in China, especially in the past when the number of foreigners is still scarce. However, we do not hold that the giggle in this case is a sneer at Frank. The solution to this case, to a certain extent, could be easily reached if both parties speak better foreign language. One obvious problem caused by the language gap is the danger of misunderstanding, especially when talk about culturally-loaded and ambiguous words and phrases. A second problem most people experience when they speak in a foreign language, especially if they don't speak the language fluently, is that they will feel less sure of themselves.

To become a good intercultural communicator, you need to be aware of how speaking in a foreign language affects you. It has long been recognized that language is an essential and important part of a given culture and that the impact of culture upon a given language is something intrinsic and

---

indispensable. The Sapir–Whorf hypothesis holds that the structure of a language affects its speakers' world view or cognition. Therefore, to reach a proficient level in the mastery of foreign languages, or English in many cases, is of great significance to introduce China. China started to attach importance to the education of foreign languages (English) in secondary schools at the end of 1980s and the beginning of 1990s. When stepping into the new millennium, we also require a growing number of students in elementary schools to learn English. Various English and other foreign languages tests such as College English Test (CET) and Public English Test System (PETS) are organized and implemented in the whole country. All of these measures greatly stimulated intercultural communication mainly in two dimensions. At the bottom level, a growing number of students begin to use English as a foreign language (still not a second language) actively in their study, work and research. Many students go to other developed countries to continue study after they graduate from high schools or colleges. At the top level, the emphasis on foreign languages spurs up the tide of learning foreign languages as a major. Foreign studies universities such as Beijing Foreign Studies University (BFSU) produced numerous talented translators, interpreters and diplomats who are very proficient at using foreign languages and mastering foreign cultures. Beijing Foreign Studies University, for example, teaches 98 foreign languages and offers education programs at different levels, including doctoral programs in foreign languages and literature, Chinese language and literature, journalism and communication, political science, law, management science and engineering, etc. up to January 2019.

4.Introducing China in a proper way: the spreading of the Chinese language

As China's economy and exchanges with the world have seen rapid growth, there has also been a sharp increase in the world's demands for Chinese learning. Benefiting from the UK, France, Germany and Spain's experience in promoting their national languages, China began its own exploration through establishing non-profit public institutions which aim to promote Chinese language and culture in foreign countries in 2004. Confucius Institutes and Confucius Classrooms adopt flexible teaching patterns and adapt to suit local conditions when teaching Chinese language and promoting culture in foreign primary schools, secondary schools, communities and enterprises.Confucius Institutes and Confucius Classrooms play a significant role in spreading the Chinese language and the Chinese culture to every corner of the world. These Confucius Institutes and Confucius Classrooms are administrated by Hanban, or Confucius Institute Headquarters, a public institution affiliated with the Chinese Ministry of Education. Hanbanis committed to providing Chinese language and cultural teaching resources and services worldwide, it goes all out in meeting the demands of foreign Chinese learners and contributing to the development of multiculturalism and the building of a harmonious world. Since the foundation of the first Confucius Institute in Seoul, Korea, up to December 31, 2018, there have been 548 Confucius Institutes and 1,193 Confucius Classrooms in 154 countries (areas). Chinese Proficiency Test (HSK), an international standardized test of Chinese language proficiency, administrated by Hanban, assesses non-native Chinese speakers' abilities in using the Chinese language in their daily, academic and professional lives.

The history ranging from the Silk Road to Zheng He, one of the pioneers in exploring the ocean engaging into inter-cultural communications in Ming dynasty demonstrated the glamor of our splendid culture. The popularity of the learning Chinese and traveling to China in the past twenty years all give us the confidence of intercultural communication.

However, the road ahead is always tough and steep. The past few years also witnessed some unhappy and negative media coverage in foreign countries. In Britain, for example, Guardian tried to stigmatize Chinese

Confucius institutes by the strategy of "selected attention"[1] in 2009. Scholars use critical discourse analysis and other criticizing weapons to reveal the hidden eyeglasses and biased ideological discrimination under the disguise of objective report. BBC, Daily Telegraph and other media also use tag Chinese Confucius institutes intentionally. Furthermore, they even call the Chinese Confucius institutes as a cultural aircraft-carrier to publicize the threat from China's rise. For example, Guardian called our institute a multibillion-pound soft power push in one of its report on December 8th, 2011. The past few years also witnessed some setbacks in the Chinese Confucius institutes in the United States. It is reported that some famous universities such as the University of Chicago would suspend the cooperation with Confucius institutes and close their Confucius Institute. When reporting and describing Chinese Confucius institutes, the U.S. media always use the following key negative key words revealed by computer-assisted critical discourse analysis: surveillance, control, constraint, propaganda, ignoring academic freedom, political taboo, too closely tied to the Chinese government, etc.

Regardless of the sophisticated factors behind these news coverages, they do remind us of the importance that we should enhance our intercultural competence in terms of Confucius Institutes. Intercultural competence is the base for intercultural communication influence while intercultural communication is the result of intercultural competence. Among various abilities of intercultural competence, the ability of intercultural acculturation is of predominant position, which is always attached enough importance to. According to the intercultural sensitivity mode proposed by Hammer & Bennet (2002), there are five stages of intercultural sensitivity development: denial, defense/reversal, minimization, acceptance, adaption, integration. The acceptance and the integration of an alien culture instead of changing it is the

---

1 Selected attention means that some newspapers in the west only choose parts of the fact or the truth to justify their argumentation in the report. These coverages seem objective and impersonal, but they are fay from the truth. The strategy of selected attention is frequently used by the west correspon-dents.

mark of the advancement of intercultural competence.

Confucius institute has to improve its intercultural acculturation, that is, to live harmoniously with the local culture instead of being just a tool of teaching Chinese language, in order to really and fully improve the intercultural communication influence of the Chinese culture. It is the people who are involved in the process of intercultural communication that are important. Four major groups of people hereby are mentioned in this process: Chinese teachers teaching Chinese in Confucius institutes, foreign students studying in Confucius institutes, foreign students studying in China and Chinese students learning in foreign countries. We should pay more attention to the feeling of these people involved in the communication to accomplish the construction of the multi-dimensional, comprehensive and diversified soft culture. The current society witnessed a change of intercultural communication modes initiated by the new media based on the new-generation information and communication technology. The Internet and the mobile Internet have been the major fronts of intercultural communication. In a mediatized environment, the spreading of the Chinese language and culture, and the spreading of the symbol of Confucius institute itself, should rely on the media. We should combine mass communication with interpersonal communication harmoniously together to renovate and refurbish methods in effects. Overseas Chinese Institutes need to work out a proper way to introduce themselves and China in an acceptable content and form. Content is, of course, very important. However, due attention should be paid to the way of story-telling, too. It is the Walt Disney company that popularizes and spreads many Chinese story, for example, Mulan, to every corner of the world, which could be a very positive example for us in story-telling.

Chinese Bridge（"汉语桥"）, a game testing the proficiency of Chinese for non-native learners, has been held annually since 2002. This activity has been conducted globally to choose the best Chinese learners and recommended them to perform in the finals, which are all broadcasted on satellite televisions and on the network. The TV audience rating is increasingly high according to the casting television station Hunan Satellite Television.

According to the Ministry of Education, China, 492,185 foreign students from 196 countries and regions choose to go to China to study Chinese and other majors in 1, 004 universities. 87.19% of the total number of these students are studying at their own expense instead of under the Chinese Government Scholarship Programs. The number reflects China's glamor as a target country of overseas study and these students, are the most convincing communication subjects of spreading our culture.

In conclusion, China has been more active and skillful in spreading the Chinese language and the culture related.

5.Introducing China in a proper way: "going globally"

The construction of the Chinese image is not a single or a static mission. The road ahead is still tough and steep. However, we have tried diversified ways of introducing China, among which the initiative of "going globally" is a successful experiment. Since the policy of reform and opening-up, we never stop attracting foreign enterprises into the Chinese market. On one hand, this initiative has reached a positive and mutual benefit for both sides. On the other hand, China has been emerged into the world globalization map quickly.

Stepping into the new century, we have the confidence and competence to go out and join in the world globalization and modernization in an active way. The complete success of the 18th and 19th national congress of the Communist Party of China (CPC) has given us the direction of development and reform. We will continue going globally and actively participating into the world construction unswervingly. Chinese enterprises, represented by Chinese state-owned enterprises (SOE), have already set their sail.

The official overseas website affiliated to People's Daily announced Overseas Communication Report for Chinese State-owned Enterprises (2019) in the beginning of 2019. The report shows that Chinese state-owned enterprises perform well according to the data from print media, websites and social media. China Southern Airlines, China Telecom, China Unicom are top three companies in the list of overseas communication report index. The news coverage of Chinese state-owned enterprises in foreign media has been increased by 13.76%. positive and neutral reports account for 82.96% of the total news coverage. Up to the end of 2018, the overall ratio of setting up the accounts in major overseas social media (Facebook,Twitter,YouTube,Instagram) has reached 47.9% with 278 active online account numbers. The account number of Chinese state-owned enterprises in Facebook has been increased dramatically by 385.2%.

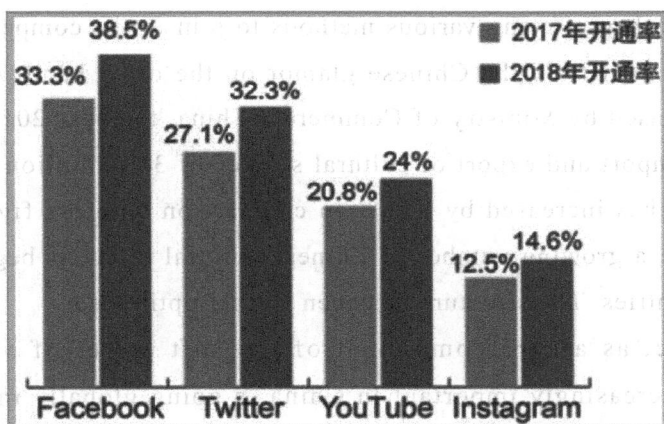

Figure 20　Data of setting up account numbers in major overseas social media by Chinese state-owned enterprises

China International Publishing Group(CIPG) have conducted international surveys of the image of Chinese enterprises for years since 2014. The investigation [1] shows that 37% of respondents hold an optimistic and positive attitude towards the China's economic prospect. 47% of respondents show their approval for China's international influence. The Belt and Road Initiative (BRI) attracts growing attention, and participation into BRI has been a consensus for citizens in most parts during the survey. The general image of Chinese enterprises has been improved dramatically and their contribution to the country and region has been highly appreciated.

1　中国外文局对外传播研究中心课题组．"2017年度中国企业海外形象调查分析报告"，"对外传播"．2017年第12期，第32-35页．

December 12th, 2018 witnessed the publishing of Investigation Report of Overseas Chinese Enterprises, released by China International Publishing Group in Beijing. Huawei and Hisense are top two companies in this list. It is our great satisfaction that Chinese private companies, in association with state-owned enterprises are showing their international prestige. The saying "made in China" has been shifting from the image of manufacturing for others to the image of high, stable and trustworthy brand. China's going out initiative has been rewarding after long construction.

With the step of going out in economy, Chinese cultural and creative products also begin trying various methods to join in the competition on one hand, and demonstrate the Chinese glamor on the other hand. According to the data released by Ministry of Commerce, China, the year 2018 saw a total volume of import and export of cultural service of 34.63 billion U.S. dollars. The number has increased by 17.8% in comparison with the figure of 2017. Furthermore, a growing number of Chinese cultural products began to export to other countries. The structure has been further optimized.

Culture, as a core component of the soft power of a country, is becoming increasingly important in China's going globally initiative. The past few years witness a quick progress in cultural export. In 2009, only 8 Chinese novels were published in the United States. The 2012 Nobel Prize in Literature was awarded to Mo Yan who with hallucinatory realism merges folk tales, history and the contemporary. After Mo Yan's award, Chinese writers such as Liu Cixin and Cao Wenxuan also won international awards for their wonderful talents in novels, which is a positive example of recognition of the Chinese writing. The years after the 18th national congress of the Communist Party of China (CPC) witnessed a popularity and prosperity of Chinese stories ranging from ancient classics to network literature due to the good stimulus of policies of the central committee. In the area of TV and film products, the number of Chinese movies going abroad has been increasingly substantially. Wanda Group, for example, has successfully grown by acquisitions or joint ventures to achieve global reach of theatre chain in the past several years. Up to 2018, Wanda Group has owned 1,470 theatres and over 15,000 film screens. TV dramas such as *Nirvana in Fire, Beautiful Life for Daughter-in-law* and *Empresses in the Palace* have been translated into English, Japanese, Korean, etc. and received high appreciation in overseas market. Traditional Chinese arts such as Peking opera, Chinese cross talk and Chinese folk dancing also received warm acclaim among the foreign audience.

No matter how many achievements we have already reached in the past, we should be sober-minded of our disadvantages and the path ahead of us. American cultural products sales account for 25% of the total volume of the world. American movies, Disneyland, Universal Studios and Grammy Awards are the best advertising of their culture. Comparatively, we should improve our cultural communication in order to better introduce China from the following perspectives.

（1）"Going globally" must be integrate with "attracting in".

It has to be acknowledged that "going globally" is not contradictory with "attracting in" initiative. A modernized China and a harmonious intercultural communication will need both. November 15th, 2018 witnessed the opening ceremony of the first China International Import Expo (CIIE) in Shanghai. Over 1,000 enterprises from more than 58 countries along the Belt and Road Initiative joined into this Expo. The principle of achieving shared growth through discussion and collaboration, the guideline of the Belt and Road Initiative, is also held high in this Expo. China now has been more skillful and proficient in coordinating and integrating "going globally" and "attracting in" moves. As is always said in the principle of the Communist Party of China (CPC), we must address ourselves to the problem of both material and spiritual civilization. We must invite the world to know China and introduce China, China in the new era to the world. By integrating "going globally" and "attracting in" initiatives, we are to build a responsible and peaceful image of a great nation, to establish the mode of achieving shared growth and mutual benefit, and to explore a new path by cooperation.

（2）"Going globally" must be based on a deep cognition of knowing ourselves.

As is said in one Chinese saying, knowing the enemy and knowing yourself, and you can fight a hundred battles with no danger of defeat. The realization of self-identity is of great importance for "going globally". The success of introducing China to the world and the effect of intercultural communication, to a certain extent, is dependent on how strong you believe who you are and what faith you hold. If Chinese ourselves do not believe in our own civilization and have not returned to cultural confidence, how can other people be convinced by our glamor of the culture? The Chinese was, is and will always be a unique scene in the world map of cultural diversity. We do not need to feel ourselves inferior to and do not need to over-beautify the western civilization. An equal appreciation based on mutual respect is the suggested attitude towards the goal of "going out globally". We must overcome the cognitive deviation in cultural development and restore our confidence in the splendid essence of the Chinese culture. We should respect the humanity and overcome alienation, trying to provide more literature and other cultural products that really move people.

（3）"Going globally" must be provided to the right people at the right place at the right moment.

China's "going globally" is not to struggle on to please west world or western people. It is the special value of the Chinese culture that attracts foreign people. Chinese philosophy, especially our combination of Confucianism, Taoism and Chinese Buddhism, provides a supplement to traditional philosophical paradigms, and could be employed to answer the current headaches in the process of post-modernity for the west. "Going globally" hereby must be provided to the right people at the right place at the right moment. We have our irreplaceablepracticability, which is an important prerequisite for the cultural dialogue.

In conclusion, an open and mature China will be more confident in implementing "going globally" and "attracting in" initiatives. We have every reason to believe that the prosperity of cultural harmony will be in front of us soon.

Section 4 Cultural practice

Cultural practice

Discussion

You are now a student studying in a European university. At the welcoming party, every student is going to introduce their own country and recommend something for others.

Which part of China are you mostly proud of ? How are you going to introduce this special part?

Please recommend one movie, one delicacy (food), and one tourist attraction that can fully represent China and the Chinese culture to the other students. Please justify your recommendation.

Section 5 Derivative development

1.Film watching

Please watch the movie *Mulan* [1] (《花木兰》, 1998) and tried to work out a short intercultural analysis of the story of the movie.

The leading role of this animation is based on the Chinese legend of Hua Mulan, who is a legendary Chinese warrior from the Northern and Southern dynasties period (420—589) of Chinese history, originally described in the

---

1　*Mulan* is a 1998 American animated musical action adventure film produced by Walt Disney Feature Animation for Walt Disney Pictures. It is based on the Chinese legend of Hua Mulan, and was Disney's 36th animated feature and the ninth animated film produced and released during the Disney Renaissance. *Mulan* was well received by critics and the public, earning Golden Globe and Academy Award nominations, and winning several Annie Awards including Best Animated Feature. A 2004 direct-to-video sequel, Mulan II, followed.

Ballad of Mulan (《木兰辞》). In the ballad, Hua Mulan, disguised as a man, takes her aged father's place in the army. Mulan fought for twelve years and gained high merit, but she refused any reward and retired to her hometown. In China, the heroine of Mulan is known to almost everyone, including young children. Therefore, she is a positive and typical representation of the Chinese spirit and the Chinese image. There are many stories, TV dramas, films adapted from the story of Mulan. However, it is the Walt Disney company that popularizes and spreads this typical Chinese story to every corner of the world.

Would you summarize the success of *Mulan* and *Mulan II* films? What can we learn from them in spreading the Chinse image?

2.Extended reading

(1)Knowing more cultures about ourselves (6): the art culture

Before we introduce ourselves to the others, the first and foremost thing is to have a correct and profound cognition of ourselves. In the ends of all the eight chapters, we add some basic knowledge of ourselves which are divided into eight sections, namely, the family culture, the food culture, the education culture, the marriage culture, the medical culture, the art culture, the consumption culture and the cyber culture respectively. We hope to help both audiences from other cultures and ourselves to have a better cognition of Chinese cultures. During these parts, the author of this book not only summarizes the traditional essence of these sections, but employs a diachronic perspective and includes the up-to-date changes.

(2)Our art cultures

The Chinese art is long standing and well established. The ancient Chinese artists have reached incredible peaks in various areas such as the Chinese painting, the Chinese architecture, the Chinese music and the Chinese opera. With the acceleration of globalization in intercultural communication, the Chinese art is showing its unique and fascinating attractiveness for a growing number of foreigners.

① The Chinese painting

The history of Chinese painting can be compared to a symphony. The styles and traditions in figure, landscape, and bird-and-flower painting have formed themes that continue to blend to this day into a single piece of music. Painters through the ages have made up this "orchestra," composing and performing many movements and variations within this tradition.

It was from the Six Dynasties (222—589) to the Tang dynasty (618—907) that the foundations of figure painting were gradually established by such major artists as Gu Kaizhi and Wu Daozi. Landscape painting started to become popular in the Sui (581—618) and Tang dynasties by the effort of Zhan Ziqian, Li Sixun, and Wang Wei. Variations based on geographic distinctions then took shape in the Five Dynasties period (907—960). For example, Jing Hao and Guan Tong depicted the drier and monumental peaks to the north while Dong Yuan represented the lush and rolling hills to the south in Jiangnan (south of the Yangtze River). In bird-and-flower painting, the noble Tang court decorative manner was passed down in Sichuan through Huang Quan's style, which contrasts with the more relaxed style of Xu Xi in the Jiangnan area.

In the Song dynasty (960—1279), landscape painters such as Fan Kuan, Guo Xi and Li Tang created new manners based on previous traditions. Guided by the taste of the emperors, especially Zhao Ji, painters at the court academy focused on observing nature combined with "poetic sentiment" to reinforce the expression of both subject and artist. The focus on poetic sentiment led to the combination of painting, poetry, and calligraphy (the "Three Perfections") in the same work (often as an album leaf or fan) by the Southern Song (1127—1279). Scholars earlier in the Northern Song (960—1126) thought that painting as an art had to go beyond just the "appearance of forms" in order to express the ideas and cultivation of the artist. This became the foundation of the movement known as literati (scholar) painting.

The goal of literati painters in the Yuan dynasty (1271—1368), including Zhao Mengfuand Huang Gongwang. This variation on revivalism transformed these old "melodies" into new and personal tunes, some of which gradually developed into important traditions of their own in the Ming and Qing dynasties. As in poetry and calligraphy, the focus on personal cultivation became an integral part of expression in painting.In the early 20th century, the Shanghai regional style was passed on to Beijing through the art of Chen Shizeng and Qi Baishi. Increasingly, by the mid-1920s, young Chinese artists were attracted not just to Japan but also to Paris and German art centers, for example, Liu Haisu and Xu Beihong.

② The Chinese music

According to the archaeological discovery of the bone-flute unearthed in Wuyang County, Henan Province, Chinese music can be traced back to 8,000 years ago. Over a long history, Chinese nation created a marvelous culture of music which also has a far-reaching influence to the country's neighboring areas. China is known as a country of music in the far ancient times; the Chinese ancient music is of great importance in the culture and etiquette of the country.

Chinese music interwove with dances in its early time, and developed into an independent art category in Xia dynasty (2000 BC—1600 BC) which is also the beginning of the times of bells and drums lasting for 1300 years. The enjoyment of music is the privilege of upper class at that time, and the content is generally the praises for the conqueror of the nature, the nobles and the governor. Percussion instrument emerged in Shang dynasty (1600 BC—1100 BC), for example, the Bianzhong (a set of hanging bronze bells for polyphonic musical sounds). And in Zhou dynasty (1046 BC—256 BC), a complete ritual music system was established.

The Chinese national musical instrument is the key part in Chinese music. With a long history standing, there are a series of national instruments developed in China. In terms of material, there are Ba Yin (Chinese: 八

音), that is, the eight categories of musical instrument in ancient orchestra, namely, metal, stone, string, bamboo, gourd, clay, leather and wood. In terms of playing skills, there are generally four kinds, percussion instruments (bells, drums, and gongs), wind instruments (flutes, Suona and Xiao), bowed string instruments (Banhu and Erhu) and plucked string instruments (Guzheng, Pipa and Sanxuan).

Broadly, there is no definite division for the music enjoyment by different people, especially in modern society. People often enjoy different kinds of music for pleasure regardless of age and background. However, different kinds of music has its own appreciation group, for example, young people prefer popular music such as pop, rock and roll and rap; middle-aged people are fond of the Chinese folk music or some popular music praising of the nation and people; while the Chinese opera or local opera are the favorite art form for the aged people. In each provinces and regions, there are also different kinds of popular music, such as the Northern Shaanxi folk songs, the songs of Huaguxi Drama in Hunan Province, Xinjiang music in Xinjiang Uygur Autonomous Region and the like. Most of these folk songs are sung by people national wide, but each is popular mostly with its local people.

③ The Chinese architecture

Chinese Architecture is great and profound with a long-standing history as well as the Chinese culture. From the early square or round shallow hole-houses to today's modern style, many wonders were built by generations of Chinese in the past 6000 years, which are astonishing with superb techniques, exquisite art designs and unique styles. The magnificent ancient Chinese architecture developed to a distinctive school of its own with unique monomer shape and delicate decorations in every part.

Wood is the main material in ancient Chinese architecture and most of the buildings are in wood frame structure. The wood frame can successfully separate the bearing structure (the wood frame) and the maintaining structure (walls).What's more, for the special properties, wood can easily adapt to different climates, effectively diminish the destroy of the earthquakes, and more importantly, it is the material to be found easily on the spot.

The ancient Chinese architecture is beautiful and graceful in appearance with distinctive features. Buildings are usually built in square, round, hexagon and octagon; key architectures are standing on platforms, a grand palace even on a three-layered platform, e.g. the Hall of Supreme Harmony in the Forbidden City.

The shapes of the roofs are rich in styles and artistic value. Slopes in four sides, six sides and eight sides are most common; the eaves with kinds of carvings and warp in different ways usually make a graceful profile of the building; ridges decorated with carvings and ornaments and tiles in colors are also adding the artistic value to the roof. The roofs are designed magnificent, which are renowned not only for the graceful appearance but also for the great practicality that the wide eaves mostly warp upside can prevent the wood structure and platform from the rains.

The upright and foursquare layout in rigorous symmetric ways of the ancient Chinese architecture come from the Confucianism and the traditional Chinese philosophy. A Chinese complex usually consists of numerous monomers, either a larger palace or a quadrangle courtyard. All buildings are facing up to the south except the ones in some ethnic areas that are limited by special landform and topography. In a complex, there is always an axis; main buildings are exactly standing on the axis while secondary buildings are on the east and west confrontations on the two sides to compose a square or a rectangle courtyard. If one courtyard cannot meet the demands, there are also back yards and side yards built according to the auxiliary axis.

Decorations are particularly important in ancient Chinese architecture. The image, color and properties of the fitments and decorations are meticulously chosen to beautify buildings. Almost every part of the building is well-decorated. The platform and steps are equipped with railings and inscriptions; beasts and birds are always set on the shaped eaves; doors and windows are engraved with colorful images and patterns; even the ceilings are designed into a shaped caisson or decorated formally in traditional patterns. Painting on architecture is a distinctive characteristic as well as an indispensable decoration on formal buildings such as palace and temple, while it is forbidden in civilian houses.

Chinese gardens are built gracefully with great artistic conceptions in three kinds, aspiring conception, immortal conception and natural conception.Aspiring conceptions are mostly in the royal gardens such as most of the scenes in the Old Summer Palace, which are built according to the Confucian theories in philosophy, politics, virtue and moral principles. Immortal conceptions are in some royal gardens and temple gardens that are built according to the theories of Confucians and Taoists that people can be immortals by ascetic practices. Natural conceptions are usually in private gardens built by scholars who follow the thoughts of Chinese philosophers Lao-tzu and Zhuang Zhou whose thoughts lie in nature, the balance and integration of human and nature, as well as all creature's relations.

④ The Chinese opera

Chinese culture is a great and extensive civilization with featured Chinese traditional opera, especially the Peking Opera, which is regarded as the national opera or the quintessence of Chinese culture. With incomparable artistic charm, Chinese opera delights people home and abroad and enjoys a particular important statue in the world, known as Three Ancient Dramas together with Ancient Greek drama and Indian Sanskrit drama.

Chinese opera was born from the ancient songs and dances, and finally completed as a mature art form after a long historical development in Ming and Qing dynasties (1368—1911). It is a comprehensive stagecraft combining folk songs and dances, dialogue and burlesque, including art fields of literature, music, dance, fine art, acrobatics, martial art and performing art. According to a rough estimation, about 360 operas exist in China. With a center criterion, each in different areas has developed to a style of its own with distinctive local features. Famous operas include Peking Opera, Shaoxing Opera, Huangmei Opera, Kunqu Opera, Yuju (Henan) Opera, Cantonese Opera, Shanghai Opera, Sichuan Opera, Shanxi Opera, Pingju Opera, Hunan Opera, Huagu (flower drum) Opera, etc.

第七章　走出跨文化商务交流的困境——基于文化间性视角

Chapter Seven
Extricating from Intercultural Business Communication Difficulty

Section 1 Lead-in

1.Question

（1）What is the most important characteristic of Chinese business negotiation?

（2）What do you think of the attitude of "economic gain" of American negotiators in the negotiation process?

（3）According to your understanding, which countries may share the same or a similar attitude towards business negotiation as China?

2.Case

（1）Case 1

As a college professor of English, Mr. Wang was in constant contact with people from English-speaking countries. Therefore, he was often asked to help introduce foreign businessmen interested in investing in China. One day, a county magistrate came and presented him with some documents concerning a project. He asked the professor to keep an ear open for potential investors. The professor agreed that it was a good project, but the sum of money being sought was staggering. Afterwards, the professor met with several foreign businessmen, among which an Australian seemed very interested in the project. Through several phone calls, he arranged a meeting between the magistrate and the investor. Realizing that a big opportunity presented itself, the magistrate assured the professor of their one hundred percent "cooperation", and told the professor that they would do whatever possible to please that investor. When the big day arrived, the investor and the magistrate met in a reception room, where about 15 other local officials were eagerly waiting. After a customary greeting and some details regarding the project, the magistrate showed the investor around the project site and its beautiful surroundings. The investor was very pleased with the project prospects and the location of the joint venture, and the atmosphere was encouraging for both the investor and the magistrate.

At 11:30 a.m., they were driven to the best hotel in this county, where they were seated in an extravagantly decorated restaurant. After a couple of minutes, the first course was served. The second followed, then the third. Before the third course was replaced by the fourth course, the investor jokingly said that their food was enough to feed an army. Misjudging the investor's joke as a compliment, the magistrate told the investor that there would be another two courses. Hearing this, the investor felt a bit uneasy, indicating that he was already full, but the magistrate kept encouraging him to eat slowly so that he could taste all the delicacies that were specially prepared for him. Although the professor had warned the magistrate against too much hospitality and extravagance, more dished were placed on the table and both the magistrate and the local officials displayed a kind of hospitality that had made the investor almost ill. At about 2:00 p.m., the investor customarily thanked the magistrate for his hospitality and left the county. But to the magistrate's bewilderment and disappointment, that meeting was their first and also last.

The foreign businessman is from Australia and knows very little about the courtesy, etiquette and hospitality in eastern culture. The county magistrate is a typical Chinese and knows little about the manners, sincerity, efficiency and value in western culture. Due to his over-eagerness, the magistrate received the foreign businessman with too much hospitality, creating a misunderstanding for the foreign investor who is concerned about with the project itself. However, the large feast and great reception makes the foreign investor hesitant toward the investment.

Is there a possibility for this negotiation to be smoother? Can you give them some feasible advice?

(2)Case 2

While I (a Chinese) was studying in America, I met an American classmate named Jimmy. One day I was eager to buy a book, but I did not have enough money, so I borrowed three dollars from Jimmy. Before he lent me the three dollars, Jimmy asked me three times, "Are you sure you will return the money to me?" Four days later, he kept reminding me about the load until I paid him back the money.

Interesting enough, weeks later he borrowed 30 dollars from me and said he would pay me back in a week. After one month, there was no sign of the money, so I reminded him. To my surprise, he said, "I'm sorry. Why don't you remind me earlier?" and returned the money instantly.

Americans don't readily give money to others nor receive others' readily. If you lent money to an American generously, and said, "Don't mention it again. You don't have to pay me back.", he would be angry and think you were looking down upon him, not believing his ability to repay the money.

If you were "I" in this case, how would you adjust yourself?

It seems that American's value of money and value of wealth are quite different from ours. They prefer to go Dutch when dining whereas we Chinese prefer to pay the whole bill by one person. Does this phenomenon indicate that Americans are stingy while Chinese are generous?

An observation of this interpersonal case may also be enlightening for us to understand the bewilderment in intercultural business communication.

(3)Case 3

TCL Corporation is a leading intelligent product manufacturer and Internet application company with over 70,000 employees in over 80 countries and regions. However, its globalized paths, especially international mergers and acquisitions, were far from satisfactory.

In 2004, TCL Corporation owned Thomson, a TV maker in France, and the phone business of Alcatel, a cellphone manufacturer in France,by acquisitions. However, one year later, TCL Corporation encountered very serious loss in these two acquisitions, which encumbered TCL's stock price. The stock price of TCL has been decreased by a large margin. This failure is so penetrating that it always appears in many case analyses in business schools of universities.

Honestly, many factors may lead to this terrible failure for this company. Among various reasons, one must be mentioned here which is TCL's ignorance of the sharp difference in business environment, business system and business negotiations between China's style and France's situation. In other words, the lack of intercultural competence of this company, to a certain extent, is a covert reason for this tragedy. For example, French workers are reluctant to speak English in communication even they have the ability. A large number of Chinese managers and workers of TCL, unfortunately, cannot speak French, which means this intercultural communication is not only money-consuming but time-consuming. Another situation that TCL did not expect was that it was never easy to sack an employee in France. Employees are protected by contracts and under the assistance of powerful trade union. On the other hand, color TV making is not a promising job for French people. Therefore, TCL was in a terrible dilemma that they cannot hire people easily or fire workers easily.

It is a pity that TCL's case is not the single case in China's enterprises' international mergers and acquisitions.

What can we learn from TCL's lesson and can we provide any suggestions from the intercultural perspective?

Section 2 Theory preparation

1.Basic concept of business negotiation

Business is the activity of making one's living or making money by producing or buying and selling products (such as goods and services).The word "negotiation" stems from the Latin word *negotiar*,meaning a process of combining divergent positions into a joint agreement under a decision rule of unanimity. It is aimed to resolve points of difference, to gain advantage for an individual or collective, or to craft outcomes to satisfy various interests. It is often conducted by putting forward a position and making concessions to achieve an agreement. The degree to which the negotiating parties trust each other to implement the negotiated solution is a major factor in determining whether negotiations are successful.

What a negotiation is designed to accomplish is seen differently by different groups of people. Before one even comes to the table, such differences in meaning of purpose of the negotiation affect the process itself, because how one defines the process of negotiating is culturally determined. In low-context culture, negotiation usually means achieving a good outcome for both parties through a discussion of reasons and facts involved. To someone from a high-context culture, negotiation has as its core element the relation between the two parties.

When negotiation specifically, the extent of cultural bias in understanding and using the term seems to depend on the explicitness of one's conception of the process. Some scholars hereby define negotiation as a process in which explicit proposals are put forward ostensibly for the purpose of reaching an agreement on an example or the realization of a common interest where conflicting interests are present. Such definition highlights some essential, seemingly intercultural, aspects of interaction, the parties' common and conflicting interests, and the ostensible goal of reaching an agreement, but the emphasis on explicit proposals may be culturally bound. Therefore, a modern definition of negotiation refers to two or more parties with common or conflicting interests who enter into a process of interaction with the goal of reaching an agreement preferably for their mutual benefit.

According to Moran and Stripp, intercultural negotiation involves discussions of common and conflicting interests between persons of different cultural backgrounds who work to reach an agreement to their mutual benefit. They further explain that negotiations take place within the context of the four Cs: common interest, conflicting interest, compromise, and criteria.

① Common interest considers that both parties in the negotiation share, have or want something that the other party has or does.

② Conflicting interests include payment, distribution, profits, contractual responsibilities, and quality.

③ Compromise includes areas of disagreement. Although a win-win negotiated settlement would be best for both parties, the compromise that are negotiated may not produce that result.

④ Criteria include the conditions under which the negotiations take place.

2.Major negotiation styles

Moran and Harris (1991) propose four major communicative negotiating styles.

① Normative. Concentrates on creating a harmonious relationship between bargainers. This style requires attention to self and other emotions and values. Appeals to emotions to reach a fair deal.

② Intuitive. Imagination solves problems. Intuitive negotiators look to the future, offer creative solutions, draw attention to prospective opportunities being created in present agreements, and follow their inspirations of the moment.

③ Analytic. Logical analysis leads to universally true conclusions. This involves forming reasons, drawing conclusions, identifying cause and effect, and weighting the pros and cons.

④ Factual. Point out facts and details in a neutral way; keep track of what has been said; and clarify the issue.

3.Negotiation strategies

Negotiation strategies are defined as plans organized to achieve a desired objective. Two universal negotiation strategies — competition and cooperation — can be summarized from negotiation literature.

① Competition negotiation strategy. This strategy is also known as contending or distributive bargaining. It is a strategy used by a negotiator to pursue his goals by persuading his opponent to concede. Competition strategy entails efforts to maximize gains and minimize losses within a "win-lose" or self-gain orientation. This "win-lose" approach highlights the negotiating tactics and tricks employed to overpower the other party and ensure victory.

② Cooperation negotiation strategy. This strategy is also known as problem solving, collaboration, or integrative bargaining. It aims to reconcile the interests of both parties, reach joint benefits, or attain "win-win" goals. The parties during negotiations will work together to find solutions that satisfy their common goals.

Section 3 Detailed analysis

1.Scanning differences of different negotiations

American negotiators assume an attitude of "economic gain" in the negotiation process. They expect others to display "American professionalism", which includes an aggressive approach. Not interested in establishing long-term relationships, they view socializing as unimportant. The American norm is to conduct business in an efficient manner, while compromises may be part of the outcome. In the eyes of the American negotiators, prestige is achieved by their ability to maneuver the debate. They are also more likely to put trust in their counterparts at the onset of negotiations. Americans tend to convey warmth, sincerity, confidence and positiveness in their communication. They are always ready to engage in bargaining, or compromise in the negotiation process. Negotiators from the United States tend to assume the English will be spoken in the sessions. They tend to more interested in logical arguments than in the people they are dealing with. They may employ threats, warnings, and continual pushiness, even if their counterparts are signaling "no". Americans tend to express their idea bluntly; silence is perceived as uncomfortable and indicative of trouble for them.

British people employ a negotiating style similar to that of Americans, but more silence is utilized and they are less egalitarian. The British negotiators interrupt less in the negotiations than their American counterparts and they have a polite yet indistinct style of negotiating. Generally, the British negotiators are regarded as kind, friendly, sociable, agreeable, flexible and responsive.

French people are more likely to distrust their counterparts in the beginning. They see themselves as more experienced negotiators. Their negotiations are conducted through formal hospitality. Their negotiation process is characterized by zero-sum game, directness and confrontational competitiveness. The French frequently employ "no" communication and often insist on the use of their own language in negotiation settings. French negotiators may be long-winded and they rationalize a great deal without bargaining or compromising. They tend to put forth all their information and establish principles of reasoning first. New information is not easily accepted. According to some scholars, the French relish debate, welcome and respect dissent. They are confrontational and competitive. To the French, negotiation involves a search for well-reasoned arguments.

Germans hold that strength lies in the bidding stage of negotiation. They do not generally agree with compromise. German negotiators are generally clear, firm and assertive in their expression. Once a bid is put forth, they are less likely to accept other possibilities. The Germans may not ask many questions in the negotiation process but will disclose a great deal and may frequently interrupt.

Japanese believe that socializing is integral to the negotiation process. They are concerned with establishing long-term business or personal relationships. Negotiators rely on the trust established between the parties involved and on an implicit understanding.

Chinese negotiators, like Japanese, feel that mutual interests and friendships are important in the negotiation process, and socializing during the negotiation process is expected. As is said in one widely-acknowledged saying in China, it is with great delights to have friends coming afar. Favorable terms are anticipated from friends. The nature of the relationship between the parties involved is critical to the Chinese negotiators.

In the Middle East, personal relationship is also an important part of negotiations. Hospitality is the first priority, and negotiations are initiated with pre-negotiation social graces. Trust and respect must be secured for negotiations to be successful.

Brazilians and Mexicans utilized the general business approach that is similar as the approach taken by Middle Eastern negotiators. Rhetoric and the grand idea pursued by Mexican negotiators. They usually do not resort to frank talk. They may play the weaker side because of the perception that Americans have sympathy for the disadvantaged— the side that needs special consideration, but at the same time, they are still extremely wary of patronizing assistance or concessions. Compromise to them threatens dignity in the negotiation process. Mexican negotiators prefer the deductive approach. More emphasis is placed on contemplation and intuition. Mexicans stand closer than Americans and Japanese; they use more physical contact to show confidence. Brazilian negotiators are very aggressive. They use a lot of commands and always show their refusal. They do not engage in silence tactics, frequent touching, or facial gazing.

It is, of course, wrong if we do not pay attention to the individual difference and the effect of global exchanges to all of the countries. However, the above-mentioned differences in negotiations of various countries in the world may help us to build a preliminary preparation before negotiations and avoid erroneous judgement during negotiations. The following figure [1] list the basic concepts of the negotiation process for seven cultural groups.

Cultural groups	General descriptions of the negotiation style
Americans	distributive bargaining, functional, direct, confrontational, competitive
Chinese	distributive bargaining with mixed integrative aspects, dysfunctional, zero-sum, indirect, avoidant, competitive
French	debate, functional, zero-sum, direct, confrontational, competitive
Japanese	contingency bargaining, dysfunctional, nonzero-sum, indirect, avoidant, collaborative
Mexicans	distributive bargaining, zero-sum, indirect, avoidant, competitive
Nigerians	distributive, functional, zero-sum, competitive, individual gain
Saudis	joint problem-solving, nondirective discussion, mixed with distributive bargaining, dysfunctional, indirect, avoidant, collaborative

Figure 21　General descriptions of the negotiation style of seven cultural groups

2.High-context culture and low-context culture

High-context cultures can be seen to prefer the use of high-context messages, in which most of the meaning is either implied by the physical setting or presumed to be part of the individual's internationalized beliefs,

---

1　Weiss, Stephen E. Negotiating with the Romans—Part 2. Sloan Management Review, (1994), 35 (3) (Spring), page 85-97.

values, and norms; very little is provided in the coded, explicit, transmitted part of the messages. Hall suggests that people from high-context systems tend to expect more of others to base their communication on common knowledge and mutual understanding. An illustration of high-context communication is the interactions among family members or between people who have maintained a long-term relationship. In such context, people involved in the communication are often able to interpret each other's message without the provision of explicit information. Communication can be based on shared understandings about their relation. Japan and China, for example, are typical examples of high-context culture.

Low-context culture means that the mass of the information is vested in the explicit code. In low-context cultures, people prefer to use low-context messages, in which the majority of the information is explicitly presented in language in communication. Low-context cultures include German, Swedish, European American, and English cultures. In low-context cultures, the population is less homogeneous and therefore tends to compartmentalize interpersonal contacts. In low-context cultures, the verbal message contains most of the information and very little is embedded in the context or the participants.

When a person from low-context culture encounters a person from high-context culture in intercultural communication, it is easy to lead to some misunderstandings even without intention of initiating cultural conflicts. Once when American former President George Bush went to Japan with leading American businessmen, he made explicit and implicit demands on Japanese leaders, which violated Japanese etiquette. To the Japanese with a high context culture, it is rude and a sign of ignorance or desperation to make direct demands. The Japanese manager, being brought up in a high-context culture, has great difficulty criticizing his employees because of his indirect language practice. Therefore, this unintentional behavior, to a certain extent, exert a negative influence on the negotiations.

3.Doing business in the United Sates [1]

Some foreign businessmen stay for extended periods in the United States and have opportunities to observe American business operations in detail. While it is impossible to list all of the characteristics of U.S. companies here, it is safe to say that the more a foreigner understands about how an organization is set up and how it operates, the more effectively he or she can work within that organization. The comments that follow represent a few aspects of American business operations that stand out in the minds of many foreign visitors.

(1) Hard work

While they may appear informal and relaxed, Americans generally work hard. They may devote long hours — as many as 16 or 18 hours per day — to do their jobs. They may consider their work to be more important than family responsibilities and social relationship. Americans use the term workaholic to describe a person who is addicted to work, one who spends as much time as possible on the job and seems to think of little else. Workaholics are by no means rare in the American business world. American executives and managers often embarrass their foreign counterparts by doing manual work or other tasks that elsewhere would be done only by lower-status people. This spirit of hard work, for Americans themselves, is a kind of professionalism, which explains the giant achievement reached by American companies.

(2) Punctuality

Promptness and schedules are important for Americans. Meetings and appointments ideally begin and end on schedule. The topic that is supposed to be addressed during the meeting or appointment is generally expected to be covered by the scheduled ending time. Delays cause frustration. Getting behind schedule is likely to be considered an example of bad management.

---

1   It is impossible to neglect the influence of Americans, American culture and American enterprises in current world business. Therefore, a special part of "doing business in the United Sates" is put here.

In keeping with their notions about the importance of using time wisely and getting the job done, American businessmen generally want to get right down to business. They do not want to waste time with formalities or with long and preliminary discussions. In fact, they are usually quite uncomfortable with purely social interactions while they are working.

(3) Impersonal dealings

Americans generally have no particular interest in getting personally acquainted with clients or customers with whom they deal. As long as they believe the other party is trustworthy in business dealings and has the ability to deliver whatever product or service is being discussed, they will proceed in a relatively impersonal manner. They value decisiveness and efficiency. For many Americans, the saying "time is money" reflects their belief that what is important is getting things accomplished as quickly as possible. German and French people are likely to engage in similar behavior, but people from most other parts of the world often find such an approach cold or otherwise uncomfortable. Even when they seem to be socializing, as at a dinner or reception with business colleagues, Americans' main purpose is more likely to be discussing business than becoming personally acquainted with other people.

(4) Quantitative reasoning

American businesspeople, probably even more noticeably than Americans in general, prefer to think and analyze in quantitative terms. They want hard data and facts and figures when they are analyzing a business situation and trying to make a decision. The assumption is that wise decisions are made on the basis of objective information uncontaminated by considerations of personal feelings, social relations, or political advantage. American executives frequently use the term "bottom line" which refers to the final entry in an accounting statement. They want the statement to show a profit. Nothing else is as important. The purpose of a business is to make a profit, and executives are evaluated on how they contribute to the company's bottom line.

(5) Writing it down

The written word is supremely important to American businesspeople. They make notes about conversations, keep files on their various projects, and record the minutes of meetings. A contract or an agreement must be written down in order to be taken seriously, and every written word in it is important. It must be the correct word, the one that clearly states each party's rights and obligations.

To Americans in business, it seems perfectly natural to consult lawyers about contracts and agreements. Lawyers are trained to select the proper words for important documents and to correctly interpret them. Americans have difficulty understanding that people from other parts of the world might feel insulted by the Americans' insistence on having written agreements, viewing the Americans' attitude as an indication of distrust.

(6) Self-improvement

The American belief in self-improvement is quite evident in the business world. Managers might attend seminars on public speaking, conflict resolution, delegation of work, or time management. Clerical staff might attend training sessions on telephone manners or spelling and grammar. Employees at any level may study videotapes about stress management or new computer software. Whole organizations might adopt some new approach to management, such as strategic planning, continuous quality improvement, or just-in-time inventory control.

(7) Behaviors in meetings

Meetings are a common phenomenon in the business world, but what actually happens in meetings varies greatly, not just from country to country but from organization to organization. Meetings can have a variety of purposes— sharing information, giving instructions, heightening employee enthusiasm and dedication, discussing issues and problems, suggesting solutions, making decisions and no doubt others. Americans like to know explicitly what the purpose of any given meeting is.

The leader's role in meetings also varies. The leader might be the one who opens the meeting, does all the talking, and then dismisses those who have attended. Or the leader may play the role of a moderator, opening the meeting and then allowing others to discuss matters and make decisions. The role of those attending the meeting differs, too. They may be expected to sit quietly and listen, to offer suggestions or comments, or even to challenge ideas others put forth.

In the ideal American meeting, the leader encourages active participation from all those who might have ideas to contribute. The people at the meeting offer ideas and information intended to help illuminate the subject under discussion. They may openly and bluntly disagree with each other. Witnessing such meetings can shock foreigners who are accustomed to more formal, hierarchical arrangements, where the leader firmly controls what takes place and participants either remain silent or mask any disagreement with others.

In American meetings, issues are often resolved by means of a vote. The majority rule is always the working rule in many meeting rooms in the Unites States. The practice of voting in meetings might disconcert foreigners who are accustomed to a system in which decisions must be unanimous or one in which the person in authority makes the decisions.

(8) Informality

Another characteristic of business life in the United States that foreigners notice is its informality. You are likely to witness much more informal behaviors than you would among colleagues at home. American businesspeople can address others by their first names, make jokes, and use a vocabulary and tone of voice suitable for informal relationships. Because they are likely to equate formality with discomfort, Americans want to encourage other to relax during their business dealings. They may dress relatively casually, and men may remove their coats and loosen their neckties if they are in a long meeting. Steve Jobs, the former CEO and founder of the Apple Corporation, always wore a casual sweater in many important occasions such as the public announcement of new products. Some companies encourage their employees to abandon coats and ties in favor of business casual dress on Fridays.

(9) Equality

Americans' notions about equality strongly influence what happens throughout business organizations. Although people at various levels are quite aware of the status differences among them, they are unlikely to overtly display superiority or inferiority. Rank-conscious foreigners often feel uneasy around the relatively relaxed and informal interactions they will see between lower- and higher-status employees.

(10) Mobility of employees

Foreign visitors may see more employees joining and leaving the organization than they are accustomed to. America is still a more mobile society than most countries (the rate of mobility may have slowed recently), so people change jobs relatively readily, and it is customary for Americans to give as little as two weeks' notice before they leave a job. It is unusual to find a strong sense of company loyalty at the lower ranks of a business, and even many executives are ready to change employers when a promising opportunity arises. Many people view their jobs as a means to earn a living, and in most cases, it does not matter to them where that living comes from. They do what they are supposed to do, according to a written job description generally, collect their pay, and go home. Supervisors are often seeking ways to enhance employee allegiance to the company, believing that employees who are more loyal will also be more productive.

4.Business etiquette

Business etiquette is a behavior standard and activity programs when people do business with others in business world, including two aspects: etiquette and ceremony. In business interactions, etiquette facilitates a professional standard of conduct that each business has in common with the other business.

Business etiquette is not just knowing what to discuss during a business dinner or how to address colleagues; it is a way of presenting yourself in such a way that you will be taken seriously. This involves demonstrating that you have the self-control necessary to be good at your job, expressing a knowledge of business situations and having the ability to make others comfortable around you. Poor business etiquette will cost you the trust of your workers and your customers, and the loss of valuable etiquette.

Each culture has its own etiquette rules, many of them unwritten. Business dinner etiquette, dress etiquette, gift-giving etiquette and so on vary greatly between countries and cultures. Intercultural business etiquette refers to the habitual form and behavior which are shaped in people's long-term business activities in the international business and it is the behavior guidance applicable throughout the world. Knowing how to behave in a variety of business situations will help build productive business relationship. Otherwise, it would be hard for intercultural business people to establish harmonious relationship in the global working environment. Nowadays, a growing number of multinational companies are founded, thus intercultural business communication becomes an important part in company's routine work. Whoever is going to work in intercultural environment should be aware of the importance of intercultural business etiquette.

（1）Intercultural business etiquette: business card exchanging

Since all business contacts require a business card, an important aspect of business protocol is to know the proper procedure for exchanging business cards. In some cultures, the act of exchanging business cards has to be accomplished with protocol. Otherwise, a big offense would be committed to your partner without your awareness in intercultural business. So, before you leave for your intercultural affairs, make sure you know the proper way to slip someone your business card.

It is important to include your position and titles or degrees in addition to your company name on your card. In China and Japan, for instance, business cards have to be offered with both hands and you are expected to study them for several seconds and never slip them in your pocket while in the giver's presence. If you have printed your card in Chinese or Japanese as well as English, then present your card with the other person's native language facing up. In the Middle East, however, you are not allowed to use your left hand when offering a business card.

Intercultural business etiquette: dressing

Good business etiquette necessitates dressing appropriately. The way you dress affects the way you are perceived, and the way you are perceived, is the way you are treated. Wearing the appropriate clothing will earn you a good first impression and set the tone for how you will be seen. The importance of dressing in business world should not be neglected.

Figure 22 Which picture is improperly dressed for men in public?

There are many variables to be taken into consideration when choosing the perfect outfit for a special occasion in Western countries. You must take ownership of the challenge by using the clues you are given on the invitation, or by the nature of the event. Improperly dressed women and men should improve their dressing language.The following clues are always considered as a reference for dressing in public.

Pay more attention to the words on the invitation letter. Sometimes there are some indications of a dress code on the invitation letter. Deciphering the notation at the bottom of the invitation is of due significance. For example, "Full Dress" in the invitation letter indicates that a woman should wear a long, formal dress, while her male companion should wear a black tailcoat, black pants, and a shirt, tie and vest which are all white. Pay more attention to the notes of the time of year, time of the day, and location indicated on the invitation letter. A beach or outdoor wedding location means that you must also take the elements into consideration. An "Afternoon Tea" calls for an outfit that is quite different from a "Cocktail Reception". The following is a short list for dressing in the Western Countries.

Requirements	Elaborate Dressing Descriptions
White Tie	Long, formal dress, jewels
Ball	Long sleeveless gown, tiara optional
Black Tie	Long dress, sleeves optional, minimal elegant jewelry
Formal	Similar to black tie
Evening	Elegant dress or pant suit
Cocktail	Elegant-looking dress in any color, not floor length
Garden	Element-appropriate dress, more casual, hosiery optional
Brunch	Shirt and blouse
Tea	Shirt and blouse

Figure 23　Dressing Dictionary in Western Countries

The dress etiquette for business women in Western countries is somewhat more complex. They should always opt for conventional and modest business attire. Women should wear a suit or dress with jacket in major cities. Wearing classic clothing and classic colors in navy, gray, ivory, and white will ensure you a confident and conservative appearance. What might be appropriate for the evening might be totally inappropriate for the daytime. Wearing a low-cut, off-the-shoulder gown for the day's social event maybe a much wrong dress etiquette. A lady would be considered vulgar indeed if she lifts both sides of her skirts, even when making her way up or down a staircase, or stepping up onto or down from a curb. It is only acceptable when she is crossing a muddy spot.

In China, on business occasion, dark in medium-colored, conservative suits with shifts and ties would be an appropriate look for men. Conservative business suits or dresses and blouses are appropriate for women. It is better to avoid low necklines, too high heels and tight-fitting or sleeveless attire. Jeans and business casual attire are not recommended at a first meeting.

It is always universally-acknowledged if you can pay close attention to personal hygiene and grooming. An unkempt appearance indicated that you do not care about yourself or respect those around you. Good grooming, especially in hair and makeup, is an important part of the overall look for business women, but excessive use of makeup should be avoided, too.

5.Phases of negotiation

The negotiation process can be divided into five phases: preparation, relationship building, opening, bargaining and closing. The first phase is preparation including gathering background information, for example, the legal and judicial systems, the financial system, the sized of the market and local standards, the availability of skilled labors, etc. Selecting team members and negotiation planning are also included in this phase. The second phase is relationship building. In this phase, the negotiating parties should get to know each other. This process usually takes the form of social events, tours, ceremonies, along with polite and informal conversations before meetings. The third phase is opening. At the beginning stage, negotiators greet each other, introduce their own positions and try to explore and understand their counterpart's intention or position in order to influence and manipulate the process of negotiation and obtain an advantageous position. The fourth phase is bargaining, which is considered the most important period in a negotiation. The success of this step often depends on how well the parties understand each other's position, the ability of each to identify areas of similarity and difference, the ability to create new options, the willingness to work toward a solution that allows all parties to walk away feeling they have achieved their objectives and the ability to recognize and use certain tactics, such as promises, threats and so on. At this stage, the negotiating parties measure their own strength and strategies against each other. Each party should identify the extent of the importance of each issue so that trade-offs can be made and compromise can be reached. A good agreement will optimize the interests of both parties, but it is more likely that one party will maximize its interests instead of the other's. The fifth phase is closing. The final stage of business negotiations involves reaching a final agreement. Normally both parties expect to reach an agreement after the negotiation, but sometimes the negotiation ends in a draw, that is, no agreement reached. Declining a deal does not necessarily mean the negotiation is a failure.

6.Intercultural negotiation variables

When you are negotiating under a mono-cultural environment, it is much easier than intercultural environment. Although there may be also diverse points in a mono-cultural environment, the negotiation process is more predictable and accurate, as the negotiators do not have to be concerned with challenges of language and other cultural differences. Behavior negotiation is consistent within cultures, and each culture has its own distinctive negotiation style.

There are many more challenges in an intercultural environment. The negotiating parties do not share the same ways of thinking, feeling and behavior. The negotiation you are so at home in can be ineffective and inappropriate when dealing with people from other cultural backgrounds. In intercultural communication, cultural variety broadens and values disperse. Many scholars have identified variables affecting intercultural negotiations, among which Stephen Weiss [1] has done significant studies on culture's effects on the negotiation process. Stephen Weiss proposes twelve variables of negotiations for intercultural comparisons and presents corresponding propositions for these variables in each of seven cultural groups —American, Chinese, French, Japanese, Mexican, Nigerians, and Saudis. The following is Stephen Weiss' summary of twelve variables.

1　Weiss, Stephen E. Negotiating with the Romans—Part 2. Sloan Management Review, (1994), 35 (3) (Spring), page 85—97.

※ **General Model**

1. Basic concept of the negotiation process

distributive bargaining / joint problem-solving / debate / contingency bargaining / nondirective discussion

2. Most significant type of issue

substance / relationship-based / procedural / personal-internal

※ **Role of the Individual**

3. Selection of negotiators

knowledge / negotiating experience / personal attributes / status

4. Individuals' aspirations

individual — community

5. Decision-making in groups

authoritative — consensual

※ **Interaction: Dispositions**

6. Orientation toward time

monochronic — polychronic

7. Risk-taking propensity

high — low

8. Bases of trust

external sanctions / other's reputation / intuition / shared experiences

※ **Interaction: Process**

9. Concern with protocol

informal — formal

10. Communication complexity

low — high

11. Nature of persuasion

direct experience / logic / tradition / dogma / emotion / intuition

※ **Outcome**

12. Form of agreement

contractual — implicit

7.Improve intercultural business communication based on intersubjectivity

Professor Shan Bo [1] holds that intercultural communication are implemented on four central questions: can I communicate? How to balance the relationship between me, us and them? How is cultural diversity and unity possible? And how to face the dual cultural role of media as both bridge and gap?

It contends that this possibility lies in shifting from the subject-object mindset of "me and other" to that of inter-subjectivity between "me and you", with inter-subjectivity being further transformed into interculturality so that a mutually beneficial cultural construct is achieved. Putting oneself in other's shoes suspends one's prejudice so that one can see and hear and then understand "the other" to get a multi-dimensional perspective of culture. Political issues of intercultural communication should be solved in light of free cultural pluralism to protect cultural diversity and the right to choose cultures but oppose taking cultural diversity as an excuse for cultural apartheid and isolation. Intercultural communication should be regarded as practical reason for seeking ethic integration among cultures, with different, historical cultural ethics being respected and diverse, interactive cultural ethic being actively constructed. A contextualized understanding of other cultures and a possible connection between cultures would reveal possible conflicts between cultures and establish a dynamic interactive mechanism in terms of cultural articulation.

Professor Shan Bo holds that any communication must be equipped with intersubjectivity. The meaning of communication does not exist in subjects, but in the inter-relation and inter-connection between subjects. Following intersubjectivity, in interpersonal communication, everyone sees others from themselves and see themselves from others. The shift from "I—The Other"

1　单波 . "论跨文化传播的可能性" .《广东外语外贸大学学报》. 2014 年第 3 期, 第 5 页 .

relation to "I—You" relation is also to transform from intersubjectivity to interculturality. Differently cultures are co-existing and co-influenced. The transcendence of the cultural ethnocentrism becomes possible. If we follow the perspective of intersubjectivity, we may draw several golden rules that are significant in intercultural business communication.

(1) Being neither humble nor arrogant. Being neither humble nor arrogant is a basic principle of the etiquette that concerns foreign affairs. You should not be a lickspittle or megalomania. It is inappropriate for you to show either inferiority or superiority. Being cordial and independent are equally important. We should uphold justice and protect our cultural benefits and dignity under all circumstances.

(2) Seeking common points while reserving differences. It will be much easier for people from different cultures to communicate and avoid misunderstanding if they observe intercultural convention and reach a consensus. Meanwhile, diversities in different cultures, for example, special etiquette, should be understood and respected. Seeking common points while reserving difference is the most viable way of communicating with foreigners. Just as is said in the proverb, when in Rome, do as Romans do. We should not set our own rules when we are someone's guest. The importance of local knowledge should never be underestimated. When we are traveling interculturally on business, we should always familiarize themselves beforehand with the local customs of the destination.

(3) Respecting one's privacy. In most Eastern countries, it is relatively usual to ask people personal questions to show concern, however, Westerners, especially English-speaking people, frown on being asked about personal matters. Our Chinese and some other Asian people like to show concern about others' health, family, kids and marriage while people in the West don't want others to interfere in these. For many western people, it is even rude and an intrusion into their privacy if you call them by their cellphone on off-duty time. As a matter fact, an email will always be the first channel used even in

a fast-rhythm social networking society. Such topics as money, age, marriage and religious belief are always forbidden zones and taboo topics for many westerners.

Section 4　Cultural practice

Cultural practice

Discussion and role-play

You are a shop assistant in one of the following shops. The intercultural practice is to sell the product in one of the shops to a foreigner in the shop. The student who plays the role of the foreigner has never been to China before and he / she does not to buy anything at beginning. However, the foreigner is triggered by the introduction of the shop assistant and becomes fascinated by the culture element embedded in the product. Please imitate a real conversation in this situation. It would be better if the verbal cultural explanation is accompanied with nonverbal symbols with the help of stage property. Your dialogue may start from the coming of the foreigner and complete with a successful transaction.

Three shops are:

（1）a silk shop

（2）a jade shop

（3）a tea shop

Since the three shops and their products are closely related to our ancient Chinese civilization, it is suggested that you'd better pay more attention to your stories instead a direct sale.

Section 5 Derivative development

1.Film watching

Please watch the movie *The Revenant* [1] (《荒野猎人》,2015) and tried to work out a short intercultural analysis of the story of the movie.

In order to understand today's America, it is important for us to have a glance at the history before and just after the foundation of the United States of America in the American Continent.

The Revenant received largely positive reviews from critics, with praise directed towards DiCaprio and Hardy's performances, the direction, and the cinematography.

You may state its reasons for winning many awards of this movie. You also need to present a deep analysis on the true implication of this movie and your understanding of the leading actor in this movie —Hugh Glass,this American frontiersman, fur trapper, trader, hunter, and explorer.

2.Extended reading

（1）Hints for doing business in China from the British Embassy in Beijing

The British Embassy in Beijing once drew some conclusions of the rules of doing business with Chinese negotiators in China. We may take these rules as are ference from the perspective of intersubjectivity.

① Cultivate guanxi

The logical development of close relationships is the Chinese concept of guanxi. According to business analyst Tim Ambler of the London Business School, the kernel of guanxi is doing business through value-laden relationships. Guanxi is the counterpart of a commercial legal system. As long as the relationship is more valuable than the transaction, it is logical to honor

---

1   The Revenant is a 2015 American semi−biographical epic western film directed by Alejandro González Iñárritu. The film stars Leonardo DiCaprio, Tom Hardy, and Will Poulter. This movie tells a story that a frontiersman on a fur trading expedition in the 1820s fights for survival after being mauled by a bear and left for dead by members of his own hunting team. It has won 3 Oscars in Academy Awards in 2016 and another 88 wins and 184 nominations in the whole world.

it.

② Take care with contracts

Chinese and Westerners often approach a deal from opposite ends. To a Westerner, starting with a standard contract, altering it to fit the different circumstances, and signing the revised version, seems straightforward. Commercial law is ingrained in our thinking. The early appearance of a draft legal contract was seen as inappropriate or more likely, irrelevant, because it carried no sense of commitment. The business clauses might form a useful agenda, but obligations came from relationships, not pieces of paper.

③ Know the tricks of the trade

Chinese negotiators are shrewd and use a wide variety of bargaining tactics. The following are just a few of the more common stratagems.

Controlling the meeting place and schedule. The Chinese negotiators will always put pressure on foreigners just before their scheduled return, which can often bring useful benefits to the Chinese side.

Threatening to do business elsewhere. Foreigner negotiators may be pressured into making concessions when the Chinese side threatens to approach rival firms if their demands are not met.

Using friendship to extract concessions. Once both sides have met, the Chinese side may remind the foreigners that true friends would reach an agreement of maximum mutual benefit. Make sure that the benefit is genuinely mutual and not just one-way.

Showing anger. Despite the Confucian aversion to display of anger, the Chinese side may put on a display of a calculated anger to put pressure on the foreign party, who may be afraid of losing the contract.

Attrition. Chinese negotiators are patient and can stretch out discussions in order to wear their interlocutors down. Excessive hospitality the evening before discussions can be another variation on this theme.

④ Play the game yourself

Foreign negotiators dealing with Chinese may find some of the following tactics helpful.

Be absolutely prepared. At least one member of the foreign team must have a thorough knowledge of every aspect of the business deal. Be prepared to give a lengthy and detailed presentation, taking care not to release sensitive technological information before you reach full agreement.

Play off competitors. If the going gets tough, you may let the Chinese side know that they are not the only game in town. Competition between Chinese producers is increasing. There may be other resources in the country for which your counterpart has to offer.

Be willing to cut your losses and go home. Let the Chinese side know that failure to agree is an acceptable alternative to making a bad deal.

Cover every detail of a contract before you sign it. Talk over the entire contract with the Chinese side. Be sure that your interpretations are consistent and that everyone understands their duties and obligations.

Be patient. Chinese generally believe that Westerners are always in a hurry, and they may try to get you to sign an agreement before you have adequate time to review the detail.

(2) Commentary of *The Revenant* by the author of this book

Please see the detail of the commentary of *The Revenant* in Chinese in the appendix part.

(3) Knowing more cultures about ourselves (7): the consumption culture

Before we introduce ourselves to the others, the first and foremost thing is to have a correct and profound cognition of ourselves. In the ends of all the eight chapters, we add some basic knowledge of ourselves which are divided into eight sections, namely, the family culture, the food culture, the education culture, the marriage culture, the medical culture, the art culture, the consumption culture and the cyber culture respectively. We hope to help both audiences from other cultures and ourselves to have a better cognition of Chinese cultures. During these parts, the author of this book not only summarizes the traditional essence of these sections, but employs a diachronic perspective and includes the up-to-date changes.

(4) Our consumption cultures

The 1960s witnessed a trend of the emergence of post-modernization society, the post-industrial society in which consumption is an important characteristic. The consumption culture has increasingly become a heated area in intercultural studies. In traditional production society, consumption is the means instead of the purpose. The early phase of consumption is characterized by emphasis on capital accumulation and frugality. The mature consumption society is a new social life in which the consumption logic represents the production logic. Consumption plays a significant role in the modern society. The production is centered on consumption. What consumption people need decides the form and content of production. The amount of consumption, to a certain extent, is an important factor to judge people's happiness index. Not only the production, but also the people, have been the slaves of consumption. The consumption dominates the whole society.

The background of consumption society leads to the study of the consumption culture. The study on the consumption culture, initiated by Baudrillard and Marcuse, carried a critical perspective which hold that the consumption society is closely associated with the fact of waste of resources, deterioration of the environment, the collapse of the community, the fracture of the tradition and the loss of the subjectivity. Therefore, the consumption culture is the very thing that should be denounced and criticized. Scholars such as Karl Marx and Max Weber all showed their deep concern of the total immersion into the pleasant sensation caused by consumption and the alienation of the people.

As a part of our life, consumption itself has its own justification in meeting the basic needs for the people. However, the concept of "consumption" that scholars criticize does not refer to the basic consumption. Their consumption is referring to the overemphasis on consumption which is a byproduct of the development of mass production and mass media. The endless pursuit of the commodities, consumption, even luxury goods will lead to a loss in the materialistic world. The consumption will hereby dominate the human being.

In the Chinese history, consumption is not our tradition. The diligent Chinese nation has a long-standing tradition of saving money. As is said in the famous saying, don't have thy cloak to make when it begins to rain. The parents will be very industrious and frugal by themselves but be well-prepared as much as they can for their children to have a better life.

The early founders of the Chinese booming economy, who earned their profit by the hard work, cheap cost and professionalism from the exportation-oriented economy. Millions of factories were set up in many cities in Canton, Shanghai, Zhejiang and Jiangsu provinces. Although these first-generation founders endure hardships and are capable of hard work and win a solid foundation, their lives are still industrious and frugal, which shows no big difference from their ancestors.

However, the current society of China does witness a trend of consumerism. Our country is better known around the world for its factory workers and exports in the 1990s. After the initiative of the reform and opening-up policy, a growing number of people began to find themselves prosperous compared with other counterparts and themselves in the past. The restrained consuming is moving into an open consumption practice. An over-consuming culture came into being in big cities in China, especially in the cities in the Zhujiang River Delta and the Yangtze River Delta. Although China is still now in the process of bounding for prosperity and in some areas, the extravagant consumption does win some die-hard fans. November the 11th, a day which is designated for bachelors to celebrate their status of being single, now has been transformed into a national, even including parts of the world, shopping festival (known as "Double Eleventh" day) both for the merchants and consumers. The 2018 Double Eleventh Festival has witnessed a total volume of 21.35 billion RMB. Not only the sellers and buyers, the companies that carried the logistics, the media that carried the broadcasting, the advertising companied all exert great effort to set this agenda of the shopping carnival before, during and after the ceremony.

Consumption, of course, is an important channel to meet personal needs and stimulate the GDP growth. "Four new China's inventions" (high-speed railway, mobile payment, bicycle-sharing and cyber-shopping), to a certain extent, push the Chinese consumption to a high level. The increasingly growing number of middle-class groups in China also make a large number of consuming behaviors possible. The newly-rich Chinese people go out of China and purchase in the globe. A quarter of a billion people have migrated from the countryside to the cities in the last 25 years, and rising incomes are spurring an expanding scale of middle class. By 2025, that middle class is expected to number 612 million, or 76% of the population, up from 43% in 2006, according to the McKinsey Global Institute. Eventually, the bourgeoisie will be dropping a greater portion of their estimated $13,000 to $54,000 annual income (adjusted for purchasing power parity) in stores, says McKinsey. In a 2007 McKinsey & Co. survey of 6,000 Chinese, two-thirds of the respondents already count shopping as a favorite activity. We benefit a lot, both physical and mentally, from the consuming process and result.

However, consumerism should never be the dominant them of our life. Why not read and discover the meaning of work and the spirit of dedication in our life?

第八章 美美与共的共同体：从想象到现实
Chapter Eight
Towards a Common Community with Shared Future

Section 1 Lead-in

1.Question

（1）Which cultural identity do America-born Chinese (ABC) belong to?

（2）People tend to put their eyes on the differences between China and the West while neglecting cultures near us or similar as ours. What is your understanding of the Japanese and Korean cultures? What can we learn from them?

（3）What is the essence of the Chinese culture? Which part of the Chinese culture could be introduced as a good supplement for the Western culture?

2.Case

（1）Case 1

Tom Chung's company in San Francisco, USA, sent him to work with one of its major suppliers in Shanghai, China. The company executives sent Tom because they thought a Chinese American would be able to develop close business relationships quickly.

Tom became friendly with a coworker, Wang Jun, who was at about his level in the company. Wang Jun enjoyed Tom's company because of a common interest in chess and because they have fun exchanging informal language lessons. Wang Jun and Tom had agreed to play a game of chess, speaking half the time in Chinese and half the time in English, on a certain Tuesday evening. In anticipation Tom had bought a new chess set made of carved marble. On that Tuesday afternoon, however, Wang Jun told Tom that he couldn't play chess that evening because his superior at work had asked him to go to dinner with him. He gave no other explanation.

Tom was irritated and thought to himself, "I'm being blown off." However, he knew enough about differences between China and the United States and asked, "I wonder if there is something cultural involved here."

Though Tom is a Chinese American, he was born and educated in the Unites States. In other words, he may get accustomed to the Western way of socialization and communication. This is the reason why he thought Wang Jun as impolite. According to Tom, Wang Jun should have turned down the dinner invitation or asked his boss to schedule the dinner another time because he had already had a social engagement ahead of time. Tom did not know that Chinese value hierarchies and was not aware of their position in the vertical relationships. With most Chinese, "My superior asked me to attend a social event" is a satisfactory explanation when breaking a previous appointment with friends, even bosom friends. In this case, Wang Jun received a request from his superior and felt the obligation to honor it. And other Chinese would act in a similar manner.

（2）Case 2

Once a woman shared her experience of returning to China after more than 15 years in the Unites States. As a newcomer, she never recognized her company's strict chain-of-command, not did she consider building up relations with her colleagues. Whenever problems arose, she would report straight to the company chairman with her plan. And soon her action caused her colleagues to disagree and superiors to lose face. As a result, people around her began to resent her and finally she quitted the job.

However, another man with the similar overseas background did otherwise. In this company, he was to head up the local operations of the Sales Department. In his first management team meeting, he presented his plans for a new direction in operations. His request was met with an uncomfortable silence, with none of the managers daring to speak up. Soon he quickly determined that his first on-the-job challenge would be to build up the managers' confidence in him, and that he had to do this individually, not in a group. By working to establish open relationships with each manager, he alleviated any fears that they would be punished for offering criticism or differing opinions. Within a year, their management team meetings were transformed into the interactive, brainstorming sessions that he intended them to be.

These cases present a sharp contrast in the results. From these two cases, what are the differences in management style of the USA and China reflected in the case?

Section 2 Theory preparation

Theory preparation: cultural adaptation

Of all of the potential problems in intercultural communication, cultural shock was first defined by the anthropologist Kalvero Oberg as "precipitated by the anxiety that results from losing all our familiar signs and symbols of social intercourse". He found that all human beings experience the same feelings when they travel to or live in a different country or culture that cultural shock is almost like a disease: it has a cause, symptoms, and a cure. Although the reactions associated with culture shock vary from normally go through four stages, shown in the U-curve, namely, ① honeymoon phase, ② rejection phase, ③ regression phase and ④ recovery phase.

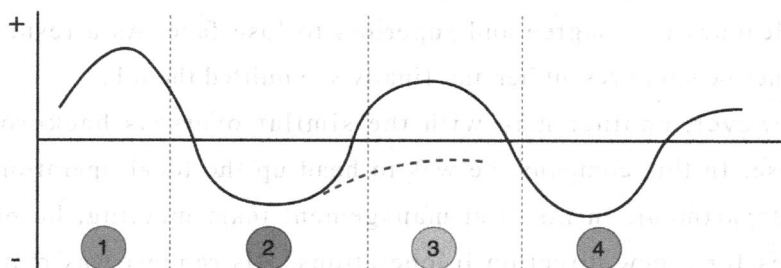

Figure 24   U-curve of culture shock and acculturation

According to U-curve of culture shock and acculturation model, people will initially have honeymoon period, and then there will be transition period, that is, cultural shock. But then, people will start to adapt (the dotted line depicted some people hated by new cultures instead). And refers to some people returning to their own places and re-adapting to the old culture.

During the first few days of a person's stay in a new country, everything usually goes fairly smoothly. The newcomer is excited about being a new place where there are new sights and sounds, new smells and tastes. This first stage of culture shock is called the "honeymoon phase". This initial euphoria phase begins with the arrival in the new country and ends when this excitement wears off.

Unfortunately, this honeymoon phase often comes to an end fairly soon. The newcomer generally has to deal with transportation problems, shopping problems or communication problems. This may lead to the second stage of cultural shock, known as the "rejection phase". It is called the "rejection" phase because it is at this point that the newcomer starts to reject the host country, noticing and complaining about the bad things that bother them. At this stage the newcomer either gets stronger and stays or gets weaker and goes home physically, or only mentally.

If you do not survive the second stage successfully, you may find yourself moving into stage three: the "regression phase". You may spend much of this time complaining about the host country / culture. You may remember only the good things about your home country.

If you survive the third stage successfully (or miss it completely), you will move into the fourth stage of culture shock called the "recovery phase". In this stage, you become more comfortable with the language and you also feel more comfortable with the customs of the host country. You are now almost adjusted to the new culture and you start to realize that no country is that much better than another— it is just different lifestyles and different ways to deal with the problems of life.

Much better, you may find yourself returning to your homeland and you may find yourself entering the fifth phase of cultural shock and acculturation, the "re-entry phase". You have "reverse culture shock" or "return culture shock", because you have been away for a long time, become comfortable with the habits and customs of a new lifestyle, and you may find that you are no longer completely comfortable in your home country. It may take a little while to become at ease with the cues and signs and symbols of your home culture.

There is a risk of sickness or emotional problems in many of the phases of culture shock. Also, because culture shock occurs over a period of time, you may not always realize that its stages are temporary. The best thing to do is to admit that you are experiencing culture shock, try to identify your stages of culture shock, and work toward becoming more familiar with the new culture.

Beyond the early adaptation experience of culture shock lies the process of long-term cultural adaptation. This idea refers to long-term acculturation which in turn refers to the process by which one culture is modified or changed through contact with or exposure to another culture. To understand acculturation is to discover interpersonal relations, the effects of prolonged culture contact, and how well individuals adapt to new cultural behaviors that are different from one's primary learned culture. Some factors are believed to be important in the log-term adaptation process.

Adaptation involves survival skills. Part of the process of acculturation is learning survival skills. The daily press of living becomes the dominant concern for a person who plans to live permanently in the new culture.

Culture adaptation assumes that attitudes and behaviors will ultimately change. In the long run, growth results from stretching and experiencing the inevitable stresses. Young Yun Kim [1] proposes that adaptation is an

---

1   Kim, Y. Y. Communication and Cross-cultural Adaptation: An integrative Theory. Clevedon: Multilingual Matters, 1988. Young Yun Kim is a renowned professor of communication at the University of Oklahoma. Her research activities mainly address two issues: the role of communication in the cross-cultural adaptation process of immigrants and sojourners; and the nature of behavior-context interface in interethnic and interracial communication.

acculturation with a progressive series of positive and negative experiences. There may be two steps forward and one step back as we move toward adaptation. We do not always adapt in a smooth, continuous process. Pictured as a coiled spring, which stretches and grows but is pulled back by its own tension, the stress-adaptation-growth dynamic ultimately depicts adaptation in the new culture. The process of adaptation is essentially a communication process in which newcomers learn, understand and acquire communication patterns of the new culture and build up relationships with the new cultural environment by various means of communication. However, long-term adaptation or acculturation does not occur in everyone's life in the same way. Some people are motivated to acculturate, while others are not. So, the challenge for intercultural communications is to recognize the dynamics of the cultural adaptation and acculturation factors and apply these principles, along with personal competences and communication accommodation to meaningful relationships.

Since intercultural adaptation skills are closely related to intercultural communication competence, let's move on to the next topic of improving intercultural communication competence, with which you can adapt to a new culture much easier and better.

Section 3　Detailed analysis

1.What makes intercultural communication possible?

Intercultural communication, as a social activity of human beings, has a long history. Global business, missionary work and explorations are all examples of intercultural communication. The history ranging from the Silk Road to Zheng He, one of the pioneers in exploring the ocean engaging into inter-cultural communications in Ming dynasty demonstrated the prosperity of intercultural communication between China and other countries. Stepping into the 21st century, intercultural has been a famous school course in many universities with the following reasons.

The improvement of science and technology transforms the pattern and the frequency of human interactions. The past two decades witnessed a dramatic acceleration of communication with the help of the transportation and communication technologies. Economic globalization enables different companies increasingly dependent on each other. The mobility in the whole world also spotlights the communication among various nationalities, colors and religions. Cross-countries traveling and cooperation become common for every citizen.

With the frequent communication between "I" and "the other", people began to reflect and rethink about the questions such as "Who am I?" or "Who are we?". When a Chinese is alone or being together with the people with the same culture, they will not easily identify what cultures features they present and what disadvantages they have. However, when they are in comparison or in contrast with "the other" culture, they will identify themselves much more clearly. People tend to comprehend and recognize the exterior world or stimulus context by the cognitive schemata stored in their brains. When the exterior stimulus context is integrated into the cognitive schemata, the assimilation will happen. When the subject is modified to get used to or accommodate the new exterior stimulus context, the adaptability will happen. If there is only assimilation, we cannot notice the difference between "I" and "the other" and self-cognitive schemata could not be developed. If there is only adaptability, the cognitive schemata will lose its stability and hereby lose the self. Only when assimilation and adaptability are somewhat balanced can we have a status of stable interaction and dialogue. Only when assimilation and adaptability are closely related can we reach the communication rationality proposed by Jürgen Habermas.

Apart from the exploration on the possibility of intercultural communication, another renowned scholar, George Herbert Mead, an American philosopher, sociologist and psychologist, should also need to be introduced to justify intercultural communication. He is regarded as one of the founders of symbolic interactionism and of what has come to be referred to as the Chicago sociological tradition. A final piece of Mead's social theory is the mind as the individual importation of the social process. According to Mead, the self is a social process, meaning that there are series of actions that go on in the mind to help formulate one's complete self. Mead presented the self and the mind in terms of a social process. As gestures are taken in by the individual organism, the individual organism also takes in the collective attitudes of others, in the form of gestures, and reacts accordingly with other organized attitudes. This process is characterized by Mead as the "I" and the "Me". The "Me" is the social self and the "I" is the response to the "Me." In other words, the "I" is the response of an individual to the attitudes of others, while the "me" is the organized set of attitudes of others which an individual assumes.Understood as a combination of the "I" and the "me", Mead's self proves to be noticeably entwined within a sociological existence. For Mead, existence in community comes before individual consciousness. First one must participate in the different social positions within society and only subsequently can one use that experience to take the perspective of others and thus become "conscious". Mead's research is a typical demonstration of intrapersonal communication, i.e. communication within and to the oneself.

Another frequently-quoted theory of the need of communication can be found in the work of Abraham Maslow, in which he described people as being driven by sets of needs arranged in a hierarchy, from the most basic at the bottom to the most refined at the peak of a triangle. Maslow's need theory may be categorized into the domain of intrapersonal and interpersonal communication of intercultural communication.

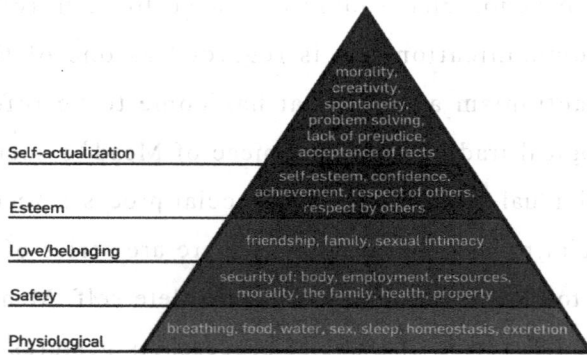

Figure 25　An interpretation of Maslow's hierarchy of needs

Maslow described human needs as ordered in a prepotent hierarchy—a pressing need would need to be mostly satisfied before someone would give their attention to the next highest need. None of his published works included a visual representation of the hierarchy. The pyramidal diagram illustrating the Maslow needs hierarchy may have been created by a psychology textbook publisher as an illustrative device. This now iconic pyramid frequently depicts the spectrum of human needs, both physical and psychological, as accompaniment to articles describing Maslow's needs theory and may give the impression that the Hierarchy of Needs is a fixed and rigid sequence of progression. Maslow developed his theory further and described human needs as being relatively fluid—with many needs being present in a person simultaneously.The hierarchy of human needs model suggests that human needs will only be fulfilled one level at a time. According to Maslow's theory, when a human being ascends the levels of the hierarchy having fulfilled the needs in the hierarchy, one may eventually achieve self-actualization. People have the need to communicate, which is clearly manifested in the Babel story. Obviously, communicating with various people from different nationalities, cultures, religions is to helpful to identify who we are and what disadvantages we have and hereby assist our self-actualization.

When our human beings evolve from primitive men, we are longing for communication and we are afraid of being alone. To a certain extent, it is communication, especially verbal communication, that distinguishes us from other animals. In modern society, the time we spend with our family members and friends in real time is becoming increasingly less due to the quick pace and mobility of the society. However, under the magnifier of the modern technology represented by the new-generation information and communication technology, we may resort to multiple talks (text talks, voice talks, video talks, etc.) to overcome digital loneliness. According to the latest data released by China Internet Network Information Center (CNNIC) on February 28th, 2019, the scale of netizens in China has reached 829 million with the popularity rate reaching 59.6%. The popularity rate via the access of the mobile Internet has surprisingly reached 98.6%.

After we are clear of the question who we are and the necessity of communication, we will further discuss whether a diversified intercultural communication is possible and how we can keep a free and harmonious relation between "I" "we" and "them".

It is universally-acknowledged that "I" is a product of socialization. Millions of "I" compose the whole society. People tend to find a group of objects who are similar as them, which is manifested in the classical saying "Birds of a feather flock together". Many "I" gather together stably and hereby form the group "we". Individual communication hereby becomes group communication. In a group communication, features of an individual are always neglected and "I", to a certain extent, is satisfied to be in this homogenizing group.

However, the East and the West show different characteristics in absorbing "I" into the group. In the Western culture, "I" am a rational being capable of any activities, thus independent and isolated self from others. Individuals are connected via the social contract. However, in the East culture, "I" am always belittled and humble. "I" exists in the relation between "I" and "the other". Social order and harmony, proper human relationships are valued. Group identity, uniformity and conformity are always appreciated.

However, just as the notion of biological diversity, cultural diversity now is also a consensus agreed by every country. Cultural diversity and conformity may exist in the process of their acculturalization. Each individual lay influence on the surrounding environment and is affected by the sounding environment. Co-culture, the third culture, marginalized culture and sub-culture are all the possible realizations of acculturation. Another possibility of cultural diversity lies in the verbal symbols. People with different languages, dialects and accents can communicate. It means that people share something in the way of thinking or cultural patterns. Diversified languages enable diversified cultures possible. Lastly, the possibility of cultural diversity could be achieved by the improvement of intercultural competence and the cultivation of intercultural personhood.

2.Improving intercultural competence

Intercultural competence is a range of cognitive, affective, and behavioral skills that leads to effective and appropriate communication with people of other cultures.Effective intercultural communication relates to behaviors that culminate with the accomplishment of the desired goals of the interaction and all parties involved in the situation.Appropriate intercultural communication includes behaviors that suit the expectations of a specific culture, the characteristics of the situation, and the level of the relationship between the parties involved in the situation.It also takes into consideration one's own cultural norms and the best appropriate, comfortable compromise between the different cultural norms.

According to Young Yun Kim, the intercultural communication competence involves the ability to communicate in all types of encounters. In entails the ability to manage various differences between communicators, cultural or otherwise, and the ability to deal with the accompanying uncertainty and stress.

Intercultural communication competence can be further divided into three interrelated categories of components, which are cognitive, affective and operational. These three parts are interdependent and simultaneously present in actual communication situations.

（1）Cognitive components

The cognitive aspect of intercultural communication is the mental capacity of comprehension and the ability to understand the meanings of various verbal and nonverbal codes. It reflects the capacity to identify and understand messages, which could be considered as a decoding competence. The cognitive components of intercultural communication further include three aspects. The first one is the knowledge of the host communication system, which refers to the proficient mastery of the languages, language-related cultural forms, and nonverbal symbols. The second one is cultural understanding. The task of acquiring intercultural communication competence entails much more than just "mastering" the language. It requires a general and deep understanding of the cultural and sub-cultural milieu that provides the context for specific situations. That is to say, a deeper-level understanding of the target culture involves knowing something about its historical, political, religious practices as well as its values, attitudes, beliefs, etc. The third part of cognitive component is cognitive complexity. Cognitive complexity deals with the structure of information processing, which is a rather abstract concept. A high-level cognitive complexity means that a person is more knowledgeable about the target culture and language and has developed a psychological orientation and the ability to identify the nuance and subtleness of the target and the interlocutor's own culture.

（2）Affective components

The second part of intercultural communication competence is the affective components that include three aspects. The first aspect is adaptation motivation, namely, the interlocutor's self-motivation of adaptation willingness or the emotional and motivational drives towards the target culture. It also means an emotional and motivational capacity to deal with various challenges. The second aspect of affective components is identity flexibility, which is reflected in a willingness to make some changes in one's original cultural habits. Identity flexibility is a basic psychological-social orientation of individuals with respect to themselves, their original culture and the target culture. This flexibility helps to engender greater openness and lessen prejudicial criticism toward new cultural experiences so that personal and social goals can be met. The third aspect of affective components is aesthetic co-orientation. This component deals with whether the aesthetic needs in the target culture will be fulfilled or the interlocutors have the capacity to participate in such experiences when they communicate with the natives of the target culture. With this aesthetic co-orientation capacity, the interlocutors are better able to empathize with the cultural products, including art, music, sports, as well as to appreciate the culture's everyday experiences of fun, joy, humor and happiness, and of anger, despair, frustration, and disappointments.

(3) Operational components

Operational components also have three aspects. The primary aspect includes technical skills ranging from basic language skills, job skills, and academic skills to skills in locating appropriate information sources and solving various day-to-day problems. The second refers to synchrony, which means that the interlocutor has to behave in a synchronized manner so as to communicate with the natives in ways that are compatible and harmonious. The last one deals with resourcefulness, which means the ability to reconcile cultural differences and come up with creative action plans to solve various problems and to accomplish personal and social goals.

The three facets of intercultural communication competence described individually in this section, namely cognitive, affective, and operational, are inseparable in reality. Altogether, they shape the overall capacity to participate in the cross-cultural communication activities. The interrelatedness of cognitive, affective, and operational components is very important in the improvement of the communicator's intercultural communication competence. That is to say, the more competent the interlocutor is in the cognitive aspect, the more he is willing to communicate with the target language. At the same time, he will be more flexible in his exchange with the target culture and will empathize more with the people from the target cultures regarding the aesthetics and psychological feelings.

3.Four-step approach to intercultural communication training

Brislin (1994) proposed a four-step approach to intercultural communication training: awareness, knowledge, motivations, and skills.

（1）Raise awareness. First, we should be aware of the importance of intercultural communication competence. The first competency requires people to move from being culturally unaware to becoming aware of the way their own lives have been shaped by the culture into which they were born. This should also be accompanied by learning to respect and be sensitive toward culturally different people. The second competency requires conscious awareness of one's own values and biases and how they affect the way one interacts with culturally different people. This can at least help people monitor their ethnocentrism. Being sensitive to circumstances implies that human beings are not infallible and that there may be certain cultural groups in which some people have a very hard time interacting. Instead of denying this difficulty, sometimes it is wiser to refer the client or business partner to someone else who is better able to serve the client.

（2）Obtain knowledge. It is unlikely that you can interpret correctly the meanings of other people's messages without proper cultural-general and cultural-specific knowledge. You will not be able to determine what the appropriate and effective behaviors are in a particular context. We should be equipped both in theory and in tools to understand a particular culture correctly.

（3）Enhance motivation. Motivations include the overall set of emotional associations that people have as they anticipate and actually communicate interculturally. Human emotional reactions include both feelings and intentions. Feelings refer to the emotional and affective states that you experience when communicating with someone from a different culture. Feelings involve your general sensitivity to other cultures and your attitudes towards the specific culture and individuals with whom you must interact. Intentions refer to the goals, plans, objectives and desires that focus and guide your choices in a particular intercultural interaction. If your intentions are positive, accurate and reciprocated by the people with whom you are interacting, your intercultural competences will likely be enhanced.

（4）Master skills. Understanding the theories and concepts in intercultural communication does not automatically lead to culturally sensitive behaviors. People who are aware, emotionally prepared, and knowledgeable about intercultural issues are not necessarily competent communicators until they also practiced the appropriate skills. Both cultural-general and cultural-specific skills could be acquired through practices.

4.Towards the construction of cultural quotient (CQ)

Cultural quotient (CQ), or cultural intelligence, is a term used in business, education, government and academic research. Cultural quotient can be understood as the capability to relate and work effectively across cultures. Cultural quotient is a person's capability to adapt as he /she interacts with others from different cultural regions. It has behavioral, motivational, and metacognitive aspects. Without cultural intelligence, both business and military actors seeking to engage foreigners are susceptible to mirror imaging. Ang, Van Dyne, & Livermore [1] describe four CQ capabilities: motivation (CQ Drive), cognition (CQ Knowledge), meta-cognition (CQ Strategy) and behavior (CQ Action).

The term is relatively recent: early definitions and studies of the concepts were given by P. Christopher Earley and Soon Ang in the book

---

1   Livermore, David (2009). Leading with Cultural Intelligence. New York: AMACOM. ISBN 978-0814449172.

Cultural Intelligence: Individual Interactions Across Cultures (2003) and more fully developed later by David Livermore in the book, *Leading with Cultural Intelligence*. The concept is related to that of cross-cultural competence.Cultural intelligence or CQ is measured on a scale, similar to that used to measure an individual's intelligence quotient. People with higher CQs are regarded as better able to successfully blend into any environment, using more effective business practices, than those with a lower CQ.

In the study of intercultural communication, cultural quotient competence could be developed and improved through three ways.

（1）cognitive means: the head (learning about your own and other cultures, and cultural diversity).

（2）physical means: the body (using your senses and adapting your movements and body languages to blend in).

（3）motivational means: the emotions (gaining rewards and strength from acceptance and success).

5.A synthesis of the East (Chinese) culture and the West culture

Many differences between the East (Chinese) and the West cultures stem fundamentally from their respective thoughts on the reality of the universe, nature, knowledge, time and communication. Based on an organic, holistic and cyclic view, the East has developed an epistemology that emphasizes direct, immediate, and aesthetic components in human nature's experience of the world. The ultimate aim of human learning is to transcend the immediate, differentiated self and to develop an integrated perception of the undifferentiated universe. That is, to be spiritually untied with the universe and to find eternity within the present moment.

The Western culture, founded on theories such as dualism, determinism, and materialism, encourages an outlook that is rational, analytic, and direct. History is viewed as a linear progression from the past to the future. The acquisition of knowledge is not so much for spiritual enhancement as for improvement of the human condition.

The different world views, in turn, have been reflected in the individual conception of self, others and the group. While the East has stressed the primacy of the group over the individual, the West has stressed the primacy of the individual over the group.

The Western world view has held to systematically describe and explain the physical phenomena. It has proved successful in technological and scientific development. However, the mechanistic world view and the corresponding communication patterns of the West are also found to be inadequate for the subtle, complicated human relationship, sometimes causing alienation between self and others. The analytical mind to the West, to a certain extent, is helpful to lead to modern science and technology, but it has also resulted in knowledge that is specialized, fragmented, and detached from the totality or reality.

The East has not experienced the alienation the West has been experiencing in recent centuries. However, at the same time, the East has not developed as much in science and technology as the West has done since its world view does not promote material and social development. It does not encourage worldly activism, not promote individuals to fundamentally change the social circumstances. Furthermore, instead of building greater ego strength and the capacity for more self-determining behavior, the Eastern view tends to work toward ego extinction. It also tends to encourage dependency and passivity since people feel locked into an unchanging social order.

Of course, the above differences are not in diametric opposition. As a matter of fact, they are different in emphasis. The contributions the West has made to the material development far exceeds the historical learning of the East. However, the aesthetic and holistic view of the East offers a deeper understanding of human experience, the natural world, and the universe compared to the Western view.

In conclusion, the Eastern and Western cultures are not completely contradictory in essence, but complementary. It is unnecessary to build a binary opposition between them. The values, behaviors, and institutions of the

West should not be substituted for their Eastern counterparts, and vice versa. The purpose of the cultural evolution is not to generate a homogeneous mass, but to gradually unfold a diversified and organic whole. This conclusion, in a sense, reiterates the necessity of intercultural communication and answers the question of the possibility of intercultural communication in the previous part of this chapter.

The following figure is a synthesis of the East (Chinese) culture and the West culture:

EASTERN (CHINESE)	WESTERN
Polymeric	Discrete
Introverted	Extroverted
Collectivism	Individualism
Holistic, Organic, Cyclic	Rational, Analytic, Direct
Confucianism, Buddhism, Taoism	Dualism, Determinism, Materialism

Figure 26 A synthesis of the East (Chinese) culture and the West culture

6.Introducing ourselves and introducing by ourselves

(1)The Chinese wisdom

Stepping into the new century, our world is perplexed by the consequence of modernity and post-modernity. The last five years witnessed several activities which are known as "post-truth" events, which may lead to the uncertainty of the world situation. Furthermore, the improvement of science and technology and the myth of the Internet still cannot alleviate people's misgivings about the future. The Chinese wisdom hereby returns to people's vision, disabuses the people and helps the world to get out of the bewilderment with its powerful and justified philosophy for the uncertain world when the traditional western view comes to a crisis in its interpretive principle.

The Chinese wisdom is mainly characterized by its emphasis on the peace and harmony. As is said by Confucius, "a gentleman gets along with others, but does not necessarily agree with them".It has been the Confucian philosophy to accommodate divergent views in the Chinese classics. Some people may misunderstand that the proposal of peace means there are no conflicts or contradictions. As a matter of fact, it is meaningless to talk about "HE" (Chinese value on peace and harmony) without conflicts and contradictions. The founder of Taoism, Lao Tzu, also proposed the importance of being peaceful and harmonious. The idea that "harmony is precious" is well-acknowledged among all Chinese.

For modern China, the Five Principles of Peaceful Coexistence has been a basic principle to deal with international affairs. We advocate peaceful talks and negotiations between laterals instead of resorting to wars. The proposal and preference of peace and harmony is not to dodge contradictions, but build a more harmonious world in dialogue and cooperation.

In a globalized world, the Chinese wisdoms is also a boon for industrialization in intercultural communication. Four decades of reform and opening-up have highlighted the importance of six kinds of "Chinese wisdom" in promoting China's unprecedented industrial development.

① First is the adherence to the principle of making progress while maintaining stability, in order to guarantee the continuous growth of industries and deepening of industrialization. Over the past four decades, China has implemented progressive reform focused on economic construction, and made great efforts to build a harmonious and stable development environment. To stabilize economic operation, China has consistently deepened reform and established a favorable relationship among reform, development and stability.

② Second is to establish the right coordination between industrial policy and competition policy, continuously improve industrial efficiency and make greater efforts to reach high-end industrialization. China has taken successive measures to coordinate the relationship between the government and market, as part of market-oriented reform, so that the market can play a critical role in resource distribution, and the government can perform its duties better. China's industrial upgrading measures are in accordance with its industrial development policy. It has achieved effective coordination between industrial policy and competition policy, and adjusted these policies to suit the actual situations, thereby effectively promoting technological progress, industrial efficiency and industrial upgrading. That industrial development and industrialization have been successful and beneficiary to China's economy is evident from the progress the country has made.

③ Third, industrial parks have played an important role in promoting rational industrial distribution and coordinated regional development. An industrial park is a modern industrial collaboration production area which includes an economic and technological development zone, high-tech industrial development zone, and an export processing zone. Which means an industrial park brings together production factors, highlights the unique features of different sectors and optimizes industrial distribution, which are conducive to promoting industrialization and transforming the development model.

④ Fourth is to follow the principle of consolidating and developing the public economy while encouraging and supporting the private economy, and cultivating an all-round, dynamic industrial development mechanism. Based on its actual national conditions, China has established socialist market economy with Chinese characteristics. This principle cultivates market players including State-owned enterprises, private enterprises and foreign enterprises, providing a coordinated dynamic mechanism for China's industrial development.

⑤ Fifth, China has not only actively participated in economic globalization to establish a sound and open modern industrial system. It has also established several special economic zones, opened 14 coastal cities to the outside world and joined the World Trade Organization. It has attracted huge amounts of foreign direct investment, introduced massive advanced technologies, and made use of overseas market resources to increase its exports that have greatly promoted industrialization.Four decades of reform and opening-up show that China owes its development miracle to the openness of its manufacturing industry. In fact, China had opened up 22 of the 31 manufacturing industries to foreign investment by 2017. Further opening up its economy to the outside world, it has accelerated its marketization process, maintained its development momentum in line with the cooperation and win-win trend in the global value chain of manufacturing, and made remarkable contributions to global economic growth.

※ Sixth, China has laid emphasis on urbanization and industrialization, because economic modernization depends on the interactive development process of industrialization and urbanization. Industrialization provides the economic foundation for urbanization, while urbanization offers excellent production factors and thus widens the scope for industrialization.China's urbanization has lagged behind industrialization for some time. But as China stepped into the middle and later periods of industrialization early in the 21st century, its urbanization process has accelerated effectively driving the industrialization process.

The "Chinese wisdom" used to propel industrial development could help other developing countries to promote their own industrialization, and as they gather experience from the process, China will advance its industrialization even further.

（2）The soft power of China

Soft power is the ability to shape the preferences of others through appeal and attraction. Joseph Nye, a professor of Harvard University, explained that with soft power, "the best propaganda is not propaganda", further explaining that during the Information Age, "credibility is the scarcest resource."

In his book Hard Power and Soft Power, Joseph Nye defines a country's soft power as "the universality of a country's culture, and its capacity to establish preferable rules and systems to control international actions." Here "a country's culture" is not only the traditional humanism, but also in a broader sense, the ideology and the superstructure, including its domestic and foreign policy. China's decision to follow a road of peaceful development and its foreign policy that serves this decision have received growing global attention and recognition and become more influential and attractive, which is the main vehicle of China's soft power.

On the road of peaceful development, China develops itself by safeguarding world peace, and promotes world peace through its own development. China boldly participates in the economic globalization, and engages in extensive cooperation for mutual benefit and common development. Since the policy of the reform and opening-up, China has maintained an average growth rate of 9% for over two decades, becoming one of the main and dynamic driving forces of the world economy. The increasingly growing China insists on an independent foreign policy, the Five Principles of Peaceful Coexistence, which serves the country on a peaceful development road.

Chinese civilization is as long as five thousand years, long standing and well established. We not only invented inscriptions on bones or tortoise shells of the Shang dynasty (16th—11th century B.C.), but enjoyed one of the first cultural prosperities early in the Spring and Autumn period and the warring States period, two thousand years ago. Many schools of thoughts were flourishing, such as Taoism, Confucianism, Mohist and Legalist, with renowned thinkers such as Lao Tzu, Confucius, Mencius and Mo Ti. Their thoughts and analects, such as "rituals and music" "benevolence and virtue" "harmony as being of primary importance" "harmony with diversity" "teaching with skills and patience", which exercised a great influence on the Chinese society and culture, are still widely-spreading now in the whole globe.

In today's complex and volatile world, traditional and non-traditional security threats have become intertwined. Many people pursue money, fame and material gains in an extreme way. What kind of thought or culture should we promote to uplift the morality and harmonize human relationship? The Chinese wisdom and the Chinese glamor of soft power may give the modern people a good guidance. Principles such as "the golden mean" and "the benevolent love others" will endow people another calm angle to deal with interpersonal and intrapersonal bewilderment. Nowadays, many foreign people learn Chinese and the Chinese culture not only for economic reasons, but also for comprehending and keeping pace with the glamor of the Chinese culture. People in Asia, for example, will maintain identity, realize self-consciousness and the sense of pride for our culture and civilization during the communicating with the Chinese culture. Now over 2,500 universities in more than 100 countries and regions covering almost 150 million population are taking the Chinese as their important foreign language.

The growing number of Confucius Institutes in various countries now provides a terrific opportunity for foreign people to comprehend the appeal of our language and culture. However, the spreading of our culture and the convergence of different cultures will never be an easy task. Compared with the world-famous US movies, music, sport and other cultural products, China lacks outstanding cultural brands that enjoy world-wide fames. The spreading of the Chinese soft power is still on the road. We should exert all our effort to renovate and refurbish methods to fulfill the real cultural harmony.The following are several tentative and feasible measures to improve our soft power effect.

First, be more confident in introducing ourselves. We have reached unprecedented achievements in the past three decades. Both our cultural strength and political strength are great. The whole world philosophy is also beneficial from Chinese's contributions in economy, culture and politics. Such notions as the Chinese Dream, the Belt and Road Initiative, the Construction of a Common Community with Shared Future, exemplify our Chinese experience in the past thirty years of development after the implementation of the reform and opening-up policy. The Chinese paradigm based on our splendid traditional civilization and magnificent current achievement is now considered a terrific studying example for a growing number of countries, especially for those under and less developed countries. The Chinese culture, was, is and will always be one of the most fantastic cultures in the world map of cultures.

Second, be more active and initiative in introducing ourselves. For decades, media imperialism has been overwhelming in the global information communication. News agencies such Reuter's News Agency and the Associated Press provide the news resources for millions of newspapers, TV stations and websites. Due to the long-existing distinction of ideology, these agencies will deliberately choose a certain amount (not the whole sample) of the news information to present an effect of stigmatizing China in a "professional" way. They turn a blind eye to the improvement of China's effort in many aspects. Instead, the reports are always focusing on the contamination of the environment and the food security, which are actually greatly improved in China. Therefore, no matter how hard the road of self-introduction is, we should exert our great effort to introduce us more actively and initiatively. On one hand, the national team, represented by China's Xinhua News Agency and China Global Television Network (CGTN) should of course shoulder the responsibility of transmitting China. On the other hand, ordinary citizens, especially those people whose jobs are closely related with international communication, for example, the journalists and our overseas travelers, should be armed with the consciousness of spreading our culture both intentionally and unintentionally. The behaviors for some Chinese people in other countries have given a bad stain on the Chinese national image.

Third, be clear that the improvement of soft power is different from that of hard power. The excellence of hard power does not necessarily equate the proficiency of soft power. In the past China, we are too eager to show our voice and image, thus paying more attention to the propaganda. The rule of mass communication and intercultural communication is not respected enough. According to the Joseph Nye, advertising and persuasion always involve some degree of framing, which limits voluntarism, as do structural features of the social environment, but extreme deception in framing can be viewed as coercive; though not violent, it prevents meaningful choice. Techniques of public diplomacy that are widely viewed as propaganda cannot produce soft power. In an age of information, the scarcest resources are attention and credibility. As Nye said, credibility is the scarcest resource. If we cannot improve the credibility of the Chinese culture, our appeal could not be well produced. Luckily, we have explored some tentatively positive attempts. Chinese documentaries such as *A Bite of China* and Chinese online literature began to appear as new instruments of attractiveness.

Fourth, we have always stepped into the era of mediatization. Everything and everyone seem to be mediatized quickly into the Net. Therefore, media ranging from TV to mobile phones have played an increasingly important role in modern cultural communication. Without a deliberate selection of news and a man-made impediment of communication, foreign audiences may find easier to access to the Chinese culture through multi-modal discourses. The Internet and mobile Internet create a user-friendly "field" for free, diversified and intercultural communication. The Chinese glamor will be further magnified and adapted to every dot of the world if we can continue improving our intercultural literacy and media literacy.

The improvement of our hard power, represented by our national comprehensive strength, has already laid a solid foundation for our soft power. It is firmly believed that if we unswervingly hold up high the banner of mutual benefit and mutual dialogue with an open attitude towards the diversity, our Chinese culture will be more flourishing, influential and attractive on the international stage.

7.The Chinese dream

The discourse of China's peaceful rise, to a certain extent, was considered to pose a challenge, even a threat to the Wester superiority. The

Chinese identity may encounter some misunderstandings when our identity comes to the frontier of the world. The Chinese dream, however, dilutes the potential threat brought by the rise. In the conceptualization of the Chinese dream, the path of the development of China is termed as "rejuvenation", which not only develops our traditional value of peaceful development and the harmony of the diversity, but also takes the perspective from the West into consideration. This discourse of the Chinese dream will be easy in reaching a discoursal and empathetic resonance among diversified people.

（1）Background: Connotations of the Chinese Dream

The Chinese President Xi Jinping first explained his vision of the Chinese Dream on November 29th, 2012, when visiting the exhibition "The Path to National Rejuvenation." National rejuvenation has been the greatest dream of the Chinese people since the beginning of modern times. It is a dream that spans generations, a dream that reflects our national interests, and a dream embraced by every Chinese. According to the quotations from President Xi Jinping, the Chinese Dream, after all, is the dream of the people. We must realize it by closely depending on the people. We must incessantly bring benefits to the people. Realizing the great renewal of the Chinese nation is the greatest dream for the Chinese nation in modern history.

We will strive to complete the building of a moderately prosperous society by 2021 when the CPC celebrates its 100th birthday, to basically achieve modernization by 2035, and to make China a modern socialist country that is prosperous, strong, democratic, culturally advanced, harmonious and beautiful by 2049, the 100th anniversary of the founding of the People's Republic of China. That is what our dream of national rejuvenation is all about. In essence, the Chinese Dream is a commitment to bringing prosperity and happiness to our country, our nation and our people. It is a dream of our country, our nation, and our people. To make our dream come true, we must follow the Chinese path to development, elevate the Chinese spirit, and boost national cohesion. The Chinese Dream is a dream of peace, development, cooperation and prosperity for all, benefiting not only the Chinese people but also the people of the rest of the world. Only by staying focused on achieving real results and making sustained and unwavering efforts can we bring our dream to fruition. The Chinese Dream is not a flower reflected in a mirror or a moon reflected in water. It is not an empty slogan. The goal of the CPC corresponds to the people's yearning for a better life and a brighter future.

（2）Making "the Chinese Dream" a reality

Since the proposal of the notion of the Chinese Dream, the past several years have witnessed the great initiative of turning the conceptualization into a reality in various dimensions. Although the Chinese Dream is a constructed concept, the frequent use of the word "we" in the discourses of the Chinese Dream in various media ranging from People's Daily to We-media, have endowed the world a connotation of reminiscence and resonance of building "a common community".

For President Xi Jinping, everyone has his or her own ideals and pursuits, in addition to this shared dream. Realizing the nation's great rejuvenation is the greatest dream of the nation. For Kenneth Lieberthal, senior researcher at the Brookings Institution, the meaning of Chinese Dream is wide ranging, with six key components required to make the dream real: a development model based on efficiency and institutional capacity; ecological urbanization; fair distribution of the benefits of economic development; political reform; reduction of governmental interference in the market; and social stability. *The Decision on Major Issues Concerning Comprehensively Deepening Reform* was adopted in response to people's concerns and requests. It requires reform to be complete by 2020, the same deadline as that of building a moderately prosperous society. Rejuvenating China, the Chinese Dream will benefit the world with experiences for other regions and countries to follow and help establish win-win relationships among world players. In China, the Chinese Dream stirs hopes and sets expectations; internationally, it provokes questions and elicits concerns. This conceptualization also brings a heated discussion and concern from the western eyes. Foreign experts believe that President Xi Jinping's overarching vision of the Chinese Dream has become a grand driver of China's continuing reform and development. The Chinese Dream differs from the American Dream in that it expresses China's collective aspirations and it differs from the Chinese dream in Chinese history by embracing the personal dreams of individual Chinese people for attaining happy, healthy, abundant and productive lives.That the entire world deriving material benefits from the Chinese Dream is apparent in a global economy. Higher standards of living mean greater consumption of goods and services in China, which works to create jobs and prosperity in a multiplier effect worldwide. China's commitment to science enables all peoples to share in China's success, often by making new technologies widely available at low costs.Misperceptions, however, can distort motivations. Western anxiety is rooted in the fear that for China to fulfill the Chinese Dream, China will become more assertive, more aggressive and more expansionist in foreign affairs, especially when dealing with smaller neighbors. Even though China's leaders avow "No matter how strong China becomes, China will never seek hegemony", there's still the worry that sometime in the future, newer reasons will emerge to belie the older promises. One never knows, foreigners fret, when the "gentle giant" will have a change of heart, when the "awakened lion" will not be so "peaceful, pleasant and civilized". The experience in the past several years proved that the Chinese Dream is beneficial not only to the Chinese people, but advantageous to the whole world. As a matter of fact, the realization of the Belt and Road Initiative, the realization of the Chinese Dream and the proposal of the construction of a common community will make possible the culture beyond the Western hegemony. The Chinese Dream will of course be merged and integrated as an important part of Chinese international communication, constructing a multi-dimensional and a responsible national image in intercultural communication.

8.Rebuilding the Chinese image in the New Era: an empirical research

Since the Belt and Road Initiative (BRI) was proposed in 2013, China and other countries along the Belt and road and countries who are interested and inspired by BRI adhered to the principle of consultation and collaboration for shared benefits to build the BRI with high quality and standards, creating great development opportunities for the world.

The joint development of the BRI complies with the intrinsic reform requirements of the global governance system. It manifests the participating countries' sense of a community with a shared future, for which they need to stick together in times of difficulty and share rights and obligations together. It provides a new idea and approach to reforming the global governance system.

The Belt and Road Initiative is an open platform for cooperation. It is guided by the principle of consultation and collaboration for shared benefits. It is a major initiative of transparency through which China shares opportunities and pursues common development with the rest of world.

As the Belt and Road Initiative cooperation enters a new stage, the Academy of Contemporary China and World Studies [1] worked with the Chinese research company Dataway and conducted a survey [2] in 2018 to learn about China's image in the eyes of the people in some countries along the Belt and Road routes.

Seventeen countries [3] were selected based on a comprehensive analysis of their economic development, geographic location, population size, land

---

1   The Academy of Contemporary China and World Studies, formerly the Center for International Communication Studies under the China Foreign Language Publishing Administration, is a state-level think-tank established in 2004, specializing in studies of contemporary China and world, translation and international discourse system, international communication and international news.
2   The survey was conducted from November 2017 to January 2018. The number of total respondents is 8,500.
3   Seventeen countries are: Russia, Kazakhstan, Poland, Serbia, Czech, Singapore, Thailand, Vietnam, Malaysia, the Philippines, Pakistan, Romania, India, South Africa, Kenya, Egypt and Brazil.

area and feasibility of implementation. In this survey, the ratio of men to women of respondents is 1:1 and the proportions of young, middle-aged and senior people are 50%, 33% and 17% respectively. The survey topics include recognition of China's overall image and evaluation of China's politics, economy, culture, science and technology, military, diplomacy, and media. The results of this survey show a three-dimensional picture of China's image among the Belt and Road participating countries. The major findings of the survey are listed as follows.

The people in Belt and Road participating countries have a high degree of recognition of China. They believe that China's political system is operating efficiently and recognize China to be an important engine for global economic development. They agree that China has a growing international influence in science and technology and culture. They have positive comments on China's active involvement in global governance. The China-proposed Belt and Road Initiatives is well known among the people, while some also believes there are challenges ahead.

78.6% of the respondents think that "China has made great contribution to world economic development"; 71.4% of the respondents agree that "China is a firm supporter of the international order with the UN at its core"; 64.4% of the respondents agree that "China is promoting world peace".

The survey showed that respondents believe that China is recognized to have great cultural strength, and it is expected to have more cultural exchanges and cooperation with other countries. 85.7%of the respondents think that China has great cultural strength; 72.5% of the respondents think that the Chinese culture is beneficial to world cultural diversity and integrated development of different cultures; 75% of the respondents support their own governments to increase cultural exchanges with China. Besides, Chinese cuisine (52.7%), tradition Chinese medicine (50%) and martial arts (46.4%) are believed to best represent Chinese culture.

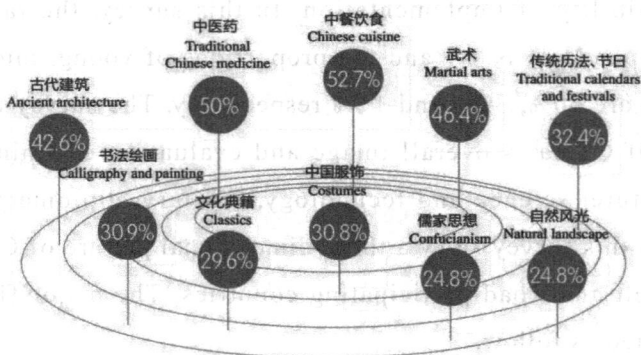

古代建筑
Ancient architecture

42.6%

书法绘画
Calligraphy and painting

中医药
Traditional
Chinese medicine

50%

中餐饮食
Chinese cuisine

52.7%

武术
Martial arts

46.4%

传统历法、节日
Traditional calendars
and festivals

32.4%

文化典籍
Classics

中国服饰
Costumes

29.6%

30.9%

30.8%

儒家思想
Confucianism

自然风光
Natural landscape

24.8%

24.8%

Figure 27   Foreingers' recognition of the Chinese culture

After many years of self-introduction, self-construction and self-improvement, the Chinese national image has been greatly improved. For us, it is satisfactory that we are more willing and initiative to participate into the world activities and sometimes chair the events. The year 2008 witnessed the success of the Beijing Olympics; the year 2014 witnessed the opening of the Asia-Pacific Economic Cooperation (APEC) Summit in Beijing; the year 2016 witnessed the opening of Group of Twenty Finance Ministers and Central Bank Governors and G20 Summit in Hangzhou, China; the year 2022 will see the XXIV Olympic Winter Games in Beijing and Zhangjiakou, China. For the Western audiences, their cognition about China has transformed from a "portrayed China" to a "real China" after the diluting of media and with the awakening of the media and intercultural literacy; the emergence and improvement of China's international construction has shifted our image from "a stereotyped China" to "a beautiful China". However, the road ahead is still filled with twists and turns. We should continue exerting all our effort to renovate and refurbish methods to fulfill the real cultural harmony.

9.Transcultural communication: towards a common community with shared future for mankind

The grand goal of intercultural communication is the realization of transcultural communication in which biases and prejudices are overcome. A community with a shared future pursues an open, inclusive, clean, and beautiful world that enjoys lasting peace, universal security, and common prosperity.The conceptualization of "a common community with shared future for mankind" is an optimal discourse of transcultural communication, which has aroused growing attention among an increasing number of people.

The idea of "a community with a shared future for mankind" was put forward by Chinese President Xi Jinping at the Moscow State of Institute of International Relations in 2013 to proclaim the aspiration of Chinese nation in establishing a harmonious world where all could live peacefully with the spirit of brotherhood.Since then, the idea has been brought up by President Xi, also general secretary of the Communist Party of China (CPC) Central Committee, several times at national and international events, including the 19th National Congress of the CPC, and won wide approval.Since Chinese President Xi Jinping made a keynote speech at the United Nations (UN) Office in Geneva titled "Work Together to Build a Community with Shared Future for Mankind" in January 2017, the idea has gained wider international recognition for offering China's solutions to cope with global challenges. This Chinese concept is increasingly turned into an international consensus.

According to the idea of common community with shared future, countries should respect one another, discuss issues as equals, and resolutely reject a Cold War mentality and power politics. Countries should take a new approach to developing state-to-state relations with communication, rather than confrontation, and partnerships, rather than alliances. It calls for settling disputes through dialogue and resolving differences through discussion, coordinating responses to traditional and non-traditional threats, and opposing terrorism in all its forms.The idea stresses promoting trade and investment liberalization and facilitation, and making economic globalization more open, inclusive, and balanced so that its benefits are shared by all.The diversity of civilizations should be respected. In handling relations among countries, estrangement should be replaced with exchange, clashes with mutual learning, and superiority with coexistence.The idea holds that humans should be kind to the environment, cooperate to tackle climate change, and protect the planet for the sake of human survival. It was seen as contributing to China's engagement with the rest of the world in pursuit of win-win results. This idea has since become a core element of China's foreign policy. It also underpins the launch of the Belt and Road Initiative. The concept of a community with a shared future emphasizes the virtue of holistic thinking, cosmopolitan ideals, and the pursuit of lasting peace and shared prosperity.

The Chinese Dream has been mature since its first proposal in 2013. It will come true via practicing upon the following principles.

(1)Seeking common ground

We live in "the global village" and share a common destiny. The outbreak of a disease jeopardizes the life of all, the economic crisis hurts prosperity everywhere, the danger of nuclear attacks threatens all nations, the operation of extremists puts the life of all at risk, and the violent death of an individual outrages the collective conscience. We live in the global village and one's pain and sufferings will hurt the feelings of all nations around the world. To put into the words of President Xi, "Everyone has in himself a little bit of others". Therefore, we have to seek common ground and promote the spirit of brotherhood to live in peace and harmony.

(2)Practicing upon international principles

To promote world peace and stability, all nations and individuals need to treat one another according to the spirit of brotherhood and respect the rights and freedoms of one another regardless of their race, color and faith. "Recognition of the inherent dignity and of the equal and inalienable rights of all members of the human family" has been declared the mainstay of peace and liberty by the Universal Declaration of Human Rights (UDHR). That is to say, all members of the human family will have to respect and protect the natural and inviolable rights and dignity of individuals and support the principle of "non-discrimination".To maintain peace and harmony, all countries have to advocate the fundamental rights, i.e., the rights to life, liberty and property, of all individuals as well as "the right to freedom of thought, conscience and religion" which are stated in the UDHR.If all members of human family respect the rights, liberty and dignity of the human person without any discrimination, there will be no room left for hostility and disagreement.On the contrary, violating international principles and encroaching on individual's rights and liberties and discriminating them on the basis of their sex, color, and race will narrow the room for peaceful coexistence. Indeed, contempt for human rights has resulted in barbarous acts throughout the history.

(3) Upholding the golden rule

Practicing upon the "golden rule" which says, "Do unto others as you would have them do unto you" is a blueprint for building a peaceful and harmonious society. The golden rule says that one must be treated on the basis of being human — no matter what faith and belief they cherish or which racial or ethnic background they belong to. This truth transcends nations and peoples and beats in the heart of billions.The golden rule is highly significant in both individual and collective life. Members of human family will have to practice upon this truth to build a utopian society with shared destiny. In fact, acting upon this truth and ethical code will put an end to one's ideological dogma and egotistic and ethnocentric mentalities and will necessarily pave the ground for tolerance, peace and harmony.

China's further reform and opening-up shows that we are intent on extending people-to-people exchanges and state-to-state friendly relations. Chinese officials are of the view that win-win cooperation, peaceful development and common prosperity will be achieved only through dialogue, partnership and mutual respect.A community with shared future is not compatible with the idea of "only my backyard" or "America first". The zero-sum game or winner-take-all mindset are contrary to a community with shared destiny in which win-win result and peaceful development are pursued relentlessly.

By calling for building a community with shared future for mankind, President Xi Jinping has issued a call for action when we come to the critical juncture of the times. His proposal, full of justice, responsibility and historical sense, is widely considered the most reasonable and pragmatic choice of mankind. This is a significant boost for all humanity. Introduced by China in Switzerland, it is being embraced by the world.

In terms of the construction of a common community with shared future for mankind adhered to the principle of peace, development, cooperation, we propose the following tentative suggestions.

① We should show great foresight and be more tolerant and open. We should learn the extraction of different civilizations. Mutual understanding, borrowing, respecting and absorbing between different cultures and civilizations are the basic guidelines. The sea can hold the water from thousands of rivers because of its capacity. We should learn from the sea and cultivate the common community together.

② We should be persistent and strong-minded to eliminate misfortunes and struggles. The scourge of war and terrorism has caused indescribable sorrow and immense suffering for nations and violated the rights and liberties of many individuals around the globe. People's rights and dignity have been violated on the grounds of their caste, color and creed. Deadly acts by radical extremists have struck a blow to global peace and left little room for the spirit of brotherhood. Only with a strong mind and a persistent spirit can we fight against the villainy.

③ We should be more creative. In the process of proposing, constructing, spreading the idea of "a common community with shared future", we have to innovate more while absorbing the traditional philosophical wisdom. We do not need to stick to the old and fixed doctrines. We are living in a vast world in which we can have our talents and innovations fully developed.

International communication is closely related with nation, power and ideology, thus being filled with the competitions of political strength.

Globalization strengthens America's super leading role in the world and causes an imbalanced opposition between the East and the West. But at the same time, globalization also brings opportunities for all countries including China and breeds the possibility of intercultural communication free from the restraint of time and space.

The Chinese globalization paradigm, represented by the Belt and Road Initiative, is to help to construct a common community with shared future for mankind. During this process, we need a special communication which could be called as the global communication with the Chinese characteristics. The essence of the global communication with the Chinese characteristics is not to assimilate other cultures, but an efficient tool to extricate these unfair and imbalance issues caused by economical and cultural hegemony. The essence of the construction of a common community with shared future is both emphasizing the comprehension of common situations, common challenges and common problems of all human beings, and the respect of differences and diversity. It is hoped that, with the help of the thinking pattern of intersubjectivity, misunderstandings and prejudices could be overcome and a common destiny of transformation, integration and progress would become possible. In the global communication with the Chinese characteristics, we are not only the pioneer who put forward this initiative, but also a powerful propellent of the construction of this common community.

Section 4 Cultural practice

Cultural practice :Discussion

Qian Xuesen, a famous scientist and Chinese academician, once proposed a famous question— Why cannot our Chinese schools generate talents?

The famous British scholar, Joseph Needham, once proposed a question why science and industrial revolution did not happen in modern China since

China enjoyed many advantages in its ancient times.

It is generally believed that Qian's doubt comes down in one continuous line from Joseph's doubt. Both doubts are trying to make detailed inquires on the Chinese education, especially science education. However, for the author of this course, these doubts also trigger our plenty of food for thought in intercultural communication.

Based on a contrastive perspective between China and the west, what is your comment on these questions and what are the possible reasons for China's inferiority in modern times? Can you provide any tentative and feasible suggestions to improve China's comprehensive power in the future? What would be the most needed measure for Chinese basic education?

Section 5 Derivative development

1.Film watching

Please watch the documentary film *Hong Kong-Zhuhai-Macao Bridge* [1] (《港珠澳大桥》,2019) and work out a short intercultural analysis based on this documentary with the production time over five years.

It would be better to introduce China in a nonfiction and polyphonic documentary instead of a direct persuasion. Despite differences among people, we do share many elements, including the same feelings towards fear, pain, magnificence, kindness, beauty and truth, which makes possible the construction of a common community with shared future and the harmony of diversity in transcultural communication.

---

1 *Hong Kong-Zhuhai-Macao Bridge* is the name for a TV and film documentary directed by Yan Dong. It has been casted in five years. The documentary TV series was broadcasted in both CGTN and Discovery Channel in 2017, received many positive comments for its documentary story-telling and the Chinese image it reflected. The documentary film with the same name will be released in May, 2019 in mainland, China.

2.Extended reading

（1）Knowing more cultures about ourselves (8): the cyber culture

Before we introduce ourselves to the others, the first and foremost thing is to have a correct and profound cognition of ourselves. In the ends of all the eight chapters, we add some basic knowledge of ourselves which are divided into eight sections, namely, the family culture, the food culture, the education culture, the marriage culture, the medical culture, the art culture, the consumption culture and the cyber culture respectively. We hope to help both audiences from other cultures and ourselves to have a better cognition of Chinese cultures. During these parts, the author of this book not only summarizes the traditional essence of these sections, but employs a diachronic perspective and includes the up-to-date changes.

（2）Our cyberculture

China has been accessed the Internet in April, 1994. According to the latest data released by China Internet Network Information Center (CNNIC) on February 28th, 2019, in China, the scale of netizens has reached 829 million with the popularity rate reaching 59.6%. The popularity rate via the access of the mobile Internet has surprisingly reached 98.6%. Almost every adult's life except sleep is closely associated with various kinds of cyber applications, such as Facebook, QQ, Wechat, YouTube and Tik Tok. Everything and everyone seem to be mediatized quickly into the Net. Therefore, media ranging from TV to mobile phones have played an increasingly important role in modern cultural communication. The past twenty-five years witness a dramatic increase in the number of users of the Internet and the trend from zero to the emergence to the booming cyber culture in China.

The Chinese cyberculture could be generally divided into three phases.

The first phase is the cyberculture in the web 1.0 period. This phase witnessed the appearance of the cyber culture, although in a dim and micro way. In this period, the data transmitted via the Internet are scarce. A majority of people still resort the radio and TV station to get the information. Very few users try to surf the Internet and email and chatting rooms are the basic forms of the cyberculture. Although the speed is extraordinarily slow, people did achieve their pleasant sensation and found their joy by disguising their names and using artificial cyber names. The anonymity of the Internet, to a certain extent, spurred up the interest of the signifiers. A small-scale discussion such as Bulletin Board System (BBS) is popular at this moment.

The second phase is the cyberculture in the web 2.0 period. This period witnessed the booming development of the cyberculture. The advancement of information and communication technology further liberates people's imagination in the virtual world. The medium of transmission has been transformed from the cable to optical fiber. The narrow-band consultation has been evolved to broad-band experience. It is increasingly easy to access to the Internet with a large number of terminals such as PC, mobile phone and pad. In the web 1.0 era, the verbal communication is largely realized by words and sentences on the screen. However, the web 2.0 era witnesses a two-way multi-modal communication containing both texts, pictures and videos.

Another distinctive feature of the cyberculture of this period is that, different from the mass communication in the first phase, users in this era are actively joining in the content production, which is called user-generated content (UGC). It seems that everyone on the Net could have the "microphone" of speaking and spreading. Traditional mass communication and opinion leaders are still existing and still powerful and convincing for their reliable source and professional knowledge and techniques. However, the social media and the social network sites (SNS) amplify individual's voice and hereby empower more citizens to shape an opinion field which makes diverse opinions and arguments existing together.

Media literacy, an important competence in the web 2.0 cyberculture, hereby comes into being. An inappropriate or even wrong utilization of the Internet produces a status of chaos. The truth is hidden and people are getting far away from it, creating a situation of "post-truth". A low media literacy and post-truth will lead to the fact that people will resort to their emotional appeal and make this emotional appeal high than a rational expression and discussion in public sphere. Therefore, the prosperity of the cyberculture in the web 2.0 period not only enjoys a group joy in the cyber world, but also implied an invisible danger or crisis of getting far away from the truth.

The third phase is the cyberculture in the web 3.07 period. This period is sharply different from the first two phases because it tries to center on the materialization of the information world while the first two phases are surrounded on the informatization of the materialistic world. The computer, the things, the data and the human beings are integrated into a big web which is known as the Internet of Things (IOT). Inspired by the IOT technology, the fifth-generation technology, the big data technology, we are quickly evolved into a ubiquitous web society in which we can access to the Internet at any time and at any venue and via any equipment. The virtual world, for the first time, is deeply integrated with the real world together and a mix reality world is hereby created. The traditional value on time and space has been completely changed. Furthermore, the appearance and development of virtual reality (VR) and augmented reality (AR) enable us to view the world in a mix and integrated way. People use both verbal symbols and nonverbal symbols to express their feelings. The pleasant sensation we acquired from the cyber world will be redefined and more connotations will be added to the scope of the cyberculture.

At last, the cyber culture does not present a binary opposition to traditional Chinese cultures. The two cultures are supplementary to each other. For example, a large number of people are accustomed to deliver their wishes to the friends and relatives via the Internet or the mobile Internet. It is not considered a deterioration of our tradition, but a new and creative inheritance and extension of our traditional Chinese culture.

附录一 跨文化研究常见术语
Appendix Ⅰ Common Termsin Intercultural
Communication Studies

1.Stereotype

Stereotyping is a very important factor that can intervene in the process of impression perception. Stereotypes can blinker people's judgements, leading them to focus on certain pieces of evidence and to overlook other contradictory evidence.

Pennington (1986) holds that stereotypes are grossly oversimplified and overgeneralized abstractions about groups of people and are usually highly inaccurate although they may contain a grain of truth.

Mackie (1973) holds that a stereotype refers to those folk beliefs about the attributes characterizing a social category on which there is substantial agreement.

Despite the widespread use of the term "stereotype", there is not real consensus among social psychologists as to exactly what they are. There are differences of opinion on the following points: how accurate or inaccurate stereotypes are in their generalizations, whether they are bad, and whether stereotypes need to be shared among a number of people rather than be held by just one person.

According to Schneider, stereotypes are simply generalizations about groups of people, and people use them on a regular basis. However, such generalizing does not always lead to accurate assessments, and one of the reasons for this is the complexity of the relationship between category and features. Schneider (2004) usefully distinguishes between three types of features:

（1）Essential features: those that are absolutely essential for category membership and that usually simultaneously preclude membership from other categories; e.g., for senior citizens / pensioners, it is essential for them to be over a certain age, and they cannot simultaneously be a senior citizen and underage;

（2）Identifying features: those that we use (but we cannot always reliably depend on) to identify category members; e.g., for pensioners we may look at their hair color, number of wrinkles, degree of stoop and so on.

（3）Ascribed features: those that are associated with a given category but are not in anyway integral to it and may be inaccurate; e.g., for senior citizens / pensioners, we may think of them as having plenty of time on their hands, as physically not very strong, and as forgetful.

One way of judging the accuracy of stereotypes is to compare a group's stereotypes of themselves with the stereotypes held by nongroup members. If there is convergence, then the stereotype could be regarded as accurate. However, even if a stereotype is empirically found to be accurate, we need to bear in mind several things. Firstly, people may differ in their evaluations (positive / negative) of a given stereotype. Secondly, stereotypes are subject to change, and so we must not assume that they are fixed and immutable. Thirdly, even stereotypes that are generally accurate can be misapplied to individuals.

2.Prejudice and Discrimination

Stereotyping is often associated with prejudice and discrimination. These concepts are interrelated but not equivalent.

A stereotype is a group of beliefs about persons who are members of a particular group, whereas prejudice can better be thought of as an attitude, usually negative, towards members of a group. It is argued that prejudice is the set of affective reactions we have toward people as a function of their category memberships. Discrimination is the treatment of a person or a group of people unfairly or differently because of their membership of a particular social group. Prejudice represents the affective or emotional reaction to social groups. Stereotypes are the cognitive manifestation of prejudice and discrimination is the behavioral manifestation of prejudice.

Many scholars argue that the cause and effect relationship between prejudice, discrimination and exclusion and inequality is complex and multi-directional. Although the interrelationship is sometimes thought of in unidirectional terms (stereotyping leads to prejudice, which leads to discrimination, which leads to exclusion and inequality), in fact, discriminatory behavior can create as well as be the consequence of prejudices. Similarly, exclusion and inequality can generate the very beliefs, attitudes and behaviors that then act to reinforce them.

3.Ethnocentrism

Ethnocentrism is the tendency to look at the world primarily from the perspective of one's own ethnic culture. The concept of ethnocentrism has proven significant in the social sciences, both with respect to the issue of whether the ethnocentric bias of researchers colors the data they obtain, and the findings from research in anthropology and sociology. Such research has revealed ethnocentrism in every culture around the world, based on a number of reasons, including religion, language, customs, culture, and shared history. It seems natural that people feel pride in the culture in which they have grown up and from which they have adopted their values and standards of behavior. The problem is that one may view other cultures not only as different, but also as inferior, with a great danger of behaving in ways that are damaging to those from other cultures. However, as increasing globalization brings different cultures together, people are learning to overcome their self-centered thinking and see human society from a broader, more inclusive perspective.

Ethnocentrism is a notion now widely used in the early twenty-first century. Coined by William Graham Sumner in the early twentieth century, the term owes what conceptual life it has to the likes of anthropology and intercultural communication. Dominant strains of these disciplines, especially anthropology, have examined the lives and cultural expressions of ethnically defined or identified groups and the misinterpretations resulting from Western perspectives.

Nevertheless, a survey of contemporary critical works on ethnicity and race, including those in critical anthropology, reveals an almost complete lack of engagement with the concept. In Anglo-American studies, the term ethnocentrism carries a largely descriptive and fleeting connotation, its meaning more or less taken for granted.

It has been overshadowed perhaps by more readily invoked characterizations or charges of racism, racialization, and ethno-racial determination. This is perhaps less the case in mainstream European social analysis, where race remains a largely taboo category and ethnic configurations and characterizations are far more readily and uncritically invoked. It is unsurprising, then, that the thickest critical engagement to be found with the notion of ethnocentrism is in French works from the late 1980s.

Ethnocentrism can be understood as the disposition to read the rest of the world, those of different cultural traditions, from inside the conceptual scheme of one's own ethnocultural group. The ethnocentric attitude assumes that one's own ethnic worldview is the only one from which other customs, practices, and habits can be understood and judged. Ethnocentrism thus is conceived critically as involving overgeneralizations about cultures and their inhabitants, others' or one's own, on the basis of limited or skewed, if any, evidence.

So, the notion of ethnocentrism is conceived as a profound failure to understand other conceptual schemes, and, by extension, practices, habits, expressions, and articulations of others on their own terms. Standing inside our own conceptual schemes, we are blinded even to the possibilities of other ways of thinking, seeing, understanding, and interpreting the world, of being and belonging—in short, other ways of worldmaking.

It would seem to follow, as many definitions in fact insist, that ethnocentrism is a claim about the superiority of one's own culture or ethnic standing. While this is perhaps a strong presumption in many ethnocentric claims, we should be careful not to make it definitionally so. One can imagine claims of inherent and inescapably culture-bound judgments about ethnically ascribed others, about inherent differences, without assumption or assertion of cultural superiority. If there is any coherence to the concept, "differential ethnocentrism" must factor into any working definition of the term as well.

Analysts or commentators usually define ethnocentrism as belief in or claim to the superiority of one's own culture, as this article suggests earlier. The universalizability claim (universalizing ethnocentrism) is considered by self-satisfied critics as revealing the poverty of extreme forms of relativism. Value universalists cannot be so smug, however. The "universality of ethnocentrism" claim on the more extreme relativistic side has its characteristic correlate among bigoted universalists too. Tzvetan Todorov revealingly defines ethnocentrism to capture just this characterization. Ethnocentrism, he writes, takes the values of one's own society without warrant as universal, as applying to all anytime, everywhere.

People always ask a question on the relation between these two extremes (ethnocentrism and cultural relativism).

Ethnocentrism is the view that one particular ethnic group is somehow superior to all others. The word ethnocentrism derives from the Greek word *ethnos*, meaning "nation" or "people," and the English word center. A common idiom for ethnocentrism is "tunnel vision." In this context, ethnocentrism is the view that a particular ethnic group's system of beliefs and values is morally superior to all others.

Cultural relativism is the view that individual beliefs and values systems are culturally relative. That is, no one ethnic group has the right to say that their particular system of beliefs, values and their worldview, is in any way superior to others' system of beliefs and values. What's right for one culture might be wrong for another and that's alright. There is no absolute standard of right and wrong by which to compare and contrast morally contradictory cultural values.

4.Culture shock

Culture shock is a term coined in the 1960s to refer to an occupational disease suffered by those suddenly immersed in a culture very different to their own. The term generally implies a negative reaction (physical, cognitive, and psychological) to moving within or between societies, but some authors have suggested it may have benefits for the individual concerned. Those who become partially, or fully, immersed in a new culture may suffer return culture shock when re-entering their own society.

This term describes the anxiety produced when a person moves to a completely new environment, especially when a person arrives in a new country where he is confronted with a new cultural environment. It expresses the lack of direction, the feeling of not knowing what to do or how to do things in a new environment, and not knowing what is appropriate or inappropriate. The feeling of culture shock is generally set in after the first few weeks of coming to a new place. People suffer a lot at the very beginning and usually suffer the following procedures.

Familiar signs and symbols are lost. Generally speaking, culture shock is precipitated by the anxiety that results from losing all familiar signs and symbols of social intercourse. People suffer little from these social activities when they are at home in their own country. However, when they are away in a foreign country, they are always at a loss over what to do and how to do it.

Familiar cues are removed. When familiar cues are removed, there is always a feeling of frustration and anxiety. People will reject the environment, which causes the discomfort and they will form a bad attitude towards the target culture.

All cultures are not exactly the same. As most people take for granted that all cultures operate and behave probably in exactly the same manner as their own, they are "shocked" or made temporarily uncomfortable by the differences and unpredictability they encounter.

Culture shock is frequently described as a series of stages that a person goes through. People will experience these stages when they are enjoying a different culture from their own culture in a new environment. In the beginning, what they experience in the new environment will make them feel excited. Soon they will feel disappointed by what they actually encounter when the sense of curiosity disappears. Then they begin to adjust themselves to the new environment and enjoy their new life. Finally, they get the sense of comfort and pleasant sensation as that in the old culture. These names of these stages are known as the honeymoon stage, the hostility stage, the recovery stage, the adjustment stage and the biculturalism stage.

（1）The Honeymoon Stage

The first stage is the incubation stage, which is also called the "honeymoon" stage, as everything encountered is new and exciting. At this stage, the new arrivals may feel euphoric and may be pleased by all of the new things encountered. Those who have just come to a foreign country will be initially fascinated with everything new. People at this stage will demonstrate an eagerness to please people around, a spirit of cooperation and an active interest in listening to people speaking. In reality, it is delightful to get along with the new arrival, but due to their enthusiasm, they frequently nod or smile to indicate understanding when they don't understand at all in fact. When misunderstanding mount up, they are likely to experience the second stage of cultural adjustment.

（2）The Hostility Stage

A person may encounter some difficult time and crises in daily life. For example, people may suffer communication difficulties if not being understood. In general, this stage is featured by frustration, anger, anxiety and sometimes depression. The initial excitement is replaced by frustration with daily bureaucracy and the weariness of speaking and listening to another language every day. The new arrivals will be at a difficult, painful stage.

（3）The Recovery Stage

The third stage of culture shock is characterized by gaining some understanding of the new culture. People will experience a new feeling of pleasure and sense of humor. The new arrivals may not feel as lost as before and start to have a feeling of direction and a certain psychological balance. At this stage, the new arrivals start feeling more positive and they try to develop comprehension of everything they do not understand. People will recover from the symptoms of the former stage, and adjust themselves to the new norms, values and beliefs and traditions of the new environment. They become generally easy to get along with the people in the target culture because they are relaxed and receptive.

（4）The Adjustment Stage

At the fourth stage, people realize that new culture has good and bad things to offer. This stage is another integration, which is accompanied by a more solid feeling of belonging. People begin to define themselves and establish goals for living. At this stage, people will feel at ease because the things that initially made them feel uncomfortable or unfamiliar are now reasonable and understandable. They should be proud because they have successfully adjusted to the new culture and mastered both cultures.

（5）The Biculturalism Stage

At this stage, people have become more comfortable in both old and new cultures. The status of biculturalism is hereby achieved. Biculturalism is viewed by some as the healthy and even ideal of adaptation in which one's original cultural world view remains intact as alternative cultural frames are required. Though a complete realization of biculturalism is hard, people are still longing for a comfortable and flexible communication among different cultures.

A person who is suffering from culture shock will generally bring about two symptoms, physically and psychologically.

Physical symptoms of culture shock include too much sleep or too little sleep, eating too much or having no or little appetite, minor illness, upset stomachaches, headaches and other uneasiness.

Psychological symptoms of culture shock include loneliness or boredom, homesickness, idealizing home, feeling helpless or dependent, feeling of irritability and even hostility, social withdrawal, excessive concern for health and security, rebellion against rules and authority, anxiety etc.

People may suffer from some or all of the symptoms due to some other factors. Therefore, culture shock is not easily sensed at the beginning without a professional knowledge about it. To be certain, no bottled remedies could be found at the pharmacy to completely deal with culture shock. However, a clear recognition and a proficient mastery of culture shock and corresponding countermeasure will make the intercultural communication more comfortable and successful. The following countermeasures are suggested to alleviate culture shock.

(1) Learn throughout your stay.

(2) Get involved in the target culture.

(3) Master simple tasks.

(4) Try to understand.

(5) Learn to live with ambiguity.

(6) Be empathetic.

(7) Be flexible and resourceful.

(8) Be humorous.

5. Acculturation

Once strangers enter a new culture, their adaptation process is set in full motion. Some of the old cultural habits are to be replaced by new ones. Most strangers desire and seek to achieve necessary adaptation in the new environment, especially those whose daily functions require them to establish what John French, Willard Rodgers, and Sidney Cobb (1974) referred to as a relatively stable person-environment fit. The adaptation process unfolds in two subprocesses, acculturation and deculturation, and involves the accompanying experience of stress. As they gradually establish some kind of working relationship with a new culture, these uprooted people are compelled to learn (acculturation) at least some of the new ways of thinking, feeling, and acting, as well as the linguistic and other elements of the host communication system. As new learning occurs, unlearning (deculturation) of some of the old cultural habits has to occur— at least in the sense that new responses are adopted in situations that previously would have evoked old ones.

Acculturation is a process that individuals undergo in response to a changing cultural context. What is related to acculturation is the more general phenomenon of cultural change. Acculturation can be conceived to be the processes of cultural learning imposed upon minorities by the fact of being minorities. If enculturation is first culture-learning, then acculturation is second-culture learning. The course of change resulting from acculturation is highly variable and depends on many characteristics of the dominant and nondominant groups. For both groups it is important to know the purpose, length, permanence of contact, and policies being pursued. Cultural and psychological characteristics of the two populations can also affect the outcome of the acculturation process.

Acculturation comprehends those phenomena which result when groups of individuals having different cultures come into continuous first-hand contact, with subsequent changes in the original cultural patterns of either or both groups.The term "acculturation" is widely accepted among American anthropologists as referring to those changes set in motion by the coming together of societies with different cultural traditions. This field of investigation is generally referred to by British anthropologists (and by British-influenced students in Africa, Oceania, and Asia) as "culture contact." In contrast with this straightforward phrase focused on the conditions under which the changes take place, the term "acculturation" and its derivatives remain somewhat ambiguous. A persistent usage gives it the meaning of cultural assimilation, or replacement of one set of cultural traits by another, as in references to individuals in contact situations as more or less "acculturated"; inconsistency is often apparent in the writings of American anthropologists with regard to whether the term is applied to results or to processes of change.

The emergence of acculturation as a significant field of study in social science may be readily traced. First glimpsed as an area of anthropological inquiry in the 1880s, it became a major focus of investigation during the subsequent eighty years. The term appears first in the writings of North Americans—for instance, W. H. Holmes (1886), Franz Boas (1896), and W. J. McGee (1898)— but they did not use it to name the same phenomena. McGee spoke of "piratical acculturation" and "amicable acculturation," meaning transfer and adjustment of customs under conditions of contact between peoples of "lower grades" and "higher grades" respectively, a distinction that was not very clear in his essay. Boas used the term in a more general way to refer to an inferred process of change as a result of which the cultures of a region become similar to one another. Boas' usage gained some currency among German ethnologists, notably Ehrenreich (1905) and Krickeberg (1910). However, the current, widely accepted usage is much closer to that advanced by McGee, even though his two "types" have never been regarded as useful. From the 1880s on, North American anthropologists concerned themselves increasingly with studying the phenomena of cultural change resulting from contacts between peoples. By 1936, however, studies by many scholars were making it clear that acculturation studies had become an important interest of anthropologists. This fact gave rise to an action in 1935 by the Social Science Research Council aimed at the better coordination of research in acculturation. The foundation appointed a committee of three prominent anthropologists and instructed them to attempt the formulation of a more systematic approach. Under the chairmanship of Robert Redfield, the committee prepared a short memorandum called "Outline for the Study of Acculturation". It sought to define the field of study that was coming to be called "acculturation" and to provide a check list of topics concerning which field data should be gathered if the phenomena defined were to be systematically investigated.

6.Cultural Empathy

Empathy is the capability to share another being's emotions and feelings in short. It is the capacity to recognize full range of emotions such as fear, pain, love, anger, etc. that are being experienced by another sentient or fictional being. The range of empathy in a sentient creature is directly proportional to the intelligence of that creature. There have been numerous peer reviewed studies that conclusively prove the existence of empathy in humans and other animals, such as monkeys, dolphins, cows, rats and other. Of all animals, humans exhibit the widest range of empathetic reactions. Recent studies have also demonstrated that while the degree, or lack of empathy, in humans is directly proportional to nurturing or lack thereof during early and mid-childhood, humans, as well as other social animals are in fact born with a natural propensity for empathy. Several such laboratory studies, concluded and ongoing, confirm that humans, as being a social and a highly intelligent animal, are soft wired for empathy.

Cultural empathy is an awareness and understanding of a culture's characteristics, beliefs and values. Intercultural empathy means trying and understanding what other person is thinking and saying and trying to understand his /her perspective by coming out of our egocentrism.

The practice of empathy by both teachers and students is an indispensable quality found in the multicultural classroom environment. Empathy is the ability of one to assume the role of another and, by imaging the world as the other sees it, predict accurately the motives, attitudes, feelings, and needs of the other. Empathy in a classroom involves two steps. First, empathic teaches are able to imagine how it must be for immigrant students to adapt to a classroom where surroundings, language, and behavior are often unfamiliar. Second, empathy involves communicating in ways that are rewarding to the student who is the object of empathic prediction.

Accurate prediction requires accepting people for who they are and thus understanding what can realistically be expected of them. The fact that you accept other people for who they are does not mean that you must agree with what they say or do. Although you may accept student's feelings, ideas, and behavior as legitimate, that does not mean you necessarily have to agree with them. Students do, however, react positively to empathic understanding—to the realization that they are not being evaluated or judged, and they are understood from their own point of view rather than from someone others'. The empathic teacher, therefore, will let students use their own cultural resources and voices to develop new skills and to critically explore subject matter.

The ability to communicate empathically requires learning specific behaviors and practices; it does not happen automatically. Intercultural scholars recommend some guidelines that we should follow in order to be an empathic communicator.

(1)Communicate a supportive climate.

(2)Attend to the nonverbal behavior as well as the verbal communication.

(3)Accurately reflect and clarify feelings.

(4)Be genuine and congruent.

7.Intercultural Sensitivity

Cultural sensitivity is being aware that cultural differences and similarities between people exist without assigning them a value—positive or negative, better or worse, right or wrong. It simply means that you are aware that people are not all the same and that you recognize that your culture is no better than any other culture.In life and work environments we frequently face situations where there is a dominant and a secondary culture. For instance, in the U.S., the European American is the dominant culture whereas Hispanic, African American and Chinese cultures are all secondary.Cultural sensitivity implies that both groups understand and respect each other's characteristics.

This is always a challenge, and even more so in large corporations.

As people become more and more culturally sensitive, they progress from having an ethnocentric orientation to a more ethno-relative worldview. Bennett holds that in general, the more ethnocentric orientations can be seen as ways of avoiding cultural difference, either by denying its existence, by raising defenses against it, or by minimizing its importance. The more ethno-relative worldviews are ways of seeking cultural difference, either by accepting its importance, by adapting perspective to take it into account, or by integrating the whole concept into a definition of identity.

Intercultural sensitivity is ability to make complex perceptual distinctions among patterns of culture. A number of scholars and experts have tried to explain the impact of cross-cultural differences on people's behavior to help reduce the intercultural risks of international business. Dr. Milton Bennett, co-founder of the Intercultural Development Research Institute, believes that the more experience a person has with cultural differences, the more that person will develop intercultural competence, becoming more effective when working across cultures.

According to Bennett's Developmental Model of Intercultural Sensitivity (DMIS), there are six stages on this path to developing intercultural competence, each characterized by certain perceptions and behavior towards the "own" and the "other" culture. The main change along the line of intercultural competence always occurs from ethnocentrism to ethno-relativism, in other words, from an understanding of your own culture as being superior to an understanding of your own culture as equal in value and complexity to any other culture. Each of the six phases of Bennett's Developmental Model of Intercultural Sensitivity are described in more detail below:

(1) Denial

When in this first stage, individuals refuse all interaction with other cultures and show no interest in discovering cultural differences. They may also act aggressively during cross cultural situations.

(2) Defense

In this stage, individuals consider all other cultures to be inferior to their own culture and will constantly criticize behavior or thoughts by someone from another culture.

(3) Minimization

When this stage is reached, individuals will start believing that all cultures share common values. They will also minimize any cultural differences by correcting people to match their expectations.

(4) Acceptance

At this stage, individuals may still judge other cultures negatively but they will tend to recognize that cultures are different and they may become curious about cultural differences.

(5) Adaptation

During this stage, individuals gain the ability to adapt their behavior more easily and effectively by intentionally changing their own behavior or communication style.

(6) Integration

This stage tends to only be achieved by long—term expatriates living and working abroad or global nomads. In this stage, individuals instinctively change their behavior and communication style when interacting with other cultures.

Progressing from "Ethnocentrism" to "Ethno-relativism" on the scale takes time, yet it is vital for the success of any business person working in what is an increasingly global economy. Becoming more interculturally sensitive can be achieved through a combination of first-hand experience with other cultures.

While the final stage "integration" is seldom reached, a combination of experience living and working in other countries and taking part in tailored intercultural training courses allows global business people to reach the "adaptation" stage, acquiring a high level of intercultural competence that will ensure they are successful working internationally.

附录二 跨文化研究文献摘录
Appendix Ⅱ Reading Literature on Intercultural Communication

Culture Is Communication

Edward T. Hall

In recent years, the mathematician, and the engineer have accustomed themselves to looking at a wide range of events as aspects of communication. A book title such as Electrons, Waves and Messages does not seem incongruous. Another book title, *The Mathematical Theory of Communication* [1], seems so appropriate that it is readily accepted, at least by the scientifically inclined layman. However, the behavioral scientists have only recently begun to examine their respective fields as communication.

The reader may wonder about the nature of the relationship between communication as I use the term and the communication theory (information theory) of the electronics laboratory. If one way it might be said that the communication theory is shorthand for talking about communication events that have already been subjected to considerable analysis, such as the phonetics of a language, orthographies, telephone and television signals, and the like. This process inevitable seems to proceed in one direction - toward symbolization. It must be remembered that when people talk, they are using arbitrary vocal symbols to describe something that has happened or might have happened and that there is no necessary connection between these symbolizations and what occurred.Talking is a highly selective process because of the way in which culture works. No culture has devised a means for talking without highlighting some things at the expense of some other

---

1 *A Mathematical Theory of Communication* is an influential work published in 1948. The author is the Claude Elwood Shannon, who is known as the father of information theory.

things. It follows that writing is a symbolization of symbols. Communication theory takes this process one step farther. The principal difference, as I see it, between the electronic engineer's approach and the approach of the cultural-communication specialist is that one works with highly compressed symbolic data while the other tries to find out what happens when people talk, before the data are stripped of all its overtones.

In considering man's total life as communication we see a spectrum covering a wide range of communication events. It is possible to observe complete messages of differing duration, some of them very short (less than a minute) and others covering years and years. In general, the study of culture deals with events of fairly short duration. The psychology of the individual in his cultural and social setting presents communication events of longer over-all duration. The study of government and political science may involve messages that take years to unfold. The following examples show how the duration of these messages can vary over a wide spectrum.

When a husband comes home from the office, takes off his hat, hangs up his coat, and say "Hi" to his wife, the way in which he says "Hi," reinforced by the manner in which he sheds his overcoat, summarizes his feelings about the way things went at the office. If his wife wants the details she may have to listen for a while, yet she grasps in an instant the significant message for her; namely, what kind of evening they are going to spend and how she is going to have to cope with it.

Or take the example of a salesman who has been trying to sell something to an important client for a number of months. The client finally agrees to take up the business with is board of directors and promises to let the salesman know the verdict in a week. The first half second of the interview that follows usually tells the salesman what he wants to know — whether he has been successful or not.

A political figure makes a speech which is supposed to be reassuring. It has the opposite effect. When the words are read,they are reassuring. Yet the total message as delivered is not. Why? For the same reason, the housewife and the salesman know what to expect. Sentences can be meaningless by themselves. Other signs may be much more eloquent. The significant components of a communication on the level of culture are characterized by their brevity as compared with other types of communication. By simply raising the pitch of the voice at the end of an utterance instead of letting it fade away, it is possible (in English) to change a statement of fact to a question. The fact that communication can be affected in so brief a time on the cultural level is often responsible for the confusion which so often occurs in cross-cultural exchanges.

As one leaves the cultural part of the spectrum and proceeds to the personality portion, the wave length increases. The analytic building blocks, instead of being sounds and the like, are whole interactions between people— mother and child, for instance. Thus, first impressions may be wrong because neither person has had a chance to reveal himself fully in a brief period. As a whole, the personality comes through rather slowly and is only fully known after years.

The portion of the communications spectrum which embraces political events is composed of units of much longer duration. Meanings must be found in the context of hundreds of years of history. In a total pattern, a government's white paper is not just another document; it may be the equivalent of a period of a semicolon or even a question mark at the end of a message that has been building up for years. The message is composed of numerous situations and acts—something which is understood by any political scientist or statesman. Diplomacy and political strategy can be seen as a kind of debate where the words cover years.

Beyond this, men like Toynbee have been trying to work out the grammar of a message which may last for several hundred years, thereby transcending the lifetime of an individual human being. They analyze the syntax of whole societies and civilizations.

The trouble that social scientists have when they talk to someone who has been working on a different part of the communications spectrum is that what one sees clearly may be a diffuse blur or a microscopic dot to the other. Yet each researcher is trying his best to establish a pattern for extracting the meaning from what he studies. In the end all these patterns are relevant to one another. The language of politics and the language of culture are a long way apart, yet each subsumes the other.

Like a telephone system, any communication system has three aspects: its overall structure, comparable to the telephone network; its components, comparable to switchboards, wires, and telephones; and the message itself, which is carried by the network. Similarly, messages can be broken down into three components: sets (like words), isolates (like sounds), and patterns (like grammar or syntax). A breakdown of messages into these components, sets, isolates, and patterns is basic to understanding culture as communication. A good deal of what follows is an explication of these terms and what lies behind them.

To recapitulate, people are constantly striving to discover the meaning of relationships between individuals and groups of individuals. The professional scholar soon learns to disregard the immediate explicit meaning of the obvious and to look for a pattern. He also has to learn to scale his perception up or down, depending upon what type of communication he is trying to unravel. This leads to an understandable occupational blindness which makes it almost impossible for him to pay close attention to communications of other types, on other wave lengths, as it were. An ability to decipher communications in a restricted area of specialization is what makes men experts. One person may be an expert in long-range events, another in short-term interactions. Further, if we return to language as it is spoken (not written) as a specialized communication system, we can learn something of how other less elaborated systems work. Most of what is known about communication has been learned from the study of language. Because the work with language has been so fruitful, there are certain analogies drawn from it which can be useful in the description of other communication systems.

In the study of languages, one can safely assume nothing. No two languages are alike; each has to be approached afresh. Some are so dissimilar, English and Navajo, for example, that they force the speaker into two different images of reality. Yet, whether a language is near or far, closely related or unrelated, there are certain steps which have to be taken in the analysis of the language in order that learning may proceed.

At first the new language is nothing but a blur of sound. Soon, however, some things seem to stand out, recognizable events recur. There are, for instance, perceived breaks or pauses, spaces which set off event from another. It is usually assumed that these breaks separate words. Actually, they may be words, or they may be sentences, or they may be something else. The point is that there is something which is perceived, and this is what the learner grasps. For the time being we will call the things which we perceive "words." This is only a convenience, however, because the word as we know it is very limited in meaning.

In the learning the new language, we discover, after having reproduced a number of words in our mouths, that the "words" are made up of sounds of various sorts, many of which are quite different from the sounds of English. Then we find that there is a way of stringing the words together that constitutes a complete utterance which we think of as a sentence.

To repeat, in discovering how a new language works and in learning that language, one starts with something akin to the word, made up of sounds, and put together in a particular way and according to certain set rules, which we call syntax. These are the basic steps and they identify the basic components of a language.

Because the terminology of the linguist is specialized and overly complex, Trager and I introduced a new set of terms which apply to all types of communication, including language. The cover terms are used to designate the three principal elements of a message. These are: sets, isolates, and patterns. The set (words) are what you perceive first, the isolates (sounds) are the components that make up the sets, while the patterns (syntax) are the way in which sets are strung together in order to give them meaning.

The idea of looking at culture as communication has been profitable in that it has raised problems which had not been thought of before and provided solutions which might not otherwise have been possible. The fruitfulness of the approach can be traced to the clear distinction which was made between the formal, informal, and the technical, as well as the realization that culture can be analyzed into sets, isolates, and patterns. It is interesting to note that the early studies of the material culture of the American Indian were originally approached in this way but became entangled in a methodological bog because the study of linguistics had not progressed sufficiently at that time to enable the worker to draw any useful analogies from the way in which language worked. The data suggested, however, that there were things like the isolate which were called traits and catch-all combinations comparable to the word which were called train-complexes.

In many instances, the earlier attempts at handling material culture founded because the living informant, if available at all, was not used properly to provide a true basis for the field worker's analysis. Somehow field work tended then, as it does today, to become contaminated by the culture of the scientist.

Like the philosophers and alchemists of the past who looked for the right things in the wrong way, many anthropologists have been searching for the essential building blocks of culture. Using the phoneme (the building block of language) as a model, they tried to discover its cultural equivalent, assuming in the process that culture was an entity, like language. Many of these efforts were based on incomplete understanding of the phoneme. In reality the phoneme is a cluster of sounds recognizable to the speakers of the language. The a as the New Englander pronounces it in the word "father," as well as its other regional variations, constitutes one phoneme. The p at the beginning of "pip" and "pop" is actually different from the p at the end, yet they are both known as allophones (recognizable variants) of the phoneme p.

The phoneme, like all other isolates, is an abstraction that dissolves into a set as soon as it is pinned down. Since this was not understood by anthropologists, the phoneme did not provide a proper mode for the rest of culture. The phoneme also represents just one structure point in a highly specialized communication system. It never pays to draw an analogy on the basis of structure points alone without reference to how the whole system behaves. The scientist has to be consistent in these things. If he is going to use a linguistic building block like the phoneme, then the rest of the system should be used too. It seems that linguistic analysis requires some adaptation before it constitutes a suitable model for the other systems of culture.

(The Silent Language, 1959)

Language, Race and Culture

Edward Sapir

Language has a setting. The people that speak it belong to a race (or a number of races), that is, to a group which is set off by physical characteristics from other groups. Again, language does not exist apart from culture, that is, from the socially inherited assemblage of practices and beliefs that determines the texture of our lives. Anthropologists have been in the habit of studying man under the three rubrics of race, language and culture. One of the first things they do with a natural area like Africa or the South Seas is to map it out from this three fold point of view. These maps answer the questions: What and where are the major divisions of the human animal, biologically considered? What are most inclusive linguistic groupings, the "linguistic stocks," and what is the distribution of each (e.g., the Hamitic language of northern Africa, the Bantu languages of the South; the Malayo-

Polynesian languages of Indonesia)? How do the peoples of the given area divide themselves as cultural beings? What are the outstanding "cultural areas" and what are the dominant ideas in each (e.g., the Mohammedan north of Africa; the primitive hunting, nonagricultural culture of the Bushmen in the south; the culture of the Australian natives, poor in physical respects but richly developed in ceremonialism)?

……

That a group of languages need not in the least correspond to a racial group or a culture area is easily demonstrated. We may even show how a single language intercrosses with race and culture lines. The English language is not spoken by a unified race. In the United States there are several millions of negroes who know no other language. It is their mother-tongue. It is as much their property, as inalienably "theirs", as the King of England's. Nor do the English-speaking whites of America constitute a definite race except by way of contrast to the negroes. Of the three fundamental white races in Europe generally recognized by physical anthropologists— the Baltic or North European, the Alpine, and the Mediterranean— each has numerous English-speaking representatives in America. But does not the historical core of English-speaking peoples, those relatively "unmixed" populations that still reside in English and its colonies, represent a race, pure and single? I cannot see that the evidence points that way. The English people are an Amalgam of many distinct strains. Besides the old "Anglo-Saxon," in other words North German, element which is conventionally represented as the basic strain, the English blood comprises Norman French, Scandinavian, "Celtic," and pre-Celtic elements. If by "English" we mean also Scotch and Irish, then the term "Celtic" is loosely used for at least two quite distinct racial elements — the short, dark-complexioned type of Wales and the taller, lighter, often ruddy-haired type of the Highlands and parts of Ireland.

……

Many other, and more striking, examples of the lack of correspondence between race and language could be given if space permitted. One instance will do for many. The Malayo-Polynesian languages form a well-defined group that takes in the southern end of the Malay Peninsula and the tremendous island world to the south and east (except Australia and the greater part of New Guinea). In this vast region we find represented no less than three distinct races— the Negro-like Papuans of New Guinea and Melanesia, and the Polynesians of the outer islands. The Polynesians and Malays all speak languages of the Malayo-Polynesian group, while the languages of the Papuans belong partly to this group (Melanesian), party to the unrelated languages (Papuan) of New Guinea. In spite of the fact that the greatest race cleavage in this region lies between the Papuans and the Polynesians, the major linguistic division is of Malayan on the one side, Melanesian and Polynesian on the other.

...

Language, race, and culture are not necessarily correlated. This does not mean that they never are. There is some tendency, as a matter of fact, for racial and cultural lines of cleavage to correspond to linguistic ones, though in any given case the latter may not be of the same degree of importance as the others. Thus, there is a fairly definite line of cleavage between the Polynesian languages, race and those of Melanesians on the other, in spite of a considerable amount of overlapping. The racial and cultural division, however, particularly the former, are of major importance, while the linguistic division is of quite minor significance, the Polynesian languages constituting hardly more than a special dialectic subdivision of the combined Melanesian— Polynesian group. Still clearer-cut coincidences of cleavage may be found. The language, race, and culture of the Eskimo are markedly distinct from those of their neighbors; in southern Africa the language, race, and culture of the Bushmen offer an even stronger contrast to those of their Bantu neighbors. Coincidences of this sort are of the greatest significance, of course, but this significance is not one of inherent psychological relations between the three factors of race, language and culture. The coincidences of cleavage point merely to a readily intelligible historical association. If the Bantu and Bushmen are so sharply differentiated in all respects, the reason is simply that the former are relatively recent other; their present propinquity is too recent for the slow process of cultural and racial assimilation to have set in very powerfully. As we go back in time, we shall have to assume that relatively scantly populations occupied large territories for untold generations and that contact with other masses of population was not as insistent and prolonged as it later became. The geographical and historical isolation that brought about race differentiations was naturally favorable also to far-reaching variations in language and culture. The very fact that races and cultures which are brought into historical contact tend to assimilate in the long run, while neighboring languages assimilate each other only casually and in superficial respects, indicates that there is no profound causal relation between the development of language and the specific development of race and of culture.

But surely, the wary reader will object, there must be some relation between language and culture, and between language and at least that intangible aspect of race that we call "temperament". Is it not inconceivable that the particular collective qualities of mind that have fashioned a culture are not precisely the same as were responsible for the growth of a particular linguistic morphology? This question takes us into the heart of the most difficult problems of social psychology. It is doubtful if any one has yet attained to sufficient clarity on the nature of the historical process and on the ultimate psychological factors involved in linguistic and cultural drifts to answer it intelligently. I can only very briefly set forth my own views, or rather my general attitude. It would be very difficult to prove that "temperament", the general emotional disposition of a people, is basically responsible for the slant and drift of a culture, however much it may manifest itself in an individual's handling of the elements of that culture. But granted that temperament has a certain value for the shaping of culture, difficult though it be to say just how, it does not follow that it has the same value for the shaping of language. It is impossible to show that the form of a language has the slightest connection with national temperament. Its line of variation, its drift, runs inexorably in the channel ordained for it by its historic antecedents; it is as regardless of the feelings and sentiments of its speakers as is the course of a river of the atmospheric humors of the landscape. I am convinced that it is futile to look in linguistic structure for differences corresponding to the temperamental variations which are supposed to be correlated with race. In this connection it is well to remember that the emotional aspect of our psychic life is but meagerly expressed in the build of language.

Language and our thought-grooves are inextricably interwoven, are in a sense, one and the same. As there is nothing to show that there are significant racial differences in the fundamental conformation of thought, it follows that the infinite variability of linguistic form, another name for the infinite variability of the actual process of thought, cannot be an index of such significant racial difference. This is only apparently a paradox. The latent content of all languages is the same— the intuitive science of experience. It is the manifest form that is never twice the same, for this form, which we call linguistic morphology, is nothing more nor less than a collective art of thought, an art denuded of the irrelevancies of individual sentiment. As last analysis, then, language can no more flow from race as such than the sonnet form.

Nor can I believe that culture and language are in any true sense causally related. Culture may be defined as what a society does and thinks. Language is a particular how of thought. It is difficult to see what particular causal relations may be expected to subsist between a selected inventory of experience (culture, a significant selection made by society) and the particular manner in which the society expresses all experience. The drift of culture, another way of saying history, is a complex series of changes in society's selected inventory— additions, losses, changes of emphasis and relation. The drift of language is not properly concerned with changes of content at all, merely with changes in formal expression. It is possible, in thought, to change every sound, word, and concrete concept of a language without changing its inner actuality in the least, just as one can pour into a fixed mold water or plaster or molten gold. If it can be shown that culture has an innate form, a series of contours, quite apart from subject-matter of any description whatsoever, we have something in culture that may serve as a term of comparison with and possibly a means of relating it to language. But until such purely formal patterns of culture are discovered and laid bare, we shall do well to hold the drifts of language and of culture to be noncomparable and unrelated processes. From this it follows that all attempts to connect particular types of linguistic morphology with certain correlated stages of cultural development are vain. Rightly understood, such correlations are rubbish. The merest coup d'oeilverifies our theoretical argument on this point. Both simple and complex types of language of an indefinite number of varieties may be found spoken at any desired level of cultural advance. When it comes to linguistic form, Plato walks with Macedonian swineherd, Confucius with the head-hunting savage of Assam.

It goes without saying that the mere content of language is intimately related to culture. A society that has knowledge of theosophy need to have no name for it; aborigines that had never seen or heard of a horse were compelled to invent or borrow a word for language more or less faithfully reflects the culture whose purposes it serves, it is perfectly true that the history of language and the history of culture move along parallel lines. But this superficial and extraneous kind of parallelism is of no real interest to the linguist except in so far as the growth or borrowing of new words incidentally throws light on the formal trends of the language. The linguistic student should never make the mistake of identifying a language with its dictionary.

(Language, 1921)

Human and Society

Larry A. Samovar, et al.

Present and Future

Intercultural communication, as you might suspect, is not new. Since the dawn of civilization, when the first humans formed tribal groups, intercultural contact occurred whenever people one tribe encounter members of another tribe and discovered that they were different. Sometimes these differences, in the absence of multicultural awareness and tolerance, elicited the human propensity to respond malevolently. However, in the pursuit of political alliances, knowledge, or commercial trade, these differences were more often recognized and accommodated. For instance, Alexander the Great was known to pay homage to the different gods of the lands he conquered and to encourage his followers to marry into the power elite families of those of Alexandria, thought to have been established in the third century B. C., accumulated texts from across the ancient world. Spices, silk, tea, and coffee made their way to Europe from China, Southeast Asia, and the Middle East via the Silk Road trade routes. Guns, modern medicine, and even bread were brought to the Far East by traders sailing from Western Europe on the voyages of discovery.

These cultural exchanges have accelerated in the past century at a dizzying pace, to the point where, as we mentioned, societies around the globe have been interwoven into a complex fabric of interdependent economic, technological, political, and social relationships. This interdependency is a salient characteristic of the world that you presently live in, and the future promises even greater interconnectivity, requiring increased cultural knowledge and language abilities. To help you understand how the challenges of the future will require you to acquire and use intercultural communication skills, we will discuss a number of areas in which global interconnectedness and the cultural dynamics of society will have a direct impact on your life.

These areas include globalization, world trade and international business, world competition for natural resources and technology and travel and so on.

Globalization

Globalization has become a term common to many languages and used in many disciplines. Some use it positively and others use if negatively. It is defined variously, depending on the user's perspective and intent. Cameron sees globalization as "the ongoing integration of the world economy." For Gannon, "Globalization refers to the increasing interdependence among national governments, business firms, nonprofit organizations, and individual citizens." From an anthropological perspective, globalization is "worldwide interconnectedness, evidenced in global movements of natural resources, trade goods, human labor, finance capital, information, and infectious diseases." The common theme resonating in these definitions is connectedness. It has become increasingly difficult to live your life without being the core of globalization, is the product of "growth in world trade and the business activity that accompanies it; dramatic improvements in telecommunications; ease of data storage and transmission; increased facility and opportunity for business and leisure travel." In order to better comprehend this transformation of the global society, let us take a minute and look at some of these forces of globalization.

World Trade and International Business

This ability to quickly move products, equipment, people, information, and securities around the world, with little concern for national or international borders, has given rise to what are commonly called transnational corporations. Their global presence and reach are sometimes difficult to comprehend. For example, McDonald's busiest location is in Munich, Germany, and the active 7-Eleven store is in Samutparkam, Thailand. Kentucky Fried Chicken is available at more than eleven thousand locations in over eighty countries. Baskin-Robbins ice cream can be purchased in over 5,800 stores, of which 2,700 are outside the United States. As of May 2007,

Toyota Motor Corporation, the world's largest automobile maker, operated "52 overseas manufacturing companies in 26 countries / regions" and marketed "vehicles in more than 170 countries / regions." General Electric collected revenues of $ 163.3 billion, employed more than three hundred thousand people, and operated in over one hundred countries in 2007. Continuing technological advances in transportation, communication, and data transfer facilitate the ability of transnational corporations to reposition manufacturing processes in regions that offer low production costs, especially for labor, and to move products and services quickly to emerging markets. Mega-corporations are expected to continue to expand in the near future, and their growth holds two principal concerns for you. First, there is a good likelihood that you will someday work for a transnational organization or one of its subsidiaries. As such, intercultural communication skills will be a critical necessity. The ability to work in a multicultural workforce and interact with people from other cultures, often in other languages, is inherent to the success of a multinational business.

A second concern will be how the economy is managed and controlled. According to Mandel, "Globalization has overwhelmed Washington's ability to control the economy." The giant commercial companies now have the capacity to exert considerable influence on local, state, and national governments and, in the pursuit of open markets and free trade, have the ability to move goods across borders with few or no regulatory restrictions. Unlike governments, these huge organizations are not transparent and are responsible only to their shareholders, which allows them considerable operational flexibility. For example, the consolidation of media outlets into a few large organizations has had a homogenizing influence on available media, and this tends to stifle constructive debate, underrepresent minority views, and discount local perspectives.

Although many of these large organizations have developed viable programs to become good corporate citizens, their main objective remains making money, and improving social conditions is a much lesser concern. Thus, governments and nonprofit organizations will need to work across borders, and this may require new international organizations, such as "global institutions for governing the world economy."

Technology and Travel

If you live in the United States, you can easily enjoy a variety of fresh fruits and vegetables that are shipped from all over the world. People living in Japan can eat blue fin tuna that was caught off the coast of Nova Scotia only days earlier and flown to Tokyo. People are now traveling widely for both business and pleasure. The U.S. Commerce Department has estimated that the United States will have as many as 61.6 million visitors in 2011. This influx of international tourists will call for service personnel trained to interact successfully with people from a wide selection of cultures. Additionally, global business will bring more and more people together from different cultures. In some cases, this contact will be face-to-face interaction, and in other instances, it will be virtual contact via electronic means. But regardless of the medium, successful interaction will require well-developed intercultural communication skills.

The technology will also expand the ability of people throughout the world to connect with each other. At the end of 2007, there are an estimated 3.3 billion cell phone subscribers in the world, and in many countries, cell phones are now perceived as necessities rather than conveniences. Cell phones are already used for voice and email communication and Internet access, and function as cameras, voice recorders, personal organizers, game devices, and music players. Japanese university students can now upload "cell phone novels" to help relieve the tedium of their daily train and bus commute, which in some cases takes up to two hours one way. As a result of cell phone's variety of uses and declining costs, the number of subscribers is expected to grow, and international phone connections are becoming more commonplace. Will you know the proper phone etiquette when traveling in another culture?

Advancing technology also promises to increase exponentially the amount of information available in the very near future. A new Internet, dubbed "The Grid," is expected to operate at "speeds about 10,000 times faster than a typical broadband connection." A recent corporate study on the future of digital information reported, "Between 2006 and 2010, the information added annually to the digital universe will increase more than six-fold…." Management and regulation of this deluge of information will require international cooperation and the establishment of mutually agreeable protocols.

Environmental Challenges

Your future will also be marked by the challenges of environmental change. For many people in the world, global warming and other forms of environmental degradation are not scientific or predictions; they are ongoing realities. For example, in the Sundarbans, a vast low-lying delta along the border of India and Bangladesh, rising waters are already destroying fields and homes. Global warming is also thought to be contributing to increased desertification in arid regions of North Africa. One result, when coupled with industrial pollution, is atmospheric dust storms "containing plant pollens, fungal spores, dried animal feces, minerals, chemicals from fires and industry, and pesticide residues."

Experts are also predicting that continued global warming will produce a worldwide shortage of water, which will affect even the United States. According to a White House report on climate change issued in May 2008, the future will be characterized by "worsening water shortages for agricultural and urban users" across the entire United States. Additionally, military experts have indicated that water problems resulting from global warming "will make poor, unstable parts of the world — the Middle East, Africa, and South Asia— even more prone to wars, terrorism and the need for international intervention." The need for intercultural communication skills to help lessen and resolve these projected problems should be quite clear.

The challenge of natural disaster response work also calls for intercultural communication proficiency. In late December 2005, an undersea earthquake created a tsunami that inundated the coastal areas of eleven Indian Ocean nations, killing an estimated 230,000 people and leaving millions homeless. In October 2005, an earthquake in the Kashmir region, which borders India and Pakistan, claimed as many as 79,000 lives and forced 3.5 million people into refugee camps. In early May 2008, a typhoon struck Myanmar (Burma) and a few weeks later an earthquake devastated Sichuan Province in central China. The death tolls in these two tragedies will probably exceed two hundred thousand; in addition, millions have lost their homes.

Programs to mitigate the human suffering caused by these calamities required international relief efforts on an unprecedented scale. Rescue teams, medical personnel, disease control professionals, logistics experts, and many other international specialists quickly converged on these areas to assist in recovery operations. Relief agencies from around the world rushed in people and supplies to help the victims. These recovery efforts will continue for extended periods. And, as you would expect, all of this work will require an enormous amount of intercultural communication. In addition to language, it is important to know the cultural norms of the people receiving aid. With experts predicting that climate change will bring more intense tropical storms and flooding to low-lying coastal areas, disaster relief work is expected to increase worldwide.

World Health Issues

Contemporary global interconnectedness also influences current and future health care concerns. Stop for a minute and think about how quickly the virus that causes AIDS traveled around the world. The recall the international coordination that was required to spread prevention awareness information across cultures. To thwart the transmission of mad cow disease, many countries had to coordinate their efforts to test and track animals, handle products suspected of being tainted, and agree on safeguards for prevention and control. A large number of national governments and international agencies are currently working to control, and find a vaccine for, a deadly strain of avian flu. This has involved the culling and killing of "hundreds of millions of birds" since 2003. It has been estimated that hundreds of millions of people could die in a worldwide pandemic should this strain mutate and become transmissible between humans. Also, the World Health Organization (WHO) is directing worldwide efforts to detect, monitor, and report on incidents of severe acute respiratory syndrome, which can be spread easily by international travels. Communication must extend across multiple cultures for these efforts to succeed.

The future promises even greater need for international agreement and cooperation to ensure safety from diseases. For instance, researches have found that the atmospheric dust clouds, which we discussed earlier in this chapter, can transport "bacteria, fungus, and viruses that may transmit diseases to humans." Global warming also promises to accelerate death rates due to diarrhea, malaria, and dengue fever among the peoples of poverty-stricken nations.

Shifting Populations — Immigration

The world's population is increasing. At about the time when many of you will begin to think about what you will do in your retirement years, the current population of approximately 6.6 billion could exceed 9 billion, according to estimates by the United Nations. Most of this growth will occur in developing nations, further straining already overburdened, inadequate social support systems. In many instances, untenable living conditions and the lack of economic opportunity will force people to look to the developed world. This could, of course, increase the waves of immigrants already moving to the developed nations, particularly Western Europe and the United States, and further change the cultural and social complexion of those nations. For example, immigrants currently make up about 11 percent of Spain's population and as much as 10 percent of Ireland's. These immigrants, arriving from Africa, the former Soviet Republics, and Eastern Europe, and the expectation of more to come, are quite naturally the subject of heated debate. From one perspective, the immigrants are seen as a threat to the long-established traditional values of the native culture, which in some cases can become a form of racism. However, on the other side of the argument, the new arrivals are seen as much-needed additions to the national economies because they supplement the shrinking indigenous workforce and pay taxes that sustain social support systems, such as retirement and health care programs, as the native population ages. Regardless of which side you take in this clash of perspectives, the situation will give rise to greatly increased intercultural communication needs.

With over three hundred million people, the United States is now the world's third most populous country, behind China and India. While population figures for the United States are expected to continue rising, and could reach 438 million by 2050, this growth is being driven by immigration, not births.

This will clearly change the complexion of U.S. society and give rise to additional cultural considerations. It is one thing to think of problems that can result when people from different cultures interact in a business or social context, but the changing demographics of the United States give rise to a host of other factors. Cultural considerations concerning medicine, education, language, cross-cultural marriages, child care, and more will come into play. Many of these considerations are already affecting American society, but the increasing demographic changes will thrust them into great prominence.

Multicultural Society

For our final look at the future, we want to discuss the growth of the multicultural society in which you will live. You are already well acquainted with the diversity of American society along ethnic lines, and we have just discussed how that diversity will continue to grow as a result of immigration. However, there is another aspect of this multicultural society. Indeed, it was a salient issue during the 2008 Democratic presidential nomination campaign. Much was made of the mixed heritage of Senator Barack Obama, whose father was from Kenya. Although Obama was born in the state of Hawaii, as a youth, he spent several years in Indonesia with his white American mother and Indonesian stepfather. The mixed ethnic backgrounds of celebrities like baseball player Derek Jeter and golfer Tiger Woods are also well known. There are, of course, many more people of mixed heritage. A 2008 report from the U. S. Census Bureau estimated that there were 4,856, 136 people in the United States whose heritage was of "two or more races." This indicates that this group has a growth rate then times faster than that of the white population, but approximately equivalent to that of Hispanic and Asian Americans. This growth is a result of surging interracial / interethnic marriages throughout the Untied States, fueled partly by greater social acceptance. These parings clearly present cultural and language problems for the husband and wife, as well as their children.

There are even signs that globalization is producing a transnational cultural group. According to Bird and Stevens, increasingly, an identifiable and homogeneous group is emerging at least within the world business community. This group neither shares a common geographic location, socioeconomic class, religion, native language nor a national culture. Yet they share a common set of values, culture and one foot in the global arena, they are members of a distinctly identifiable and emerging global culture. In some cases, they appear to share more in common with others active in the global village than with those of their own national culture. They are members of what we identify as the emergent global culture.

You may well have the opportunity to interact with or become a member of this new cultural group during your professional career. These first few pages contain only a few of the endless examples of how society is transforming as the world becomes metaphorically smaller. We believe these examples should convince you of the many and varied changes that you will confront during your adult life. In addition, as we previously mentioned, a constant theme associated with these changes is the interconnectedness of contemporary society. This interconnectedness means people of different nationalities and ethnic origins, many speaking different languages and holding different convictions, must learn to work and live together, despite the likelihood of conflict. We hope, therefore, that by now you have recognized that you are faced with a requirement to expand and improve your cultural awareness and intercultural communication competence. If so, then you are ready to begin your study of intercultural communication.

(Communication Between Cultures, 2010)

Paradox of Translating

Eugene A. Nida

Translating is a complex and fascinating task. In fact, I. A. Richards has claimed that it is probably the most complex type of event in the history of the cosmos. And yet, translating is so natural and easy that children seem to have no difficulty in interpreting for their immigrant parents. These children normally do well until they have gone to school and have learned about nouns, verbs and adverbs. Then they often seem tongue-tied because they try to match the words and grammar rather than the content.

Because of experience in learning a foreign language in school, most persons assume that literalness in translating means faithfulness to the text, even though close, literal renderings are often seriously misleading. In English, for example, the repetition of a word usually implies emphasis, but not in Bahasa Indonesia, where repetition only signals plurality. In the Quechua dialect of Boivia the suffix -runa marks the preceding non as plural, but in conversation Quechua speakers use the suffix only at the beginning of a section and do not constantly repeat it, as is the case with the plural suffix in Spanish. Accordingly, a literal translation which represents every plural-s in Spanish by the Quechua suffix -runa is regarded by Quechua speakers as being not only strange but even an insult to the intelligence of hearers.

Because of the many discrepancies between meanings and structures of different languages, some persons have insisted that translating is impossible, and yet more and more translating is done and done well. Those who insist that translating is impossible are usually concerned with some of the more marginal features of figurative language and complex poetic structures. the use of figurative language is universal, but the precise figures of speech in one language rarely match those in another.

It is true that in some languages one cannot say "My God", because native speakers insist that no one can "possess" God, but a person can speak about "the God I worship" or "the God to whom I belong." Translating is simply doing the impossible well, regardless of the objections of such famous authors as Goethe, Schleiermacher, and Ortega y Gasset, who insisted that translating is impossible and yet did not hesitate to have their own writings translated.

Another paradox of translating is reflected in the contention that translating is valid but paraphrase is wrong. In fact, all translating involves differing degrees of paraphrase, since there is no way in which one can successfully translate word for word and structure for structure. In Spanish "me fui" is literally "I went myself," in which me is a so-called reflexive pronoun, but this Spanish phrase can often be best translated into English as "I left right away" or "I got away quickly." In English, as well as in most other European languages, one speaks of the "heart" as being the center of emotions, but in many languages in West Africa a person "loves with the liver" and in some of the indigenous languages of Central America people talk about "loving with the stomach". Since languages do not differ essentially in what they can say, but in how they say it, paraphrase is inevitable. What is important is the semantic legitimacy of the paraphrase.

A further paradox occurs in the widespread view that a translator should first produce a more or less literal rendering of the source text and then proceed to improve it stylistically. Style, however, is not the frosting on the cake, but an integral part of the process of interlingual communication. It must be built into the text right from the beginning. It is usually better to aim first at a stylistically satisfactory rendering or the source text and then reviews it carefully to "tighten it up" by analyzing and testing the correspondences. A few errors in the correspondences of lexical meaning are much more excusable than missing the spirit and aesthetic character of the source text.

Since translating is a sill which generally requires considerable practice, most people assume that it can be taught, and to an extent this is true. But it is also true that really exceptional translators are born, not made. Potential translators must have a high level of aptitude for the creative use of language, or they are not likely to be outstanding in their profession. Perhaps the greatest benefit from instruction in translating is to become aware of one's own limitations, something which a translator of Steinbeck's of Mice and Men into Chinese should have learned. Then he would not have translated English mule-skinner into a Chinese phrase meaning "a person who skins the hide off of mules".

For many people the need for human translators seems paradoxical in this age of computer. Since modern computers can be loaded with dictionaries any grammars, why not let computers do the work? Computers can perform certain very simple interlingual tasks, providing there is sufficient pre-editing and post-editing. But neither advertising brochures nor lyric poetry can ever be reduced to the kind of logic required for computer programs. Computer printouts of translations can often be understood, if the persons involved already know what the text is supposed to say. But the results of machine translating are usually in an unnatural form of language and sometimes just plain weird. Furthermore, real improvements will not come from merely doctoring the program or adding rules. The human brain is not only digital and analogic, but it also has a built-in system of values which gives it a componential and incalculable advantage over machines. Human translators will always be necessary for any text which is stylistically appealing and semantically complex—which includes most of what is worth communicating in another language.

The most difficult texts to translate are not, however, highly literary productions, but rather those texts which say nothing, the type of language often used by politicians and delegates to international forums. In fact, a group of professional translators at the United Nations headquarters in New York City have insisted that the most difficult text to translate is one in which the speaker or writer has attempted to say nothing. The next most difficult type of text is one filled with irony or sarcasm, since in a written text the paralinguistic clues to the meaning are usually much more difficult to detect than when someone is speaking. And perhaps the third most difficult type of text is a book or article on translating in which the illustrative examples rarely match. In fact, a book on translating almost always requires extensive adaptation.

One of the most surprising paradoxes of translating is that there is never a completely perfect or timeless translation. Both language and culture are always in the process of change. Furthermore, language is an open system with overlapping meanings and fuzzy boundaries—the bane of logicians but the delight of poets. The indeterminacy of language is part of the price that must be paid for creativity and for the new insights which come through symbolic reinterpretation of human experience.

Some people imagine that the greatest problem in translating is to find the right words and constructions in the receptor of target language. On the contrary, the most difficult task for the translator is to understand thoroughly the designative and associative meanings of the text to be translated. This involves not only knowing the meanings of the words and the syntactic relations, but also being sensitive to all the nuances of the stylistic devices.

As one struggling translator summed up his problems, "If I really understood what the text means, I could easily translate it."

Perhaps the least understood paradox of translating is the general assumption that a person who knows two languages well can be a good translator or interpreter. In the first place, knowing two languages is not enough. It is also essential to be acquainted with the respective cultures—one of the important reasons for the title of this book Language, Culture and Translating. Persons may be able to speak two languages perfectly but not have the capacity to write well, which means they can never become skilled translators. Moreover, merely speaking two languages in a competent manner does not mean that persons can become first-rate interpreters, whether in consecutive or simultaneous circumstances. In addition to knowing a language, an interpreter must have a quick mind to organize and formulate a response. The test for potential interpreters at the Maurice Thorez Institute in Moscow involves an assigned topic, one minute to prepare a short speech on the topic, and one minute to speak.

The least understood paradox of language is the parallax of language, that is, the fact that language not only represents reality but also distorts it. For example, people use the terms sunset and sunrise when they know full well that the sun does not actually set or rise, but that it is the world which is rotating. Similarly, people call certain large-eared seals sea lions, although they are in no sense lions. Even when a word is wrongly understood, many persons tend to give it credence. For example, people still cite the adage "The exception proves the rule" as a means of justifying exceptions, when proves should be understood only in the sense of "testing."

Some people think of a language as being a picture or map of reality, and they seldom take the time to realize that pictures and maps inevitably involve selectivity and distortion. Both pictures and maps suffer from parallax, but people generally get used to such skewing of reality and even have special devices for calculating the errors in maps and photographs of the earth's surface. Unfortunately, they often do not recognize the parallax in language, and they accept verbal formulations as being absolute truths. They talk about the Holy Roman Empire, when in reality it was not holy or Roman or an empire. More recently there was the German Democratic Republic, which from the viewpoint of democracies in the West was neither democratic nor a republic in the generally accepted meanings of these terms. Some people no longer speak about agreements being broken; they simply use the word inoperative. And armies are no longer supposed to retreat; they just regroup. Similarly, stock markets no longer fall; they merely consolidate.

(Language and Culture, 2009)

Managing Differences Abroad

Susan C. Schneider & Jean-Louis Barsoux

Interpersonal Skills

Interpersonal skills are often identified as crucial, if not the most important. The ability to form relationships helps the manager integrate into the social fabric of the host culture. Not only does this satisfies the needs for friendship and intimacy, but also facilitates the transfer of knowledge, and improves coordination and control. Establishing relationships and building trust allows the expatriate manager to tap into critical information, thus reducing the stressful uncertainties surrounding both work and personal life.

While many companies acknowledge the importance of interpersonal skills, it is rarely seen as a critical criterion for selection. In practice, expatriate managers are primarily selected on their strong track record at home, that is, their reputation for getting the job done. Companies also send abroad those who have been identified as "high fliers" for the purpose of career development. Either way, expatriates are most often chosen based on technical or conceptual abilities rather than interpersonal skills.

Those having been placed on the fast track often arrive on assignment ready to prove themselves, to make their mark. Thus, they tend to be quite focused on the task and on achieving the objectives set by corporate headquarters. As assignments may last only 18 months, they have to move quickly to make things happen. This can create tension with the local staff, who refer to them as "birds of passage", laying low waiting for this latest arrival to fly off again, until the next one arrives, with yet another personal agenda.

Time pressures and a strong task orientation can interfere with the need to build relationships and to establish trust. Often local staff feel exploited, as instruments to achieve goals that are not their own. This exacerbates feelings of mistrust and resentment towards head office. In fact, some experts argue that successful expatriates actually need to have low task orientation.

The need for more people-oriented managers is confirmed by the personal director for the European division of ICI, a British chemical company, who looks for people who are good at getting along with colleagues at home. This is deemed essential for the simple reason that any problems a manager has in dealing with colleagues will be magnified in a foreign setting, where much more effort is needed to build understanding and trust. The former co-chairman of Unilever, Floris Maljers, agrees by stating, "We tend to look for people who can work in teams and understand the value of cooperation and consensus". Thus, the ability to get along with others is considered to be an important passport to international business.

Nevertheless, a survey conducted of US companies that post staff internationally found that the most important employee selection criteria remain technical expertise (95 percent of respondents), employee interest in the assignment (88 percent of respondents) and personal flexibility (84 percent). Interpersonal skills do not seem to be high on the list.

Linguistic Ability

Linguistic ability is also important as it helps to establish contact. However, having total command of the other language may not be feasible and may be less important than trying to develop a feeling for what matters to others, picking up bits of "conventional currency" : local expressions, information, and interests.

On short overseas assignments in particular, efforts to speak the local language may have more symbolic than practical value, but the impact is highly significant. It indicates an eagerness to communicate and connect with host nationals. A resolute unwillingness to speak the other's language can be very damaging in that it may be taken as a sign of disdain, or un unwarranted display of power.

Motivation to Work and Live Abroad

Motivation to work and live abroad has been shown to be a key ingredient to the successful adaptation of the expatriates and their families. This is manifested as cultural curiosity. Expatriates and their families should be selected based on a genuine interest in other cultures and new experience. For Swedish managers, wanderlust was rated as their top motive for going abroad.

Ability to Tolerate and Cope with Uncertainty

Ability to tolerate and cope with uncertainty and ambiguity is also needed. Action often has to be taken on the basis of insufficient, unreliable and / or conflicting information. Circumstances change unexpectedly, the behavior and reactions of local employees may be unpredictable, so that the international manager has to be able to adapt almost instinctively. This requires, first of all, acknowledging that uncertainty and ambiguity exist, that everything is not as straightforward as it seems, and that multiple perspectives are possible. The ability to do so encourages dogmatic thinking and rigid behavior, which interferes with the flexibility and resourcefulness necessary for responding effectively. Top executive at Colgate asked to identify the kind of executive who worked best in an international setting cited the main attribute to be flexibility. The consensus was that you don't always go by the book.

Faced with the threat of greater uncertainty and ambiguity of international assignments, managers need to keep to principles while remaining flexible. Research has shown that under conditions of threat, managers tend to engage in efforts to impose greater controls, restrict information flows, and revert to well-known behavior. This can result in stereotypical responses, not necessarily well-adapted to the situation at hand. In these circumstances, expatriates may more often need to let go of control, to "go with the flow."

This is quite difficult especially when managers are used to being rewarded for being in charge and staying on top of things. This is particularly evident in cultures where control over the environment is an underlying assumption. Indeed, the success of Japanese company strategies (as in the case of Honda) was often attributed to their flexibility which enabled them to capitalize on unexpected opportunities. This flexibility comes from their readiness to adapt rather than to impose controls over changing circumstances.

Patience and Respect

Perhaps even more crucial for the international executive are patience and respect. Patience is necessary, not only because different cultures have different rhythms, but also because it takes time to "learn the ropes". Expatriates have to avoid the temptation constantly to benchmark the new culture against the home culture, but must instead try to understand the local reasons for the way things happen. While having patience and respect may be the golden rule of international business, it seems to be the one most often broken.

Cultural Empathy

Respecting the behavior and ideas of others requires empathy. Some individuals find it easier to appreciate the thoughts, feelings and experiences of others. Focused listening and non-judgmental approach help managers to understand the other person's viewpoint. But one's capacity for empathy is deeply rooted in one's character and may not be a skill easily acquired.

Narcissism, which evolves from one's psychological development, interferes with the capacity for empathy. Narcissistic managers often treat others as mere extensions of themselves making it difficult to recognize, let alone appreciate, the attitudes and behavior of others, especially those who are different. These managers see others as objects or instruments to satisfy their own needs, or as mirrors to reflect their own glory. In their efforts to prove their worth, they fail to take into consideration the needs and the value of others.

Strong Sense of Self

On the other hand, expatriates do need a strong sense of self, or ego(healthy narcissism). This allows interaction with another person or culture without fear of losing one's own identity. This also enables the expatriate to be self-critical and open to feedback. It permits expatriates to respond appropriately to failure, treating it as a learning experience rather than as a narcissistic injury, a blow to their self-image which can undermine their self-confidence.

A strong ego also reinforces the ability to handle stress. This is particularly critical in an environment where the manager is deprived of familiar surroundings and social support. The anxiety created by the uncertainties and frustrations of international experiences needs to be appropriately handled, rather than triggering dysfunctional coping devices, such as alcohol abuse.

Creating "stability zones" — hobbies, diaries, favorite pastimes, meditation, or religious worship— can provide refuge into which the expatriate can temporarily withdraw and get refueled. Taking time-out is vital because it reintroduces the element of choice and control over the rhythm of involvement with the new culture and enables the manager to regain a sense of perspective, "observing ego."

Sense of Humor

Finally, a sense of humor is one quality which is often cited but only in passing. Humor is actually important on two levels: as a coping mechanism and for relationship building. Retaining a sense of humor is seen as a way for managers to buffer the frustration, uncertainty, and confusion they are bound to encounter in an unfamiliar environment. Humor provides a way of distancing oneself from the situation, to regain a sense of perspective. Also, "the ability to laugh at ones' mistakes may be the ultimate defense against despair," or in the words of one oil industry veteran, "The first few months in an international posting can seem like one long round of social gaffes and management blunders.

Humor can also be used proactively to break the ice, to establish a link with others, and to deal with sensitive issues. A well-timed bit of humor can put people at ease, break the tension in an interaction, allowing a more open and constructive discussion to follow, and to say what might not be said otherwise.

Besides connecting with people, humor can serve to create the space for an "emotional time-out," to let off steam and alleviate tension. One person noted for his humor in international relations was Henry Kissinger. He made humor a tool of diplomacy. His banter inspired banter in others and usually led to a more relaxed atmosphere in the private, formal discussions or negotiations with world leaders. The humor opened the door to more frankness and less ritualized recitations as well. In that regard, Kissinger lightened the whole heavy international diplomatic scene.

But it must be remembered that what is considered funny in one culture does not necessarily translate to another. British humor often involves poking fun at oneself and others, dosed with a bit of sarcasm and wit (sometimes biting). In France, "se moquer" ("to mock" self or others) has a different, more pejorative, connotation. Thus, teasing or making fun of someone may be experienced as humiliation. For Asians this type of humor does not adequately "save face," or protect self-esteem

In Latin America, teasing and joking at work are pervasive. Not only does humor "grease the wheels" of the organization, but can be used to keep people in line — an acceptable way to convey feedback. It can also serve as a safety valve: the more powerless, the more joking.

Humor can also be used to reinforce the power distance, in the form of "put downs", or one-upmanship. French comedy, for example, often depicts situations where different social classes are forced to interact. In the UK as well as in France, humor is often based on intellectual or linguistic prowess — witticisms or "jeux de mots", that is, plays on words or double meanings. This demands a high level of language sensitivity which excludes most foreigners, even the most fluent. Humor, such as "inside jokes", can also reinforce notions of who's in and who's out. Thus, the use of humor has great potential for facilitating or destroying cross-cultural interactions.

Most of the above skills and competencies, traditionally considered crucial for expatriate effectiveness, are equally valid for those who deal with foreigners at home. The experiences of expatriates provide important lessons for handling this diversity. However, international management is no longer the exclusive domain of expatriates.

(Managing Across Cultures, 1996/2002)

媒介融合背景下中国文化软实力国际传播模式探析[1]

Exploration on the Mode of International Communication of the Chinese Cultural Soft Power under the Background of Media Convergence

李炜炜

（北京邮电大学人文学院外语系，北京 100876）

摘要：移动互联网等新兴信息技术的发展促进了媒介融合，在一定程度上实现了新媒体和传统媒体的有效互动，为中国文化软实力国际传播提供了新

---

1 本文发表于 2015 年第 1 期《现代传播》，在收录进本书的时候作者略有调整。

渠道和新空间,同时也构建了中国互联网文化强国等新课题。建构有中国特色的中国文化软实力传播路径,丰富中国文化和中国形象国际传播模式,是贯彻党的十八大和十八届三中全会精神的要求,将为深化文化体制改革、建设社会主义文化强国营造良好的国际舆论环境。

　　关键词:媒介融合、文化软实力、文化强国、传播模式

　　当今世界的竞争不是单纯军事实力或经济实力的较量,而是包括以文化、人才、创新能力等在内的综合国力的竞争。其中,文化鉴于其重要性,常被称作是文化"软实力"。我们国家一直以来就非常重视中国文化软实力的建设、提升和传播的问题。在文化兴国和产业报国的信念指导下,研究者很早就从多个角度来探讨中国文化软实力发展的问题。北京大学中国软实力课题组从2005年起就开始研究中国软实力的课题,其研究成果《文化软实力战略研究》已于2008年12月付梓出版;中国文化软实力研究中心于2009年7月22日在湖南大学成立;原中宣部理论局副局长、中国文化软实力研究中心主任张国祚教授主编的《中国文化软实力研究要论选(第一卷)》于2011年11月3日发布。研究者发现,有效传播能力的欠缺是中国文化软实力提升的一个重要掣肘。因此,借助媒介融合这一"东风",分析中国文化软实力传播的可行性路径,探讨中华文化独特魅力的展现手法,研究中国好故事的国际叙述形式,加大对内对外有效传播力度,营造良好的国际国内舆论环境,对于正在实现中华民族伟大复兴和全国建设小康社会的当今中国,有着重要的现实诉求和理论意义。

　　"软实力"最早出现于1990年,由美国哈佛大学肯尼迪学院教授约瑟夫·奈提出。"软实力"这个概念一出现,便受到了世界各国政治领袖、专家学者和媒体的广泛关注。约瑟夫·奈认为,"软实力"简单说就是一种能够影响他人喜好的能力,是通过非强制手段获取结果的能力。[1]

　　在经济全球化和跨国相互依存的时代,软实力显得越来越重要。在经历了三十多年经济高速增长之后,中国接下来的高速增长需要更加巨大的超越性的动力,即创新的动力。而只有科学技术和文化发展等各方面全面协同创新,才有可能产生如此巨大的动力。2013年12月30日,习近平总书记在主持中共中央政治局第十二次集体学习时强调,提高国家文化软实力,关系"两个一百年"奋斗目标和中华民族伟大复兴中国梦的实现。中共中央"十二五规划"

1　[美]约瑟夫著:《美国注定领导世界》,刘华译,中国人民大学出版社2012年版,第28页。

建议提出"推动文化发展大繁荣,提升国家文化软实力"。党的十八大更是把增强国家文化软实力作为整个文化要求的一个总领性的要求写进报告。

激发全民族文化创造力,提高国家文化软实力,是党的十七大以来国家发展的总体战略组成部分,其实质是"社会主义核心价值体系"。中华文化的伟大,绝不仅是因为体量巨大,也不仅在于其所呈现出来的极其多样化的形式,而是在于内在的强大感召力和吸引力,这些伟大的历史文化遗产不仅构成了"社会主义核心价值体系"的宝贵资源,也是构建社会主义文化强国源源不断的动力。

一、中国文化软实力传播现状

当今世界,和平是主流,但各领域内的竞争却暗流潮涌;在思想传播的阵地,西方发达国家与我们的斗争之激烈和残酷丝毫不逊于短兵相接式的近身肉搏,信息技术的极速突破更加剧了这一阵地战况的激烈程度。然而当前中国思想传播阵地与西方发达国家相比还显得苍白。且不谈国际政治经济旧秩序的存在使得西方国家把持"游戏规则",中国等发展中国家处于被动应对地位等老生常谈的客观因素,中国传播阵地的苍白,主要在于主导思想尚未完全在各类新兴阶层人群中进行主动传播,而且我们的执政党对互联网监管举措和思想言论引导尚处于初级阶段。我们可以从对内传播和国际传播两个角度来看中国文化软实力的传播现状。

1. 对内传播

从对内传播的角度来看,Web2.0 时代的互联网与生俱来的开放性和交互性,加上互联网信息海量化、碎片化、娱乐化的特征使得在互联网中成长起来的新一代没能系统地理解源远流长的中华文化,自然就很难形成深刻的文化认同感,再加上互联网受众对大众传播的"选择性抵触"和"吐槽"的常态化,我们很多积极的、正能量的元素没能很好地被受众理解、接受和贯彻。

一方面,中国社会分层的加剧,不仅催生了基于不同利益的新兴阶层(如私营企业主、白领阶层等),而且也在加剧各个阶层之间的利益差异,孕育产生新的思想传播阵地。作为唯一执政党的中国共产党肩负着各个阶层的较高期望,对于各个阶层,尤其是新兴阶层的政治、民主、文化等回应滞后有可能进一步加剧社会对主导意识的抵制。文化的浸染与传承不仅需要政府的引导,更需要全社会、全民族的合力创造。

另一方面,互联网、移动互联网等信息技术的日新月异也在不断创造新的思想传播阵地。新兴技术的发展让传统意义上的受众不再是被动的接受者,而是成为瞬间"传播",甚至"攻击"的发起者。尽管我们正在加快网上办公、电子政务等改革的脚步,政府微博政务微信的数量也在不断增加,但是对于新兴信息技术浮于表面、形式化的应用和管理肯定不能满足需求,也不能真正解决问题。

2. 国际传播

历史上,从丝绸之路到四大发明再到郑和下西洋,中国的文化传播分享了我们对世界的认识,加深彼此的了解和互信,中国文化的国际传播有着悠久历史。从《马可·波罗游记》到18世纪风靡欧洲的"中国风",再到当前欧洲持续涌现的"汉语热",都说明世界各国对中华文明的向往。特别是近20年,中国经济蓬勃发展,使得世界各国对包括思想、价值观、发展道路、社会制度在内的中国"大文化"产生浓厚兴趣,渴望与中国人民分享体验,共同面对彼此互通的各种问题。2011年,坦桑尼亚国家电视台在黄金时段播出中国电视剧《媳妇的美好时代》,受到当地观众热烈欢迎。一位坦桑尼亚女观众说:"这部连续剧很有意思,能让我们了解中国文化和社会,最重要的是,它讲述中国正在发生的变化,而且是通过我们的语言。"

尽管成绩斐然,但我们不得不承认传统的中国符号国际传播囿于时间、地域、语言、国民性格以及传播成本等限制传播效果并不理想。从2008年北京奥运会伊始,我国提升自身软实力的工作开始加强,如放宽外国记者在境内采访的限制,希望借助国际媒体提升中国影响力;投放国家形象广告进行国家公关等。然而,这一系列举措的传播效果似乎并不尽如人意。如在2011年曾亮相纽约时报广场的国家形象广告仍过于偏重"宣传"的概念,在文化情感上造成了一定的隔阂,再加上投放时机为西方后金融危机的大背景下,一直持有零和博弈思维的西方受众难免会曲解我们的国家形象公关。

总的看来,中国文化软实力的国际传播有以下几点不足:

1. 抛弃媒介帝国主义的观点不说,我们的中国文化软实力传播当中说服、宣传成分还比较大,外国受众,尤其是欧美受众对我国优秀文化知之不详,甚至屡有误解,国际传播手法还需提升。

2. 文化贸易逆差仍然较大。尽管2014年初统计数字表明我国在出口贸易总额方面首次超越了美国,跃至全球首席,但文化贸易逆差与美国相比仍然太大。以美国受众为例,他们了解比较多的节目还是中国的功夫电影系列,且主要就是集中在李小龙、成龙等寥寥可数的几位明星身上,来自中国的文化元素大多还是名胜古迹、功夫等碎片化的表意符号。因此,中国文化产业"走出去"步伐亟须加快,中华文化的深厚底蕴和丰富资源还需深入挖掘。

3. 文化产业总量还不够大,水平还不够高,集中度不足,缺乏知名品牌,且存在盲目发展的苗头,规划、引导、调控、法规建设有待进一步加强。

二、媒介融合的契机

正视中国文化软实力传播的现状和不足,我们需要借助媒介融合这一契机,实施"弯道超车",加速发展。

根据中国互联网信息中心(CNNIC)2014年2月份发布的数据,截至2013年12月中国网民规模已达到了6.18亿,上网普及率达到45.8%,手机网民规模达到了5亿,网民和手机网民数量皆为全球第一;全国企业使用互联网的比例达到了83.2%。根据艾瑞咨询数据显示,2013年中国移动互联网市场规模达到了1059.8亿元,同比增速81.2%。数字表明,移动互联网在中国正进入高速发展通道。新兴信息技术的发展进一步实现了新媒体和传统媒体的有效互动,促进了媒介之间的进一步融合,媒介融合不仅给予中国文化软实力传播提供了新渠道和新空间,同时构建了中国互联网文化强国的新课题。

对于今天的中国媒介而言,中国文化软实力传播是不可回避的课题;对于研究中国文化软实力而言,媒介动力是无法忽略的前提。我们谈中国文化软实力的互联网传播,不得不提媒介融合;谈媒介融合,就不得不提新媒体。

新媒体这一概念由美国哥伦比亚广播电视网技术研究所所长戈尔德马克(Goldmark)在1967年首先提出[1]。新媒体是一个相对的和宽泛的概念,是利用数字技术、网络技术,通过互联网、无线通信网、卫星等渠道,以及电脑、手机等终端,向用户提供信息和娱乐服务的传播形态。我们可以从四个层面来看新媒体的内涵:

1. 新理念:新媒体的出现消解了传统媒体的边界,造成了一种"到处是中心,处处无边缘"的状态;它还消解了国家之间、社群之间、产业之间的边界;它还消解了发送者与接受者之间的边界。

---

1 廖祥忠:《何为新媒体?》,《现代传播》,2008年第5期(总第154期),121-125.

2. 新模式：随着技术的不断革新,新媒体传播的性质已经从广播变成了窄播；传播对象经从大众进化成了分众；传播工具从窄带升级成了宽带。新的模式一定会对社会产生深远影响。

3. 新效应：新媒体和社会化媒体的出现使新媒体的人际传播特性变得更加显著。根据罗杰斯的创新与扩散理论[1],有效的大众传播与人际传播的结合是创新信息传播的最佳途径,同时也是促进社会态度变迁的重要传播渠道。社会化媒体使很多信息在传播过程中被赋予了人际传播时所具有的信源可信度及说服力。

4. 新价值：媒体的基本价值形成的基本条件包括：载体具备一定的受众、具备信息传递的时间、具备传递条件、具备传递受众的心理反应空间条件等。而新媒体则需要定义其独有的核心价值,从 Web1.0 时代的"只读"为主,到 Web2.0 时代的兼顾读写,双向互动,到 Web3.0 时代的全方位互联互通,新媒体对于传统媒体的价值构成了一定挑战。

新媒介和传统媒介的融合、互联网,尤其是移动互联网的兴起给了我们提供了绝佳的机会。不同于传统媒体环境下大众传播的线性,新媒体和社交媒体呈现出一种"多对多"的叠加式放射性传播,在互联网的每一个节点上人人既是下载者,也是上传者。内容共享、平台延伸之后的新老媒体融合传播效果更好,传播成本却更低,可以获得较高的信源可信度和较好的说服效果。

媒介融合背景下的新媒体有利于促进主流传统媒体的改进,促使主流媒体更加关注反映民众关心的话题,更"接地气",主流传统媒体可以作为人们信息交换与传播的平台发挥其社会服务价值。而新媒体则可以延伸主流传统媒体优秀的内容,形成良性互动。

截止到 2013 年底,中共中央各部门网站开通了 20 余个。中央纪委、中央统战部、中联部、中央外宣办等部门开设了官方网站。还有一些部门主办了网站,例如中国文明网、中国长安网等。在中国文明网上播出的"讲文明、树新风"公益广告系列之"图说我们的价值观"等广告以可爱的卡通形象配上朗朗上口的诗歌,同时在中央电视台、中国网络电视台等台网联动同步播出,取得了较好效果。

1　E. M. Rogers and F. F. Shoemaker. Communication of Innovations: A Cross-Cultural Approach. New York: Free Press, 1971, p. 178−179.

三、中国文化软实力的传播模式

中国文化软实力传播是任重而道远的工程,需要文化界、传媒界、国际关系界等多方合计,全社会、全民族合力方能奏效。我们在此探讨中国文化软实力传播路径,旨在在媒介融合的背景下来提供一些基本路径,希望以此为契机将中国文化软实力真正做到实处,扎实推进。

1. 传播载体

从传播载体方面,政府和社会需要增加投入,加强我们的国际传播能力建设,以提高社会主义先进文化影响力,加快构建先进的现代化传播体系;加快数字化转型,建设融合媒介的集成播控平台,实现台网有机联动,扩大有效覆盖面;切实推进电信网、广电网、互联网三网融合,创新业务形态,发挥各类信息网络设施的文化传播作用,实现互联互通。

2. 传播内容

传播文化价值的根本是"以人为本",只有讲"好故事"才能真正打动人心。习近平总书记指出,提高国家文化软实力,要努力展示中华文化独特魅力。要使中华民族最基本的文化基因与当代文化相适应、与现代社会相协调,以人们喜闻乐见、具有广泛参与性的方式推广开来,把跨越时空、超越国度、富有永恒魅力、具有当代价值的文化精神弘扬起来,把继承传统优秀文化又弘扬时代精神、立足本国又面向世界的当代中国文化创新成果传播出去。

中华文化源远流长,儒释道三教互补千年传承没有断代的独特文化魅力,收录进《世界遗产名录》的几十处世界文化遗产……我们并不缺内容,关键是要适应现代传媒发展变化,及时调整故事叙述的方式,做到"中国故事,国际叙述"。

一方面,我们需要加强党报党刊、通讯社、电台电视台和重要出版社建设,进一步完善采编、发行、播发系统,提高新闻信息原创率、首发率和落地率,以提高内容构建的质量;另一方面,尽管工业化时代鼓励快节奏和批量生产,但在人文内容的制造和传承方面,可能还是需要坚持人文化成,润物无声的培养模式,不要功利冒进,加快广大受众的人文素养和媒介素养培养功在当代利在千秋。

3. 传播模式

只是传播投入的加大、传播手段和内容的丰富还不足以使中国文化形成软实力,播散到全世界,如何表达、通过何种途径表达才是问题的关键所在。纵观全球,中华文化传播最好的介质当数我们的饮食文化,因为美食的传播可以不著一言,唯舌尖感知即可;而诸如中国民族医学和中国经典文艺等传播在域外囿于种种原因却常常受冷。如此种种说明中国文化走向世界不能仅凭热情,我们需要切实提高和优化传播的形式与途径:

(1)加快建设中国互联网文化强国的步伐。作为一个具有优秀文化传统的文明古国,中国在对全球文化输出的贡献方面义不容辞。在全球信息贫富差距拉大、信息获得与输出愈发不成比例的背景下,获得信息的人会更加富有,缺乏信息的人更加贫穷。中国文化借助互联网的强势崛起,可以改变当下信息社会的"不平等"状况,使全球互联网文化和谐健康发展。互联网文化强国的提出与实现,可以推进信息化与工业化的融合,开创出更卓越的生产方式,提升我们的文化自信,为中华民族的伟大复兴做出贡献[1]。加快互联网平台上中国文化软实力的传播力度,组织做好优秀文化作品的译介工作,加快优秀作品从传统媒体到新媒体的平移,切实利用好网络视频、博客、微博、微电影、社交媒体等形式,并积极应对来自新媒介的反馈。

(2)加快语言、翻译、跨文化传播等方面人才的培养。莫言获奖需要感谢《蛙》的译者陈安娜女士(瑞典人,笔者注)。中国戏曲等文艺形式海外传播的尴尬局面也和我们相关人才匮缺有一定关系。面对21世纪全球化趋势,人才培养应具备通识基础和全球视野,我们需要制定全球化时代杰出人才的培养路线图,着力培养具有全球领导力的优秀人才。

(3)抛弃自我中心论的观点,加大向发达国家,尤其是发达国家的跨国传媒企业学习的力度。为什么同样是源自中国文化的故事别人展现出来就可以既取得口碑传播效应,又可以实现商业价值最大化,而我们就不行?尊重受众、理解受众恐怕是有效传播的前提。不仅东西方受众价值观迥异,就是欧美之间,甚至操同一官方语言的文化价值取向都有出入。所以我们的"I-oriented"(以自我为中心)宣传心态必须转变成"U-oriented"(以用户为中心)的传播模式。以英国为例,这是一个非常喜欢读书的民族,所以通过平面媒体,尤其是中华经典的文本翻译来传播对于英国受众正确理解、欣赏和接纳中华文化

1　曾静平、李欲晓:《中国互联网文化强国的理论探讨》,《现代传播》,2009年第6期(总第161期):111-113.

就尤为重要。值得一提的是,于 2014 年 4 月 8 日在伦敦伯爵宫会展中心开幕的第四十三届伦敦书展(世界第二大书展,笔者注)就见证了超过三十家中国出版社参展,仅中国国际出版集团就带来了 700 多种图书参展,其中不乏《中国梦》《中国红》《习近平治国大思维》《中共十八大:中国梦与世界》《我们这 30 年——一个记者眼里的中国改革开放》《中华人文》《符号江苏》等设计与语言皆符合英国受众的好作品。

(4)重视鼓励民间符号和民间文化"走出去"。鉴于中西方意识形态的差异和西方媒介对中国文化别有用心地"抹黑",西方受众对于中国官方推出的文化传播常常呈现出"选择性不注意"和"选择性不接触",因而难以取得应有效果。但是像姚明、李娜这样的民间符号的国际传播却常常能取得让人意想不到的良好效果。2014 年第三次晋身澳大利亚网球公开赛决赛的李娜最终收获了继法网之后又一个大满贯冠军,在颁奖晚会上李娜用极其流利的英语回答记者提问,并用非常幽默的口吻调侃自己的丈夫姜山,赢得了现场观众阵阵热烈掌声。李娜的表现不仅不像某些媒体所批评的那样——说李娜不用汉语回答问题,不爱国云云——如果李娜真是如这些媒体所说,对于现场绝大多数的英语国家观众而言传播效果就要大打折扣了,正是像李娜、姚明、朗朗、丁俊晖这样的一个个民间符号的优秀表现见微知著,细流汇海,将中华优秀文化传向各地。2008 年 8 月 1 日,新华书店在美国纽约法拉盛开设的第一家海外分店剪彩开业,书店从营业以来吸引了大批读者,有的特地从外州开车数百公里前来选购图书,其中最受欢迎的是健康养生、学习中英文以及各种生活百科类的图书,在中国几乎人手一册的《新华字典》的销量也相当不错。

(5)以更加宽广的胸怀海纳百川,吸引更多的外国友人在中国或自己的国家学习汉语、了解中国、传播文化。截至 2012 年,我们已在 108 个国家和地区建立了 400 所孔子学院和 500 多所中小学孔子课堂,世界上有 4000 万人通过不同途径在学习汉语,这对中华文化的国际传播是一个契机。我们还可以积极利用"慕课(MOOCs)"等新兴媒介技术形式将孔子课堂、中国文化学习"空中化""实时化""互动化"。著名的"汉语桥"世界大学生中文比赛由国家汉办主办,是各国学习中文的大学生展示汉语水平和中国文化知识及才艺的大型国际性赛事,旨在激发各国青年学生学习汉语的积极性、增强世界对中国语言和中华文化的理解。第十二届"汉语桥"比赛于 2013 年 7 月 17 日在湖南开幕,比赛的主题正是"我的中国梦",主办方湖南卫视也派出几路人马组成摄制小组对美国、泰国、南非、德国、法国、澳大利亚、日本、韩国、加拿大这九个赛区进行了全程跟踪拍摄,传播过程尽显大国担当和文化自信。

（6）加强中国文化软实力的智库建设。文化软实力要上升到国家战略的高度来发展,需要全社会的智力贡献。构建全社会的立体化智库对于中国文化的国际传播意义非凡。我们已经取得了可喜成绩:2014年2月26日,中国人民大学公共外交研究院揭牌成立,这是国内高校首个以公共外交为研究主题的研究院,将以公共外交为核心推动协同创新,为社会各界提供公共外交咨询服务,致力打造成为中国公共外交的重要智库;为积极服务国家文化"走出去"战略,提升中华文化国际影响力,北京外国语大学联合国内外高校、政府部门、行业产业、国际学术机构,坚持"中国情怀、国际视野",成立了中国文化"走出去"协同创新中心。今后我们要继续加大对于此类智库和活动的投入力度,要以高等学校为主要阵地,融各方之力,加速公共外交研究和中国文化软实力传播研究。

四、结语

随着媒介技术的不断进步,社交媒体网站的出现以及以手机为终端的移动网络迅速普及,实现了互联网对权威的"消融"和对弱势群体的"赋权"。然而,中国文化软实力的互联网传播还是任重道远,我们需要警惕"伪话语平权",中国文化软实力的传播不会一蹴而就,我们只有讲"好故事",讲好"好故事",积极利用好媒介融合的契机,尊重传播的规律,才能实现中国文化软实力的大发展、大传播。

当大数据遭遇人性：兼论技术的断层与无奈[1]

When Big Data Encounter Humanity: on the Fault and Incapability of Technology

李炜炜

（北京邮电大学人文学院外语系，北京 100876）

1　本文发表于2017年第12期《陕西学前师范学院学报》,在收录进本书的时候作者略有调整。

摘要：在数据科学滥觞之初，"模型推动运营"还是"数据推动运营"就是学术界争论的焦点。时至今日，在"算法统治世界"的话语喧嚣中，我们依然需要清醒。当大数据遭遇人性，我们该如何应对技术的断层与无奈。在越来越多的人文社会科学都宣称进行大数据研究转向的语境下，我们更需要逆流而思，冷静分析大数据方法热下的人文社会科学研究方法的大作为。

关键词：大数据 人性 技术 研究方法

随着信息技术的深入，加上各种媒体报道议程设置的推波助澜，越来越多的人知道了"数据"和"大数据"的概念。且不说专业从事数据技术与运营的专业人士，就连数学能力较为薄弱的很多人文学者现在也是言必称"大数据"，一时之间，大数据成了产业运营和学术研究的标准配置，大数据好像成了万能灵药，更有媒体不遗余力地鼓吹"21世纪最重要的战略资源是数据"。作为一篇研究方法的论文，本文无意对大数据技术进行刻意吹捧或诋毁，只想从更加客观和理性的角度出发来审视大数据方法，尤其基于互联网的人文社会科学研究中的大数据方法的不足以及改进之道。

一、"大数据"概念的滥觞与发展

"大数据"的概念首先源自于未来学家阿尔文·托夫勒[1]（Alvin Toffler）《第三次浪潮》（1980）一书，但大数据发展的物质基础则是始于21世纪信息量的爆炸性增长。计算机公司首先推进了数据计算能力，但是大数据真正勃兴还是得益于营销公司对于市场与用户孜孜不倦的渴求。随着传统营销学的经典"漏斗式"销售模型在精细化、个性化的用户需求面前式微，基于移动互联网的用户画像的"数据推动运营"模式在大量公司流行开来。在"数据推动运营"模式的感召下，不仅互联网公司痴迷于数据采集与数据分析，就连房地产企业和汽车销售公司等也纷纷加入数据家族，优质低价地将顾客的信息转卖给任何感兴趣的个人或实体。笔者日前在买房时，房地产中介就强行安装某一客户端应用（不安装无法交易），结果就是不仅姓名等信息清晰可见，就连住址、单位、位置、银行卡号与交易密码等个人可识别信息（PII, Personal Identifiable Information）也得拱手托出，宛如"透明人"。

大数据的应用外延并不仅限于商业领域，早在2012年的时候，美国前总统奥巴马就宣布启动"大数据研究和发展计划（Big Data Research and

---

1　阿尔文·托勒夫著. 第三次浪潮 [M]. 黄明坚译. 北京：中信出版社，2006: 19-25.

Development Initiative)"[1]，以提高美国的科研、教育与国家安全能力，这是继 1993 年美国宣布"信息高速公路"计划之后的又一次重大科技发展部署。美国政府认为大数据是未来信息时代的重要资源，战略地位堪比工业时代的石油。

学术界对于大数据的探索则主要集中在自然科学领域，2008 年 *Nature* 出版了专刊"Big Data"，2011 年 *Science* 推出关于数据处理的专刊"Dealing with Data"。与自然科学研究领域关注大数据对超级计算、互联网技术、生物制药的钟爱不同，人文学科更多是在介绍大数据方法对于人文社会科学研究范式的影响，如彭兰[2]、喻国明[3]、曾凡斌[4]、黄升民[5]等。

在众说纷纭的大数据解读中，产业和学界、自然科学和社会科学都比较公认的认知是大数据的"4V"特征，即，数据规模大（Volume）、数据种类多（Variety）、数据要求处理速度快（Velocity）、数据价值密度低（Value）。和传统的数据处理流程相似，大数据也是从"数据获取—数据分析—数据显示—数据处理"的流程来进行数据处理的，比较特殊的是大数据除了包括传统的数字和结构化数据以外，还包括了很多从文本或评论采集而来的文字和其他非结构化数据，以及通过传感器从物体上采集回来的物联网数据。大数据是一个介于云计算和人工智能中间的产物，因为大数据必然要求传统算法向云计算算法演进，而随着数据量的增加，计算机的深度学习（Deep Learning）能力也越来越强，从而在人工智能的路上又迈进了一大步。

二、大数据方法的不足

1. 大数据技术本身的不成熟

尽管大数据的呼声不绝于耳，但是毫无疑问，绝对的技术至上主义和计算神学[6]是偏激的。既然大数据是一种技术，我们不妨首先就从技术角度来分析大数据技术本身的不成熟。

1　David Reinsel, John Gantz. The Digital Universe in 2020: Big Data, Bigger Digital Shadows, and Biggest Growth in the Far East, 2012, 12.
2　彭兰．"大数据时代：新闻业面临的新震荡"[J].《编辑之友》，2013(1): 6.
3　喻国明．"传播学研究：大数据时代的新范式"[J].《新闻记者》，2013(6): 22.
4　曾凡斌．"大数据对媒体经营管理的影响及应对分析"，[J].《产业论坛》，2013(2): 21.
5　黄升民．"大数据时代，电视如何作为"[J].《南方论坛》，2013(3): 21.
6　计算神学认宇宙是一台量子计算机。在大数据时代，计算能力和数据不再是问题，计算神学变成了主流意识形态。经过大数据修正过的计算神学试图将一切问题简化成数据处理。

以大数据的第一个公认的标志性参数"数据规模大（Volume）"来看，目前很多宣称使用大数据的研究只能被称之为"较大的数据研究"，其规模远远不够。机器学习的原理是通过海量数据来从事深度学习的。举个例子来说，AlphaGo 之所以打败了围棋高手，是因为在之前的屡战屡败中，AlphaGo 积累了大量与高手对弈的数据，在这过程中其实现了深度智能学习。所以，如果不想 AlphaGo 胜利，方法很简单，不要请高手与其对弈，不要为其积累大量博弈数据就好了。能够被称之为大数据的数据量至少需要有超过 100TB 的数据量，且需要包括非结构化数据等多维数据，目前我们很多人文社会科学研究的大数据应用的数据规模远未达到"大数据"的量级。

其次，人工智能技术自 20 世纪 70 年代提出之后，沉寂了将近 30 年，直到近些年大数据算法的优化才又使其火爆了起来。原因很简单，技术本身并不成熟。计算机可以进行每秒钟数十亿次的计算和自动驾驶飞机，却学不会简单的骑自行车。因为驾驶飞机的技术是程式化的，而骑自行车却需要瞬间的反应以及相应的平衡力。在人工智能界，比较公认的结论是包括 AlphaGo 在内的机器人其实只是实现了弱人工智能，实现强人工智能的数据量还远远不足。

此外，人们现在已知晓大数据推送的不足，但从技术上尚无法克服，信息茧房效应就是不足之一。作为对现代社会信息过载的一种自我保护，多数用户顺从地接受了可以节省他们信息获取成本的个性化信息推送算法。"今日头条""一点资讯""天天快报"等新闻客户端主打的个性化新闻噱头的弊端已经日益显现。在企鹅智酷面向用户的调查中，认为个性推荐能完全满足获取资讯的用户为 15.2%，另有 70.3% 的用户认为满足程度为一般。认为个性推荐的内容太少（32.6%）和认为它会让视野变狭窄的用户（32.3%）比例相当，而认为推荐内容不准（30.7%）和推荐内容低俗（29.4%）的比例也相当[1]。

而且，很多用户都有这样的经验，我们可能是出于对"标题党"的好奇而点击的一条资讯可能在客户端引发后续的无限推送（美其名曰"猜你喜欢"），并且机器抓取的同类资讯常常是过时的信息，这不仅违反了新闻是"新近发生事实的报道"的定义，更与"阅读是为了发现未知世界"的初衷背道而驰，使得新闻价值无法体现，也使得我们在被大数据建构的碎片化、肤浅化和娱乐化的"媒介景观"中作茧自缚，无法提升媒介素养，信息辨识能力不强，失去批判的

1　彭兰."智媒化：未来媒体浪潮—新媒体发展趋势报告(2016)"[J].《国际新闻界》，2016(11): 6.

本能。

2. 大数据技术对于人性的不可知

相对于技术本身的掣肘,大数据技术对于人性的不可知更是让人唏嘘。我们人类的大脑尽管在数学计算速度上无法和机器相提并论,但是大脑懂得人性。人们擅长反射彼此的情绪状态,擅长侦测出不合时宜的行为,擅长用情绪为事物赋予价值。在可预见的未来,这恐怕都是大数据无法企及的高度。

在营销学中,人们津津乐道的案例是"即食通心粉"。按照大数据分析,消费者在烹饪即食通心粉的时候会加上一点洋葱,于是体贴的通心粉厂家就发明了一个新产品,在即食调料包里为消费者加上一些洋葱。但在实际销售时,没有加洋葱的通心粉却比加了洋葱的新产品卖得更好。尽管大数据分析了人们的行为数据,也得出了即食通心粉与洋葱之间的相关性关系,但是大数据却忽视了一种人性:家庭主妇在给家人烹制即食通心粉的时候,有一种没有尽到家庭主妇职责的内疚感,为了消除这种内疚感,她们会选择在烹饪通心粉时,加入一点自己准备的洋葱,表明这顿饭是自己精心准备的,自己不是一个偷懒的、不称职的家庭主妇,所以她们选择购买没有添加洋葱的即食通心粉。对消费者的深刻洞察不是来自于量化的研究数据和书面的研究报告,而是来自于与消费者的直接、深度接触中,比如街头暗访、消费行为的观察、与目标人群的谈话等等更接地气、更原生态的研究方法,这不是冰冷的数据符号、人群标签所能替代的。与量化研究不能取代质性研究一样,大数据方法也不能取代研究假设。

计算机数据分析擅长的是测量社会交往的"量"而非"质"。数据科学家可以测量出你在微信上的互动数量,但是他们不可能捕捉到你心底在读朋友圈里分享的圈文时的情感。因此,在社交关系的决策中,我们不能一味地相信机器。

美国社会学家库利认为,人的行为很大程度上取决于对自我的认识,而这种认识主要是通过与他人的社会互动形成的,他人对自己的评价、态度等等,是反映自我的一面"镜子",个人通过这面"镜子"认识和把握自己[1]。因此,人的自我是通过与他人的相互作用形成的。从这个意义上说,基于大数据技术

1　查尔斯·库利著. 人类本性与社会秩序 [M]. 包凡一、王湲译. 北京:华夏出版社,2015:13-28.

的用户画像画出来的可能是"镜中我",而非"本我"。美国著名社会学家戈夫曼也认为人生就是一出戏,社会是一个大舞台,社会成员作为表演者都渴望自己能够在观众面前塑造能被人接受的形象[1]。如果微博和微信等媒介中呈现出来的大都是"更好的"的伪装的自己,那么这肯定不是真实的社会状态。当媒介呈现的景观与真实的社会反差巨大的时候,对于缺乏媒介素养的青少年而言绝非利好。

此外,就算算法是机器的力量,但决定算法的还是人。最典型的例子就是使用不同搜索引擎搜出来的排序结果常常并不一致。算法的常见陷阱是它会带来偏见与歧视,而我们却常常对此一无所知。所以,在大数据算法时代,人还是需要保持自身对现实世界的洞察力与判断力。

3. 大数据技术对于隐私的侵害

相比起大数据对于人性洞察的无力,大数据技术对于隐私边界的侵蚀则是公认的事实。如今国际主流研究将信息隐私权看作一项社会权利。它的本质是"信任",核心在于分享个人信息后依然能够保留某些控制。但是个性化信息服务与隐私通常是相矛盾的。

从技术层面来看,目前的技术是无法保证绝对的隐私安全的。互联网的底层技术支撑是通信网,在量子通信没有普及以前,基于光纤的通信技术无法保证绝对的网络安全和信息安全。

现在大数据通常和移动互联网交织在一起,因此在互联网时代并不凸显的个人位置信息数据在移动互联网的环境下变得异常活跃。无处不在的无线网络 (SSID)与有线通信网络一起编织起成一张巨大的"泛在网",在这张网里,人们没有隐私,近乎"裸奔"。更加让人担心的是,人们似乎并不满足于人机互联,人们通过传感器接入了物体、通过移动的虚拟现实 (VR) 和增强现实 (AR) 设备构建场景,我们在实现万物互联的理想之时,也将自己置身于隐私被暴露和售卖的时代桎梏之中。

对于大数据时代对隐私的侵蚀引起的伦理问题,现在国际社会已经有了较多的技术手段和立法手段来进行规避和处理[2]。但在笔者看来,切实提升个人的媒介素养以及养成对个人隐私的保护意识才是此类问题得以解决的王

1 尔文•戈夫曼著 . 日常生活中的自我呈现 [M]. 冯钢译 . 北京 : 华夏出版社 , 2008: 11.
2 截止到 2017 年 3 月 , 我国尚没有一部直接明确的隐私权保护法律。

道。正如联合国教科文组织在2013年12月发布的"媒体和信息素养(Media and Information Literacy)"评估框架中所提到的那样,"每一个居民都需要和理解媒体和信息供应者的规则,以发挥他们在社会中的功能,了解更多来自虚拟世界的机会和威胁,学会管理资源"。[1]

鉴于大数据时代个人隐私保护的困难程度,已经有人提出"遗忘"的必要性,甚至有观点称"被遗忘是人的一项基本权利"。尽管实施起来还是困难重重,但是我们欣喜地看到越来越多的用户逐渐了解了隐私保护的意义,像Snapchat这样主打"阅后即焚"的保护隐私的产品风靡也说明了这一趋势。有时候,笔者甚至认为现在技术整合复杂多维数据尚有难度,政府和企业一些数据由于不开放而导致的"信息孤岛"现象常被人认为是不足需要攻克,但从隐私保护的角度来看,这又何尝不是一种另类之"幸"呢?

三、大数据技术在人文社会科学研究中的应用和挑战

传统的人文科学研究方法主要是定性研究和量化研究。量化研究秉承实证主义的传统,主要使用基于统计学和概率论的方法来进行实验和调查,各种问卷与量表是量化研究中必不可少的分析手段。定性研究则更多地是从人文主义和理论建构的基石出发来收集人们的感受、见解与经历等资料,故而研究手段常常是参与观察与深度访谈。与量化研究主要使用演绎推理不同,定性研究常使用归纳推理法,带有浓郁的思辨色彩。

鉴于学科的分野以及研究方法的差异,传统的人文学科,如文学多使用定性研究,而社会学科,如社会学则多诉诸量化研究。但是,进入到"数据推动学术"之后,人文学科和社会学科皆出现了不同程度的"数据转向"热。跟自然科学走得比较近的量化研究方法对大数据方法的狂热程度更强,"数据主宰一切""算法统治世界"之类的声音不绝于耳。从研究范式到具体方法,从人才培养到产学联合,大数据对人文社会科学研究产生了深远的影响。

从具体操作从面来说,与传统人文科学领域中的基于假设或模型的小网络小抽样不一样,大数据研究方法使用的是面向复杂网络的全样本分析。由于集成了自然语言处理技术、分词抓取技术、语料库语言学技术,现在的大数据研究可以更加快捷地分析人们的情感语义特征,从而使得用户画像更为准确,

---

1　陶媛. "联合国教科文组织发布全球媒体和信息素养评估报告"[J].《世界教育信息》,2014(3)：78.

也就使得个性化的推介变得可能。

以新闻学为例,大数据在新闻上的应用涵盖了根据业务板块的需求定制发稿模板、数据自动抓取与采集、稿件自动生成等,那么传统意义上基于采编模式的新闻研究与新闻教育就需要更新。早在 2011 年,用 Narrative Science 软件写作的新闻稿件已出现在一些美国媒体上。2016 年里约奥运会期间,机器写作的新闻体育报道更是大行其道,占据了数字化媒体的版面。除了体育新闻之外,财经新闻也是数据新闻和机器写作的先驱者,国内领先的互联网巨头腾讯网的财经新闻机器写作已经颇具规模。国内也已经有高校开设了"数据新闻"专业。相比于火爆的新闻业务方向的研究,对传统新闻学理论研究,尤其是新闻史论的研究则更加式微。

对于广大的人文社会科学研究者而言,其数据处理的能力本来就偏弱,更没有必要迷信大数据,鼓吹所谓的"大数据转向"。

具体来说,只有数据其实是没有意义的,不管是学术上的意义,还是商业上的意义。数据的价值无法充分发挥,并不仅仅是数据质量问题或是数据分析能力问题。问题的关键原因之一,还在于一门重要学科——运筹学(Operations Research)在学术界和产业界的稀缺。运筹学不同于数据科学,是一门致力于研究由数据到决策的科学。如果说数据科学旨在理解数据中的规律,运筹学则是将理解的规律为最后的决策服务,从而给决策者带来效益,以体现自身的价值。但在国内,学界和业界的合作尚未起步。作为学术水平要求较高的交叉学科,国内运筹学长期面临着人才匮乏的尴尬。多年来,中国都没有自己的优化求解器(solver),主要靠海外购买或者使用海外的开源求解器。

鉴于此,大数据学和运筹学等一众复杂的技术将会是人文社会科学研究者路上难以逾越的一道巨坎。那么,在大数据时代,人文社会学科,尤其是重实证和调查的社会学科难道就难有作为了吗?答案很明显是否定的!如果将大数据热看成一种"能指狂欢",那么原始数据本身可能也只是一种隐喻,数据从来都不可能是"原始"的,数据总是依照某些人的倾向和价值观念而被构建出来的。数据分析的结果看似客观公正,但其实价值选择贯穿了从构建到解读的全过程。人文社会科学的研究者完全可以摒弃自己不擅长的数据采集和分析,选择和自然科学研究者,尤其是运筹学研究者主动对接、深度合作,实现研究方法的跨学科交叉融合与协同创新,自己专攻价值判断,使用深描等研究方法来阐释意义,将量化研究与定性研究进行深度融合,以便获取更准确、更严谨、更有解释力、预测力和指导价值的研究成果。

四、结语:技术的断层与无奈

历史上,诸如麦克卢汉等学者思想家常过分强调技术的加持,著作中常充盈着技术乐观主义的气质。但是,我们知道,不管在技术的演进还是在历史的更迭中,人才是最重要的常量。人性是健康、成熟技术的底线,没有对人性的尊重,技术一定是处于断层之中,充满无奈。而这个健康、成熟就体现在人道主义,其核心是对每个个体生命权、自由权的尊重,这个尊重是一切核心价值观的前提,没有对个体的尊重,不可能创造现代文明。很多人文社会科学研究本来就是基于人性的深刻洞察,因此,人文社会学科在应用大数据方法时,要不忘初心,只有将人和人性至于整体性的技术图谱和生态中进行系统考查,才会有惊人的发现和深刻的研究。

电影《荒野猎人》的跨文化解读[1]

Intercultural Interpretation of *The Revenant*

李炜炜

（北京邮电大学人文学院外语系，北京 100876）

《荒野猎人》(*The Revenant*)是 2015 年亚利桑德罗·冈萨雷斯·伊纳里多执导的剧情电影,由莱昂纳多·迪卡普里奥、汤姆·哈迪、威尔·保尔特 、多姆纳尔·格利森、保罗·安德森等主演。《荒野猎人》根据迈克尔·彭克同名长篇小说改编,故事讲述 19 世纪一名皮草猎人休·格拉斯(Hugh Glass)被熊所伤并被其他猎人抢走财物抛弃荒野,猎人经历痛苦奇迹存活后开始复仇的故事。2016 年 2 月 29 日,该片在第 88 届奥斯卡金像奖同时获得最佳导演、最佳男主角和最佳摄影奖。该片在全球范围内一共揽获了 88 项大奖和 184 项提名。

早就看过了《荒野猎人》(*The Revenant*)的预告片,忙忙碌碌,直到今天(2016 年 3 月 20 日)才看到了《荒野猎人》的全貌。在长达长 2 小时 36 分钟

1　本片是 2016 年 3 月 20 日作者接受媒体采访时的一段发言整理，在收录进本书的时候作者略有调整。

的影片中,莱昂纳多·迪卡普里奥饰演的男一号台词竟然不到几十句,如此走心的表演,配以大胆的自然景观广角镜头和令人惊艳的一镜到底的拍摄手法,给我们呈现了堪称教科书级别的摄影,唯美且震撼,该片获得今年奥斯卡最佳摄影奖名至实归。

在影片北美上映初期,鉴于莱昂纳多在《泰坦尼克号》之后长达 20 年的悲情奥斯卡,有铁杆影迷就担心小李会不会在片中用力过度而导致与小金人再次失之交臂。而只靠落基山脉的壮美取景和"老姜"加"劳模"的阵容,显然不足以打动挑剔的奥斯卡评委。某种意义上而言,在复仇的噱头之外,该片讲述的其实是第一代北美移民挑战和征服荒野的故事,所要传递的荒野精神正是成为美国人对抗欧洲古典传统的砥柱,也是塑造美国身份认同和民族自豪的重要源泉。而今日的美国正渴望重拾荒野精神,致敬那曾经的过往,走出大变革时代的迷惘,并更从容地走向未来。

有人批评说,《荒野猎人》是德波尔口中所说的景观电影,只靠宏大的场面,唯美的画面来阐释导演的理念,尤其是超现实主义的画面描写和逼真的声音,对观众的视觉产生强烈的视觉冲击,从而使观众陷入暂时的"沉醉"之中。人们的理性原则终会屈从于欲望法则,人们会在这些导演的引导下最终沦为一个"图像的囚徒"。联想到最近另外两部热映的影片(《功夫熊猫 3》(*Kung Fu Panda 3*, IMDb: 7.5 分)和《疯狂动物城》(*Zootopia*, IMDb: 8.4 分),反观国内电影的票房则粉丝和 IP 效应双双失落,中国电影观众正在学会用脚投票,曾经在资本市场和票房市场都无往不利的"粉丝经济""话题炒作"等招数已经不再好使,越来越多的诚意制作则走上逆袭之路。因此,在我们不得不感慨,好莱坞的金字招牌不仅仅来自其领袖全球的拍摄技巧,而且将艺术与商业、经验和批判、技术与人文、历史与未来、剧本和叙事等要素有机地结合起来,敬畏自然,直指人心,激荡心扉。影片可以跨越异质的语言和文化,但人们心灵深处的真善美始终如一。不忘初心,方得始终。从这个角度而言,中国影人还任重道远。